the way we cook

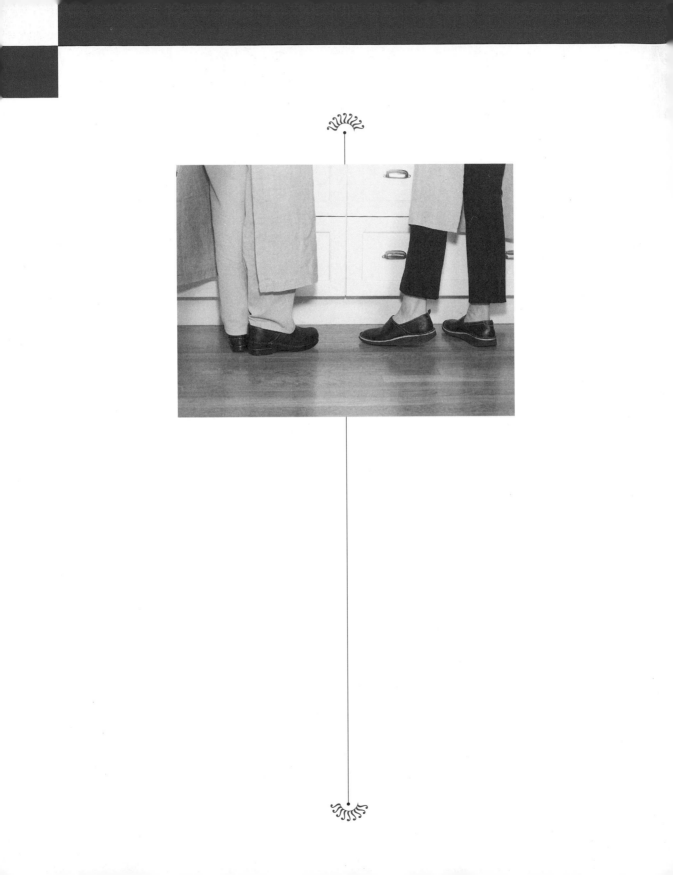

Sheryl Julian & Julie Riven

the way we cook

Recipes from

the New American

Kitchen

Photographs by Karen Wise

Houghton Mifflin Company

BOSTON NEW YORK 2003

For information about permission to reproduce selections from this book, write to Permissions, Houghton Mifflin Company, 215 Park Avenue South, New York, New York 10003.

Visit our Web site: www.houghtonmifflinbooks.com.

Library of Congress Cataloging-in-Publication Data is available.
ISBN 0-618-17149-5

These recipes appeared in slightly different form in the *Boston Globe.*

Book design by Anne Chalmers
Photographs by Karen Wise
Food styling by Julie Riven and Sheryl Julian
Prop styling by Heidi Fielwell
Accessories courtesy of La Cafetière, 160 9th Avenue, New York, New York

Printed in the United States of America

VB 10 9 8 7 6 5 4 3 2 1

For our mothers

Doris Guren Julian

and

Ghita Henderson Riven

Wise and generous women who taught us

all their golden rules for life,

which include:

⟨∾∾⟩

Take a warm sweater.

Get a good night's sleep.

Make sure there's plenty to eat.

acknowledgments

꿍꿍꿍

We've been writing about food for so long that you would think the path from columnists to book authors would be easy and maybe even a little graceful. But it was abrupt. We never thought about writing this book until Alison Arnett, the *Boston Globe*'s restaurant critic, who made the template for the column twenty years ago when she was an editor, ordered us one day to set the wheels in motion. With constant prodding from Alison, we met Rux Martin of Houghton Mifflin and Doe Coover of the Doe Coover Agency. We four became laughing accomplices, shaping the ideas on these pages. We loved those "work" sessions. Doe is instinctive and generous about people; Rux is delightful, and when she massages a manuscript, it's a joy to follow her editing.

Michael Larkin was the *Boston Globe Magazine* editor when the column was established, and many people shaped it over the years, including Jan Freeman, the first copyeditor, Mimsi Beckwith, Fiona Luis, Bennie DiNardo, Louise Kennedy, Ann Cortissoz, and Barbara Pattison. The witty David Cohen cares deeply about getting it right.

The tech team at the *Boston Globe* couldn't have been more helpful (especially considering our computer pho-

bias): Paul McGeary, Stephen Shepard, and Mary Ellis among them.

When things got tight with the book schedule, Alison and Amy Graves took over as food editors.

Julie Michaels gave remarkable, animated advice, as usual; Gail Banks and Sandra Shapiro read and cheered relentlessly; Corby Kummer, who sent us to Rux, offered wisdom and encouragement in large doses; the talented Judith Barrett offered the title.

We watched photographer Karen Wise balancing herself like a ballerina on the top of a stepladder in Julie's kitchen, breathing carefully so her camera wouldn't shake. We love her work. Ingrid Lysgaard, in Sheryl's kitchen, cooked and baked and always laughed. Kim Abrams, who assists us in other cooking projects, rescued us at the computer and in the kitchen.

The Eustises, Fairbanks, Kursons, and Solomons reminded us how much we enjoy a lively table of friends.

Steve and Barry and our children, David, Tony, Peter, Asher, and Jennifer — marvelous eaters — could not have been more enthusiastic.

Thank you all for launching the "we" in *The Way We Cook*.

contents

introduction

We are two women — friends, colleagues, and coauthors of a long-running cooking column in the *Boston Globe* — who collect recipes and love to spend time in the kitchen. For the past twenty years, we've been talking to other cooks. We'll drive three hundred miles to interview someone we heard about who makes a great apple pie. And a creamy, crusty mac and cheese? We'd go anywhere to find a good one.

We look for recipes that might introduce you to something you've never tried or dishes that are so familiar they seem to fall off our pages and into your pots — simple, honest food that's typical of a culture. We're excited when we stumble on a better method for a favorite dish, like butterflying chicken, which produces a succulent roast bird in a flash (see Herb-Roasted Flattened Chicken, page 192). We're partial to recipes that use just half a dozen beautiful ingredients, ones that allow the taste to shine through without adornment. Fresh Corn "Risotto," for instance, is

simply corn, cream, and fresh herbs, a takeoff on the classic Italian risotto, and the results are dreamy. Roast Side of Salmon — with a mere handful of ingredients — is a spectacular dinner for company.

Our mission isn't to reinvent cooking but rather to offer dishes that are so pared down they're elegant. Equally often, we gravitate toward ordinary, family-style meals — ones you'd never find in restaurants. We're not restaurateurs, and we don't think people at home, taking time from busy lives, should pretend they are either — not even for one night.

The recipes in this book have other things in common. They often reflect the seasons, with lighter dishes for warm weather and heartier ones for cold months. Most aren't new, but simply modernized. They all give you the most for your effort. We'd never ask you to spend the afternoon in the kitchen without feeling confident that you'll be pleased with the results.

When someone shares a recipe with us, we go to the stove and make it exactly as the cook instructed. Then we might lower an oven temperature, take out a step that doesn't seem necessary, or streamline a method. We try to make the recipe as efficient and forgiving as possible, so you can bend and adapt the ingredient list and still have success. Our readers write, call, and stop us in the supermarket aisles to tell us that they like our recipes because they're straightforward but not simplistic, contemporary without being fussy. They say our food is so dependable that it can be made for the first time just before guests are due to arrive.

That's because we know we're writing for home cooks. Many of us don't have much time, and we want to get the most out of the few hours we devote to grocery shopping and cooking. When the phone is ringing and the kids are wondering when dinner will be ready, or a guest is at the door, or you've just come home frazzled after a bad day,

complicated recipes (make that complicated anything) are out of the question.

When we talk about *The Way We Cook*, we're talking about the way *you* cook, the way you eat today, what excites you, what you want when you're sitting at the kitchen table, and what you're willing to do when it's time to celebrate. We think you're accomplished home cooks who know your way around the kitchen, but if you don't, there are many recipes on these pages that won't frighten you. We think you entertain and experiment, eat out, and watch what you eat. We also think you have a stable of good recipes you've depended on for years. But like all good cooks, you probably like to drop one or two recipes every season and add some new ones.

Look at these recipes, and put a line through any ingredients you don't like. Go right to the dishes that interest you, and cook them until they're yours. Use our years of experience to make your time at home and at the kitchen table more pleasurable.

appetizers

We grew up in the era of cocktail parties, when everyone served the same menu: old-fashioneds and sour cream dip with crackers, cheese balls, shrimp with cocktail sauce, and pigs in a blanket. We're quite attached to those dishes, and you'll find variations of most of them in these pages.

Most modern hosts, however, don't follow such set patterns when they entertain. They're often wondering at the last minute what to serve as a little nibble with wine before dinner and whether or not to make a first course. In that sense, we're no different from anyone else. We let dinners revolve around the main course, then plan the dessert, and finally "the befores." When there's no time left to cook, we often revert to what we know best, then run up to take a bath and dress just before the doorbell rings.

Sheryl often dashes out for olives and good pita, dependable standbys. For many years, she tore the pita into pieces and toasted them with olive oil and coarse salt to make Pita Crackers. Now, the thin rounds have become Pita Pizzas with Goat Cheese and Scallions, which are just as easy, but look more impressive.

She's made Tuna Pâté with Capers for almost every guest who has walked in the door, except during the summer and fall when smoked bluefish is available and she purees it into Smoked Bluefish Pâté. All fall and winter, guests get Sweet Potato Oven Fries with Homemade Ketchup or Pink Yogurt Sauce because you can cut up the potatoes and they won't turn brown if you set them aside until it's time to roast them.

Julie often has Spicy Pecans in a little glass bowl on her coffee table and Devils on Horseback (roasted dates with bacon and cheese) rolled up and ready to cook when the guests come. One year when she was rummaging through a flea market, she happened upon some old cooling racks and bought them to make Stovetop Toasts, which she serves with a soft goat cheese or with Broiled Eggplant Caponata.

Sometimes we serve something substantial in the living room before dinner — like Miniature Croque Monsieur, small versions of the melting French ham-and-cheese sandwiches, and then skip a first course at the table. Or, we bring the first course into the living room, offering Summer Tomato Soup in Teacups, which are easy to hold and sip, or Mini Crab Cakes, which need small plates and forks.

For years, it bothered us that we didn't have our appetizer routine settled, that it varied for every dinner and every season, and that even though we were the hosts, we didn't know which variation was about to unfold. Now we're happier with our own system of come-what-may. One of these days, we'll probably revive the old-fashioneds.

appetizers

spicy pecans

You can eat these spicy pecans by the handful. This recipe, from Susan Markson of Wayland, Massachusetts, is warm with cumin and hot from cayenne pepper. The nuts are coated first with egg whites, then roasted in a buttery pan until they absorb the butter and turn crisp.

2	**large egg whites**
	Pinch of coarse salt
1	**teaspoon cayenne pepper, or more to taste**
1	**teaspoon ground cumin**
4	**cups pecan halves**
½	**cup sugar**
4	**tablespoons (½ stick) unsalted butter**

Set the oven at 350 degrees.

In a large bowl, beat the egg whites and salt for 1 minute with an electric mixer. Add the cayenne pepper (if you want the nuts to be spicier, add up to 2 teaspoons) and cumin and beat for 1 minute more.

Stir in the nuts and sugar with a large metal spoon, making sure all of the nuts are coated with the egg-white mixture.

Place the butter on a rimmed baking sheet and transfer it to the hot oven. Leave the pan for about 1 minute — only until the butter melts — then quickly remove from the oven. Spread the pecans on the baking sheet in a single layer and stir to coat them with the butter.

Return the pan to the oven and bake the pecans for 30 to 40 minutes, stirring every 10 minutes, or until the nuts are golden brown and have absorbed the butter.

Remove the nuts from the oven; they should be crisp and dry. If they're still moist, they're not done. Stir them again, and set them aside to cool. Store them in an airtight container for up to 3 weeks (if they last that long).

THE WAY WE COOK

curried deviled eggs

Deviled eggs made a comeback recently, which we were happy to see since we had never stopped serving them. All the ingredients are in the fridge or pantry — this is only a small part of the appeal — and you can vary the filling ingredients infinitely, as long as mayonnaise is included. Because the eggs and their piquant fillings are substantial, they used to be cocktail party standbys. This filling is seasoned with curry powder and has lots of red-onion crunch.

6 **eggs, hard-cooked (see page 293)**
2 **tablespoons finely chopped red onion**
3 **tablespoons mayonnaise**
2 **teaspoons fresh lemon juice**
1½ **teaspoons curry powder**
   Pinch of cayenne pepper
½ **teaspoon coarse salt, or to taste**
½ **teaspoon freshly ground black pepper, or to taste**

   Finely chopped scallions or chives

Peel the eggs and slice them horizontally. Carefully remove the yolks and set them in a small bowl. Cut a tiny slice from the rounded ends of the whites so that they sit flat on a platter. With a fork, mash the yolks with the onion, mayonnaise, lemon juice, curry powder, cayenne pepper, salt, and black pepper. Add more mayonnaise or lemon juice, if you like.

When the mixture is thoroughly blended, spoon the yolk mixture into the shells, mounding it slightly. Sprinkle the tops with the finely chopped scallions or chives and serve.

note: To make in advance, arrange the eggs on a platter, cover them with wax paper and a damp paper towel, and refrigerate; they will stay moist for half a day. Garnish with scallions or chives before serving.

tuna pâté with capers

Sheryl has been serving this tuna pâté for twenty-five years, and even though it contains canned tuna, one of the most familiar ingredients on the American table, most of the time, guests don't know what's in it. It should be very smooth, be pleasantly hot from cayenne, and have a slight piquant taste from the capers and lemon juice. The pâté must be made with tuna in oil (good brands are imported from Italy). Let it mellow for at least half a day before serving it at room temperature, spread on crackers or Pita Crackers (page 13).

- 1 **can or jar (6–7½ ounces) light tuna in oil, drained**
- 8 **tablespoons (1 stick) unsalted butter, at room temperature**
  Pinch of cayenne pepper, or to taste
  Squeeze of fresh lemon juice, or to taste
- ¼ **cup capers, drained**

In a food processor, pulse the tuna and butter until the mixture is smooth. Add the cayenne pepper and lemon juice and pulse again to mix them in thoroughly.

Taste the pâté for seasoning and add more cayenne or lemon juice, if you like. Add the capers and pulse for 30 seconds, just to distribute them but not mash them.

Transfer the mixture to a small bowl and smooth the top. Press a piece of plastic wrap directly onto the pâté, then cover the top of the bowl with another piece of plastic wrap so the mixture won't dry out. Refrigerate the pâté for at least several hours or as long as a few days and serve.

smoked bluefish pâté

When the blues are running during the summer, we eat bluefish as often as we can. Dark and silvery-fleshed, it's rich in oils and almost meaty. Bluefish right off the boat is mild and delicate, so some people will only eat it the same day it's caught. Many recreational fishermen (Julie's husband, Barry, is one) own backyard smokers, and smoked bluefish has become so popular that it's available in markets throughout the summer and fall. We make it into a pâté with cream cheese, lemon juice, and red onion, then spread it on Pita Crackers (page 13) or Stovetop Toasts (page 12).

½ **pound skinless, boneless smoked bluefish (or use smoked trout)**

4 **ounces cream cheese, at room temperature**

2 **tablespoons fresh lemon juice**

1 **tablespoon Dijon mustard**

2 **tablespoons finely chopped red onion**
  Pinch of cayenne pepper

½ **teaspoon coarse salt, or to taste**

½ **teaspoon freshly ground black pepper, or to taste**

Flake the bluefish, discarding any skin and bones.

In a food processor, pulse the bluefish and cream cheese until they are smooth. Turn off the motor and scrape down the sides of the work bowl several times.

Add the lemon juice, Dijon mustard, onion, cayenne pepper, salt, and black pepper and pulse again until the mixture is smooth. Taste for seasoning and add more salt and pepper, if you like.

Transfer the pâté to a serving bowl and smooth the top. Cover with plastic wrap and store in the refrigerator for at least 2 hours and for up to 1 week.

lebanese tabbouleh with loads of mint

Tabbouleh, the Middle Eastern salad of cracked wheat and chopped vegetables, is served with triangles of soft pita, often alongside several other appetizers such as hummus, the popular chickpea spread. Guests use the pita as scoops for the grainy salad. This tabbouleh, from a talented Lebanese-born cook in the Boston area, Seta Yapoudijian Keshishian, is made with a lot of lemon juice (the bulgur is soaked in lemon juice and water), tomatoes, parsley, mint, and Aleppo pepper. The pepper, sold at Middle Eastern markets, has a warm heat. Chop the tomatoes and bell peppers finely so they blend into the cracked wheat. Fine-grain bulgur (also known as cracked wheat) is available at Middle Eastern markets. You can also use medium-grain bulgur.

½   cup fine-grain or medium-grain bulgur (cracked wheat)
¼   cup fresh lemon juice
¼   cup water
 1   bunch scallions, finely chopped
 1   bunch flat-leaf parsley (about 1½ cups leaves), finely chopped
½   bunch fresh mint leaves (about 1 cup), finely chopped
½   red or green bell pepper, cored, seeded, and finely chopped
 2   ripe plum tomatoes, peeled, cored, and finely chopped
 2   teaspoons ground Aleppo pepper or 1 teaspoon freshly ground black pepper, or to taste
 1   teaspoon coarse salt, or to taste
¼–⅓   cup olive oil, or to taste

In a medium bowl, combine the bulgur, lemon juice, and water. Stir well and set aside for 15 minutes, or until the bulgur absorbs the liquid.

Add the scallions, parsley, mint, bell pepper, tomatoes, Aleppo or black pepper, and salt. Drizzle the salad with enough oil to coat it. With two forks, fluff the mixture until all of the oil is mixed in. Add more oil, 1 teaspoon at a time, if you like, until the cracked wheat and vegetables are coated to suit your taste.

Spoon the tabbouleh into a serving dish. Serve at once or cover with plastic wrap and refrigerate for up to several hours before serving.

broiled eggplant caponata

Many eggplant dishes are too oily because the slices absorb so much oil during their preliminary cooking. Instead of frying the eggplant, we broil it, which works very well for this Sicilian sweet-and-sour relish. After the diced eggplant is broiled, it's mixed with tomatoes, raisins, capers, and balsamic vinegar. Spoon it onto Stovetop Toasts (page 12), or serve it as a relish with chicken or grilled fish.

1	large (1½ pounds) eggplant
	Olive oil, for sprinkling
2	tablespoons olive oil
½	red onion, finely chopped
1	garlic clove, finely chopped
4	(¾ pound) ripe plum tomatoes, peeled, seeded, and chopped
2	tablespoons capers, drained
½	cup golden raisins
¼	cup balsamic vinegar
	Pinch of sugar
3	tablespoons chopped fresh oregano
¼	cup chopped fresh parsley
½	teaspoon coarse salt, or to taste
½	teaspoon freshly ground black pepper, or to taste

Preheat the broiler.

Cut the eggplant into ¼-inch pieces. Sprinkle them with oil and spread them on a rimmed baking sheet. Broil them 10 inches from the element for 20 minutes, turning several times, or until the eggplant is tender. The pieces should be charred. Set aside.

Heat the oil in a large skillet. Add the onion and cook over medium-high heat, stirring often, for 10 minutes, or until softened. Add the garlic and tomatoes and cook, stirring often, for 5 minutes.

Add the eggplant to the pan with the capers, raisins, vinegar, sugar, and oregano. Cook the mixture over medium heat for 1 minute, stirring often.

Add the parsley, salt, and pepper. Taste for seasonings and add more salt, pepper, or capers, if you like. Stir thoroughly and transfer to a bowl. Cover with plastic wrap and refrigerate for at least 1 hour for the flavors to mellow.

To Peel and Seed Tomatoes

Core fresh tomatoes and dip them into a saucepan of boiling water. Leave them for 10 to 20 seconds (summer tomatoes take less time than winter ones), then lift one out. Rub your fingers along the skin to see if it moves slightly. If it does, it's ready to peel. Remove all the tomatoes from the water and plunge them into ice water or run very cold water over them.

When they are cool enough to handle, peel the skin away with a paring knife (top right).

To seed the tomatoes, halve them horizontally, and squeeze each half so the seeds pop out (bottom right). Or, scoop out the seeds with your finger or a spoon. For a hearty soup, leave in the seeds.

molded chicken liver pâté

Every week, when we buy whole chickens, we add the liver to a container in the freezer until there is enough to make this pâté. It's the classic mixture, made with lots of butter, flamed with brandy, and pureed in a food processor until it's creamy. We line a small bowl with plastic wrap, pack the liver into the bowl, and let it chill until firm. Then we turn out the molded pâté and surround it with cornichon pickles, rounds of cucumber, and commercial crackers or Pita Crackers.

1   **pound chicken livers**
6   **tablespoons (¾ stick) butter, at room temperature**
1   **teaspoon coarse salt, or to taste**
½   **teaspoon freshly ground black pepper, or to taste**
2   **tablespoons brandy**
⅛   **teaspoon freshly grated nutmeg, or to taste**
¼   **teaspoon allspice**

   Cornichon pickles, for serving
   Cucumber rounds, for serving
   Pita Crackers (page 13), for serving

Trim the chicken livers of all fat and spread them out on a plate lined with paper towels to dry. Dry livers won't splatter as much when they hit the hot butter.

Heat 2 tablespoons of the butter in a large skillet. Add the livers and sprinkle them with the salt and pepper. Cook over high heat, turning often, for 8 minutes, or until the livers are cooked through. Add the brandy to the pan, tip the pan away from you, hold a lit match to the mixture to ignite it, and let the flame die. Set the pan aside until the livers are completely cool.

In a food processor, pulse the livers with all the scrapings from the bottom of the skillet. Add the nutmeg, allspice, and remaining 4 tablespoons butter.

Pulse the mixture, stopping the motor to scrape down the sides of the work bowl, until the pâté is smooth. Taste for seasoning and add more salt and pepper, if necessary.

Line a deep 3-cup bowl (or 2 smaller bowls) with plastic wrap and pack the pâté into the bowl, smoothing the top with a blunt knife. Fold the plastic wrap over to encase the pâté completely. Slide the bowl into a plastic bag and secure the opening.

Refrigerate for at least half a day to allow the flavors to mellow or for up to 5 days.

Before serving, turn the pâté upside down onto a large platter. Lift off the bowl and then peel off the plastic wrap. Let the pâté sit at room temperature for 30 minutes. Surround the pâté with cornichons and cucumber rounds and serve with Pita Crackers.

stovetop toasts

You can take any savory spread — or even a few roasted red peppers — set them on rounds of toasted bread and make something quite nice to accompany a glass of wine. If that bread isn't ordinary toast but rather heavenly golden, crusty rounds, wouldn't that be better? Toaster ovens and old-fashioned toasters make perfectly acceptable toast, but we discovered another way. We set the bread on a wire rack over a gas flame, so the toast is singed as well, good enough to eat without a spread or topping. The idea, of course, is as old as fireplace cooking. But we stumbled on it when Sheryl bought a perforated steel stovetop toasting pan some years ago in France. The toaster goes directly onto the heat and the bread is set on it to brown. Camp-stove toasters, sold in camping-equipment stores, are similar. We use racks from yard sales and set them directly on a gas burner — only gas does this successfully. Rub the toasts with garlic and sprinkle them with oil, or serve them plain as delicious crackers.

1 **French bread, thickly sliced**
1 **garlic clove, cut in half**
Olive oil, for sprinkling
Coarse salt, to taste

Toast the bread on both sides on top of the stove or under the broiler. Rub the bread with the garlic, then sprinkle it with the oil and the salt. Serve at once.

note: If serving these toasts with a spread, oil them lightly, if you like, or leave them plain.

pita crackers

If we have a few minutes before guests arrive, we make these simple pita crackers. Like Stovetop Toasts, you can serve them as is or use them as crackers for a spread. Use any pita you can find. If you have access to a Middle Eastern grocery store, buy the large loaves or try the whole-wheat loaves, which make heartier crackers.

2   **large (12-inch) pita rounds or 4 medium (6-inch) rounds**
    Olive oil, for sprinkling
    Coarse salt, to taste
    Chopped fresh herbs, such as rosemary, oregano, or thyme,
      for sprinkling (optional)
    Freshly grated Parmesan cheese, for sprinkling (optional)

Set the oven at 375 degrees.

To separate the double layer of pita, cut into the outside circumference of the pita using scissors or a serrated knife. Gently separate the two layers. Tear the bread into irregular shapes. Place them on a baking sheet rough side up.

Sprinkle them lightly with oil and salt. If you're adding herbs or Parmesan cheese, sprinkle some on top.

Toast the bread for 8 to 10 minutes, or until the crackers are golden brown. (They go from golden to burned quickly.) Transfer the pitas to a serving platter.

Store the cooled crackers in a plastic zipper bag for up to 2 days.

rye crackers

When we put these crackers on the hors d'oeuvre menu, we might serve a little cheese to go with them, but nothing else. Made from rye and all-purpose flours, butter, and milk, the crackers are thin — they're rolled right on the baking sheet — dark and chewy. They look professionally made, but they're a cinch. We got this recipe from Ingrid Lysgaard, a Danish-born chef who teaches pastry making at Boston University.

- 1 **cup rye flour**
- ½ **cup all-purpose flour, plus more for rolling**
- 1 **teaspoon salt**
- 6 **tablespoons (¾ stick) unsalted butter, cut into pieces**
- 6 **tablespoons cold whole milk**

- 1 **egg white, beaten with 1 teaspoon water, for the glaze**

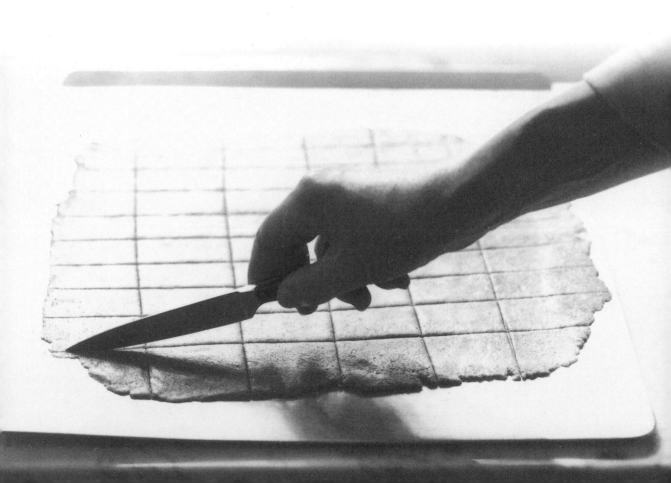

In a food processor, combine the flours and salt. Pulse for 5 seconds. Sprinkle the butter over the flour. Process until the mixture resembles sand. With the machine running, pour in the milk. Mix just until the dough forms a ball.

Turn the dough out onto a lightly floured board and shape it into a smooth, flat cake. Wrap it in foil and refrigerate it for several hours.

Set the oven at 400 degrees. Butter a 14-by-16-inch baking sheet.

Remove the dough from the refrigerator and place it in the center of the baking sheet. Press it with the heel of your hand to make a 6-inch cake.

Lightly flour the dough. With a rolling pin, roll it into a rectangle about 12 by 14 inches. If the edges are jagged and the sides not quite even, that's OK.

With the tines of a fork, pierce the dough all over the surface. Using a pastry or pizza cutter or a knife, make 5 vertical cuts and 9 horizontal cuts to form 60 crackers (left). Brush the dough with the egg white mixture.

Bake the crackers for 20 to 25 minutes, or until they are brown. If some of the crackers are beginning to get too brown on the edges, remove them early and transfer them to a wire rack to cool. Cool all the crackers on a rack and store in an airtight container.

rosemary biscuits with smoked turkey and cranberry relish

Sheryl often makes rosemary biscuits to serve with soups or roast chicken. They're always on the Thanksgiving table and, the following day, are made into little sandwiches similar to the ones here. A sweetened version of the dough is used to make Strawberry Shortcakes (page 314). Chopped rosemary is added to the dough in the food processor, and the dough is rolled into a rectangle, cut with a knife into small rectangles, and sandwiched with smoked turkey and cranberry relish.

{ **FOR THE ROSEMARY BISCUITS**
- 3½ **cups all-purpose flour, plus more for rolling**
- 1 **tablespoon baking powder**
- 1½ **teaspoons salt**
- 12 **tablespoons (1½ sticks) unsalted butter, cut into pieces**
- 3 **tablespoons chopped fresh rosemary**
- 3 **tablespoons sugar**
- 1¼ **cups whole milk**

Set the oven at 425 degrees. Line a baking sheet with parchment paper.

In a food processor, combine the flour, baking powder, and salt. Pulse once just to combine.

Add the butter and pulse just until the mixture resembles coarse crumbs. Add the rosemary and sugar and pulse just to mix them in.

Remove the processor lid and pour the milk over the flour. Pulse the mixture just until it forms large clumps. Do not let it come together to form a dough.

Dust a counter with flour. Turn the clumps out onto the counter and cut through them half a dozen times with a pastry scraper or a blunt knife until they come together to form a dough. With your hands, gently shape the dough into a square. Then flatten the square.

With a floured rolling pin, roll the dough to a ½-inch-thick, 8-by-10-inch rectangle. Make 2 lengthwise cuts and 4 crosswise cuts in the dough to form 15 biscuits (left). Set them on the baking sheet.

Bake the biscuits for 25 minutes, or until they are golden brown. Transfer them to wire racks to cool. While the biscuits are baking, make the relish.

note: To make in advance, let the biscuits cool completely (don't split them for sandwiches). Cover them with a clean kitchen towel. They'll stay fresh for half a day. To serve hot, wrap the biscuits in foil, shiny side inside. Warm them in a 350-degree oven for 10 minutes, or until hot.

❊} FOR THE CRANBERRY RELISH
1 cup fresh whole cranberries
Grated rind of 1 orange
½ cup sugar

In a food processor, chop the cranberries with the orange rind and sugar. Transfer to a small saucepan. Bring the mixture to a boil. Turn the heat to low and cook the cranberries just until they are softened and give up their liquid. Transfer the relish to a bowl. Set aside until ready to use.

❊} TO ASSEMBLE
8 thin slices smoked or roasted turkey breast

Split the biscuits in half. Spread a little of the relish on half of a biscuit. Top with a small slice of turkey breast. Close the sandwich. Repeat with the remaining biscuits and serve.

pita pizzas with goat cheese and scallions

We used to reserve pita bread for Middle Eastern dips, but lately we've begun to use it for other things, including these "pizzas." We heat the bread briefly, then top it with goat cheese and bake it quickly. You can also use pot or farmer cheese, mascarpone, or Jack cheese and scatter the rounds first with chopped tomatoes or slivered bell peppers. The goat cheese pizzas are one of our favorite instant hors d'oeuvres.

4 **medium pita breads**
4 **ounces fresh goat cheese**
   Olive oil, for sprinkling
1 **bunch scallions, finely chopped**
   Coarse salt and freshly ground black pepper, to taste

Set the oven at 400 degrees.

Place the pita rounds on a baking sheet. Heat them for 2 minutes. Dot them with cheese and return them to the oven for 5 minutes, or until they are warmed through and the cheese is hot.

Sprinkle the rounds with the oil, scallions, salt, and pepper. To serve, cut each round into wedges.

miniature croque monsieur

The French ham-and-cheese sandwiches called croque monsieur, which are crusty and brown with melted cheese spilling out at the sides, are just as delightful in miniature. We use regular white sandwich bread, French mustard, good ham, Gruyère cheese, and thin slices of ripe pear. The ham should be smoky, the mustard hot, and the pear sweet, just right with the melted Gruyère. Roll the bread first with a rolling pin, which flattens it slightly. Then build the sandwiches and fry them in a skillet like grilled cheese sandwiches. Cut them into squares and serve with red wine.

8 **slices fresh white sandwich bread**

1/4 **cup Dijon mustard**

4 **thin slices (4 ounces) flavorful ham, such as Black Forest or Westphalian**

1 **ripe Bartlett, Anjou, or Bosc pear, cored, seeded, and very thinly sliced**

4 **thin slices (4 ounces) Gruyère cheese**

4 **tablespoons (1/2 stick) butter, at room temperature**

Set the oven at 300 degrees.

Place the bread on a counter. With a rolling pin, roll it out as if you were rolling out dough. It should flatten but not tear. Spread the mustard on each bread slice.

Top 4 of the slices with ham, pear, and cheese. Set the remaining slices on top. With a serrated knife, cut the crusts off the sandwiches.

Spread the top side of each sandwich with a thin layer of butter.

Heat a large, nonstick skillet over medium-high heat. Place one or two sandwiches buttered side down in the hot pan. Brown the sandwiches for about 5 minutes, or until they are golden on the bottom.

While the sandwiches are cooking, spread a little butter on the sides facing up. Flip the sandwiches and brown the remaining side until the cheese melts and the sandwiches are hot. Keep the sandwiches warm in the oven, while you cook the remaining sandwiches in the same way. Transfer all of the sandwiches to a cutting board and slice each into quarters or thin rectangles. Serve at once.

gougères

Traditionally used to make éclairs or cream puffs, choux (pronounced *shoo*) paste is mixed in a saucepan and beaten hard. When you add grated Gruyère cheese to the dough, it becomes gougères. These cheese puffs are served hot as a nibble with a glass of wine before dinner. If you have a pastry bag with a plain round tip, use it to pipe the batter onto the baking sheets. Otherwise, shape them with a spoon. They'll puff nicely either way.

1   **cup all-purpose flour**
1   **teaspoon coarse salt**
1   **cup water**
8   **tablespoons (1 stick) unsalted butter, cut into pieces**
5   **large eggs, beaten to mix**
2½   **ounces Gruyère cheese, grated (1 cup)**

1   **large egg, beaten with 1 tablespoon water and ¼ teaspoon salt, for the glaze**

Set the oven at 400 degrees. Line two baking sheets with parchment paper.

Stir together the flour and salt in a medium bowl. Bring the water and butter to a boil in a medium saucepan. As soon as the butter melts and the water is rolling, remove the pan from the heat. Stir in the flour mixture until the dry ingredients are moistened and there are no lumps.

Return the saucepan to a burner set on medium-low and continue beating the dough for 30 seconds or until it comes away from the sides of the pan in one mass.

Reduce the heat to low and continue stirring the dough for 2 to 3 minutes to dry it out slightly. Remove the pan from the heat. With a wooden spoon, begin beating in 4 of the eggs, 2 tablespoons at a time. After each addition, beat the dough well.

Add the fifth egg, 1 teaspoon at a time, until the dough is very shiny and soft enough to fall gently off the spoon. (Leftover egg can be used for the glaze.) Beat in all but 3 tablespoons of the cheese.

Fit a pastry bag with a ½-inch plain round tip and pipe the dough onto the parchment in thirty 1½-inch mounds, leaving space around each. Or spoon the batter onto the parchment.

Using a pastry brush, coat each mound with the egg mixture. Dip a finger into the remaining egg and then smooth the tops. Sprinkle the remaining cheese on top.

Bake the gougères for 45 minutes, or until lightly browned.

Serve hot or transfer the gougères to a rack to cool and serve at room temperature within half a day.

onion tart

Made in a tart pan with a removable base, this onion tart — nothing but sautéed onions, bacon, and thyme baked on a sour cream pastry — can be cut into wedges and served as a first course garnished with a little salad. Alternatively, you can make a free-form tart (page 23). Or, double these proportions so they fill a professional-quality jelly-roll pan and cut the tart into big squares. The larger version is ideal for a reception.

FOR THE DOUGH

1½   **cups all-purpose flour, plus more for rolling**
1   **teaspoon salt**
8   **tablespoons (1 stick) unsalted butter, cut into pieces**
1   **large egg, lightly beaten**
¼   **cup sour cream**

In a food processor, pulse the flour and salt just to combine. Scatter the butter on the flour and pulse again until the mixture forms coarse crumbs.

In a small bowl, mix the egg and sour cream. Add the egg mixture to the flour. Pulse just until the dough forms large clumps; do not let it come together to form a ball.

Turn the dough out onto a lightly floured counter and shape it into a flat, round cake. Wrap the dough in foil and refrigerate it for 20 minutes.

On a lightly floured counter, roll the dough into a 12-inch round. Lift it onto the rolling pin and ease it into a 10-inch tart pan with a removable base. Turn the top edge of the dough onto itself like a hem.

Prick the bottom a dozen times and set the tart on a baking sheet. Refrigerate while you prepare the filling.

VARIATION
Free-Form Onion Tart

✳} FOR THE FILLING

4 **bacon strips**
1 **tablespoon butter**
2 **large onions, coarsely chopped**
½ **teaspoon coarse salt**
   Freshly ground black pepper, to taste
4 **tablespoons chopped fresh thyme**

To make the onion tart without a tart pan, roll the dough to a 12-inch round and turn in about ½ inch of the edge all around to make a raised border. Set the free-form tart on a parchment-lined baking sheet. Fill and bake as directed.

In a large skillet, fry the bacon, turning once, until it is golden brown. Remove it from the pan and transfer it to paper towels. When it is cool, crumble the bacon.

Discard the fat and wipe out the skillet. Melt the butter in the skillet, and cook the onions with the salt and pepper over medium heat for 15 minutes, or until they begin to brown at the edges. Stir in the bacon and thyme. Set aside to cool.

Set the oven at 400 degrees.

✳} TO ASSEMBLE

Spread the onion mixture in the tart shell. Bake the tart for 35 minutes, or until the pastry is golden.

Let sit for 10 minutes, then set the tart pan on a small bowl so the rim falls off. Use a wide metal spatula to slide the tart onto a flat platter or board. Cut the tart into wedges and serve.

honey-roasted chicken wings

If there are lots of kids in the crowd or you're worried about fussy eaters, you need a dependable recipe for chicken wings. Use the miniature drumstick part of the wing (sometimes called drumettes or Buffalo wings), if you can find them. Or use "party wings," whole wings with the smallest pieces removed. Otherwise, buy whole wings and cut them in half with scissors.

1	1-inch piece fresh ginger, peeled
½	cup hoisin sauce
½	cup orange juice
1	tablespoon vegetable oil
1	tablespoon toasted sesame oil
4	garlic cloves, finely chopped
1	tablespoon Dijon mustard or prepared Chinese mustard
	Freshly ground black pepper, to taste
16	chicken wings (3 pounds), halved, or 32 drumettes
½	cup honey

Using a fine grater, grate the ginger against the grain into a small mixing bowl. Stir in the hoisin sauce, orange juice, oils, garlic, mustard, and pepper.

Place the chicken wings in a baking dish and pour the marinade over the wings, tossing them in the mixture so they are coated all over. Cover the dish with plastic wrap and refrigerate for at least 4 hours or for as long as overnight.

Set the oven at 375 degrees.

Remove the wings from the marinade and place them in a single layer on a rimmed baking sheet. Pour the marinade into a small saucepan.

Roast the wings for 30 minutes, turning them once halfway through cooking.

Meanwhile, add the honey to the marinade and set the saucepan over medium heat. Bring to a boil and sim-

Kitchen Shears

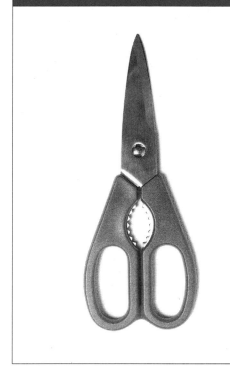

We find kitchen shears more convenient than knives for many tasks. Scissors are handy for trimming the edges of pastry, for cutting cooked potatoes into uniform pieces, for crushing tomatoes in a bowl, for snipping the stem ends off green beans, or for cutting cooked pasta to fit the lasagna pan. Any heavy-duty shears will work. We're partial to the ones made by Henckels (and everyone in our households knows that the shears are never used for paper or plastic). Fancier "half-hole" poultry shears, which have a tight spring and a half-moon shaped notch so you can cut through chicken bones, don't work any better than strong scissors.

mer, stirring often, for 8 minutes, or until the mixture is syrupy. Remove the wings from the oven.

Turn on the broiler. Broil the wings 12 inches from the broiling element, watching them carefully, for 2 minutes on a side, or until they are crisp. Brush them with marinade and serve at once.

mini crab cakes

Good crab cakes have as little filler as possible. This recipe uses bread crumbs and cornmeal to hold the crabmeat and eggs together. The crab cakes are delicate and therefore a little hard to handle. You drop them off the end of a spoon, and they spread quickly into 2½-inch rounds to make several bites. To serve as an hors d'oeuvre, you'll need small plates and forks. For a first course, make them larger (page 27) and serve with Pink Yogurt Sauce (page 32).

   2   large eggs
 ⅓   cup whole milk
   1   cup fresh white bread crumbs (see page 29)
 ⅓   cup yellow cornmeal
  12   ounces fresh lump crabmeat
   3   tablespoons grated raw onion
   1   cup fresh corn kernels (optional — see page 113)
       Pinch of cayenne pepper
 ½   teaspoon coarse salt, or to taste
 ¼   teaspoon freshly ground black pepper, or to taste
   3   tablespoons butter

In a medium bowl, combine the eggs and milk and beat them for 1 minute with a fork. Stir in the bread crumbs, cornmeal, crabmeat, onion, fresh corn (if using), cayenne pepper, salt, and black pepper. Cover the bowl with plastic wrap and refrigerate for 20 minutes.

Set the oven at 250 degrees.

Remove the crab mixture from the refrigerator and stir well. Melt 1 tablespoon of the butter in a large non-stick skillet. Use a soup spoon to drop 6 heaping mounds of the mixture into the pan, leaving room around each one. With the back of the spoon, flatten the cakes slightly and smooth out the edges to form neat cakes. If a few of the fresh corn kernels stray from the cakes, tuck them back in.

MAKES 8 CRAB CAKES

Prepare the crab cakes as directed for Mini Crab Cakes.

Use 2 tablespoons butter for half the batter. Place 4 mounds of butter in the skillet, flatten with a spoon, and fry for 5 minutes per side, or until the patties are golden brown. Use two forks to turn the patties over. Melt 2 more tablespoons butter and repeat with the remaining batter. Keep the patties warm as directed.

Cook the cakes over medium heat for 3 minutes per side, turning them halfway through cooking, or until they are golden brown and cooked through.

Transfer the crab cakes to a baking sheet and set them in the oven to keep warm. Use the remaining butter to fry the remaining cakes in the same way, making only 6 cakes at a time. Serve immediately.

note: These cakes may be made ahead of time and reheated just before serving. Reheat them in a 350-degree oven for 10 minutes, or until they are hot.

roasted asparagus
with panko bread crumbs

Julie's sister-in-law, Arlene Jacobs, a talented cook in New York, makes these with thick crunchy asparagus spears (thin spears won't hold the coating). She coats them in a mustard mayonnaise first, then rolls them in Japanese panko bread crumbs (see page 29), which are crispier than regular white crumbs. Use unseasoned dry white bread crumbs if you can't find panko.

- ¼ **cup mayonnaise**
- 2 **tablespoons Dijon mustard**
- 1 **teaspoon fresh lemon juice**
- ½ **teaspoon coarse salt, or to taste**
- ¼ **teaspoon freshly ground black pepper, or to taste**
- 1 **cup Japanese panko bread crumbs (see above)**
- 1 **pound thick asparagus spears, fibrous stems snapped off (see page 247)**
- 2 **tablespoons olive oil**

Set the oven at 450 degrees.

In a large, shallow bowl wide enough to hold the asparagus, whisk together the mayonnaise, mustard, lemon juice, salt, and pepper. Put the bread crumbs in another shallow bowl.

Oil a large rimmed baking sheet. Roll the asparagus in the mayonnaise mixture, then in the bread crumbs to coat them all over. Transfer the asparagus to the prepared baking sheet and sprinkle them with the oil. (The asparagus can be covered and refrigerated at this point and left for several hours before roasting.)

Roast the asparagus for 12 to 18 minutes, turning halfway through cooking, or until the crumbs are golden brown and the asparagus are tender but still have some bite. Sprinkle with salt and serve at once.

Bread Crumb Basics

The coarse white bread common in Japan, called **panko**, makes coarser, slightly sweet bread crumbs. They're more appealing than ordinary bread crumbs because they're crunchier and form a light crust or topping on a dish. Panko crumbs are available at most Asian markets or Japanese specialty stores. Use them for gratins (see page 254) or to coat fish (see page 156).

We use **fresh bread crumbs** to give ground mixtures structure, dry bread crumbs for coating.

To make fresh bread crumbs: Begin with a loaf of stale white bread. Cut it into thick slices and let the slices sit at room temperature for several hours.

Break each slice of bread into several pieces.

In a food processor, pulse the bread until it is reduced to coarse crumbs. Store the bread crumbs in an airtight container or in a plastic zipper bag in the freezer for up to 2 weeks.

To make dry bread crumbs

Cut a loaf of stale white bread into thick slices and dry them in a 250-degree oven for 30 minutes, or until the bread is crisp. Let cool to room temperature. Follow the instructions above for grinding to make fine crumbs, then store in the refrigerator.

vegetables with anchovy dipping sauce

This is our version of the popular sour cream dip that was standard at our parents' cocktail parties when we were kids. We mix the sour cream with mayonnaise now and add lots of anchovies, garlic, and parsley. The vegetables are seasonal: in the summer, you have your pick, and ideally, everything is raw, which saves time. A winter platter might include radishes, baby carrots, and cauliflower cut into florets.

FOR THE SAUCE

2 **cups fresh Italian parsley leaves**
3 **scallions**
3 **garlic cloves**
8 **flat anchovy fillets**
Generous squeeze of fresh lemon juice
1/2 **teaspoon freshly ground black pepper, or to taste**
3/4 **cup mayonnaise**
1/4 **cup sour cream**

Place the parsley, scallions, garlic, anchovies, lemon juice, and pepper in a food processor and pulse until finely chopped.

Add the mayonnaise and sour cream and pulse just until the sauce is smooth. Transfer it to a small serving bowl and cover tightly with plastic wrap. Refrigerate the sauce for at least 4 hours or for as long as 1 day, then prepare the vegetables.

❈⁓ FOR THE VEGETABLES

3 pounds small red or white potatoes

3 pounds slender green beans, trimmed

3 pounds asparagus spears, fibrous ends snapped off (see page 247)

2 pounds baby carrots

4 pickling cucumbers

In a large saucepan fitted with a steamer insert, steam the potatoes over several inches of boiling water, covered, over high heat for 15 to 20 minutes, or until they are tender when pierced with the tip of a knife. Remove from the pan and set aside to cool.

Add more water to the steamer so it comes up to the level of the insert. Steam the green beans, covered, over high heat for 3 minutes (they should still be bright green). Remove from the steamer and transfer to a bowl of ice water.

Add more water to the steamer. Steam the asparagus, covered, over high heat for 2 minutes (they should still be bright green). Remove from the steamer and transfer to the bowl of ice water.

Cut the potatoes into quarters. If the carrots are large, halve them lengthwise. Peel the cucumbers and slice them thickly on an extreme diagonal.

Arrange the vegetables on a platter in clusters — put the potatoes in three clusters on the platter, the green beans in three clusters, and so on. Cover the platter with wet paper towels and then with foil. Refrigerate the vegetables for up to 4 hours.

Serve with Anchovy Dipping Sauce.

sweet potato oven fries with homemade ketchup or pink yogurt sauce

Sweet potatoes don't turn crisp in the oven like baking potatoes do, but the edges caramelize a little and the flesh is meaty. Cut the potatoes into wedges, so you use all the skin and flesh. Pass a yogurt sauce seasoned with cocktail sauce (which turns the yogurt pink) or a simple homemade ketchup to dip them into. Make either sauce ahead of time and arrange the sweet potatoes on baking sheets in advance, but don't bake them until the last minute.

FOR THE PINK YOGURT SAUCE

- 1 **cup plain yogurt**
- 1/2 **cup sour cream**
- 3 **tablespoons grated onion**
- 1/2 **teaspoon ground cumin**
- 2 **tablespoons spicy bottled cocktail sauce, or to taste**
  Generous dash hot sauce
- 1/2 **teaspoon coarse salt, or to taste**
- 1/4 **teaspoon freshly ground black pepper, or to taste**

Combine the yogurt and sour cream in a small bowl. Add the onion, cumin, cocktail sauce, hot sauce, salt, and pepper. Stir thoroughly, then cover with plastic wrap and refrigerate until ready to use. Stir again just before serving.

Serve with Sweet Potato Oven Fries.

FOR THE KETCHUP

- 1 **tablespoon vegetable oil**
- 1 **red onion, finely chopped**
- 8 **ripe plum tomatoes, peeled, cored, and finely chopped**
- 2 **garlic cloves, finely chopped**
- 1/2 **teaspoon coarse salt, or to taste**
- 1/2 **teaspoon freshly ground black pepper, or to taste**
- 1/4 **cup balsamic vinegar**
- 1/4 **cup packed dark brown sugar**
- 1 **tablespoon grated fresh ginger**
  Pinch of ground allspice

Heat the oil in a heavy-bottomed saucepan. Add the onion and cook over medium heat, stirring often, for 10 minutes. Add the tomatoes, garlic, salt, and pepper, and cook for 1 minute, stirring.

Stir in the vinegar, brown sugar, ginger, and allspice. Bring to a boil, reduce the heat to low and simmer for 1 hour, or until the tomatoes are soft and the mixture has thickened. If it still seems too thin, continue cooking until it holds its shape. (Homemade ketchup will never thicken as much as the commercial variety.)

Remove from the heat and transfer to a small bowl. Let cool and use at room temperature, or store in an airtight container and refrigerate for up to 1 week.

note: For a smoother ketchup, puree it in a food processor.

❊⟩ FOR THE SWEET POTATO OVEN FRIES

4 **large sweet potatoes, scrubbed but unpeeled**
   Olive oil, for sprinkling
1 **teaspoon coarse salt, or to taste**
½ **teaspoon freshly ground black pepper, or to taste**

Set the oven at 400 degrees. Grease a rimmed baking sheet with some oil.

Use a sharp knife to quarter the potatoes lengthwise. Cut each quarter into thirds or fourths to make thick spears.

Place the spears flesh side up on two large baking sheets. Drizzle with the oil (about 3 tablespoons), and sprinkle with the salt and pepper. Roast the potatoes for 35 to 40 minutes, or until they are cooked through.

Serve immediately, giving the yogurt sauce or ketchup a stir just before serving.

devils on horseback

Devils on horseback have been around for as long as the English have been sipping sherry at teatime. They're made by wrapping bacon around chicken livers or plumped pitted prunes. Our devils are made with dates and stuffed with cheese. In the oven, the bacon turns crisp, the cheese melts, and the textures are dreamy together.

24 **large dates**
1/4 **pound Italian Fontina or raclette cheese, rind removed**
12 **strips bacon, halved crosswise**

Set the oven at 450 degrees.

Using a sharp paring knife, make a slit down one side of each date to expose the pit. Remove and discard the pits.

Cut the cheese into 24 pieces that will fit into the dates. Place the cheese inside the dates and pinch the dates back together. Wrap a piece of bacon around each date and secure with toothpicks.

Set the dates seam side up on a rimmed baking sheet. Roast for 20 to 25 minutes, until the bacon is crisp and the cheese melts.

Use tongs to transfer the dates to a plate lined with paper towels. Cool slightly and serve.

ceviche

Freshly caught fish is the only choice for ceviche because it is served raw after marinating in lime juice. Striped bass works especially well, but you can also use other fish, though nothing oily. Garnished with avocado and served on lettuce, this dish is perfect as an appetizer on a breezy summer night. You can also turn it into a lunch dish (preferably served overlooking the water). In that case, it will serve four. This recipe comes from fisherman Ron Murphy of Cape Cod, Massachusetts.

- 1 pound skinless, boneless striped bass or other nonoily white fish, such as flounder or scallops
- 1 cup fresh lime juice (about 5 limes)
- 1/2 red bell pepper, cored, seeded, and thinly sliced
- 1/2 green bell pepper, cored, seeded, and thinly sliced
- 1/2 red onion, thinly sliced
- 2 garlic cloves, finely chopped
- 1 teaspoon coarse salt, or to taste
- 1 jalapeño pepper, cored, seeded, and finely chopped

- 8 large romaine lettuce leaves
- 1/4 cup olive oil, or to taste
- 2 ripe avocados, cut into very thin slices
- 1/4 cup coarsely chopped fresh cilantro

Combine the striped bass, lime juice, red and green bell peppers, onion, garlic, salt, and jalapeño pepper in a shallow bowl. Turn the fish in the marinade. Cover with plastic wrap and refrigerate for 1 to 2 hours.

To serve, arrange the lettuce on a platter or on four salad plates. Use a slotted spoon to transfer the ceviche to the lettuce.

Drizzle with oil, garnish with avocado, and sprinkle with cilantro.

marinated shrimp in white wine vinaigrette

Sheryl's father was a career Army officer, so her parents often went to "Hail and Farewell" parties to send off the officers who were transferred and to welcome those just arriving. From then on for her, big platters of shrimp have been associated with great parties. This version is made by marinating cooked shrimp in a dressing of white wine vinegar, olive oil, ginger, garlic, and horseradish. In Sheryl's family, two pounds of shrimp do not go very far, but perhaps your guests will hold back. (Purchasing cooked, peeled shrimp cuts back on the preparation time.)

2	pounds jumbo shrimp
1/4	cup chopped fresh parsley
1	shallot
1	garlic clove
1	1-inch piece fresh ginger
1/8	teaspoon sugar
2	tablespoons white wine vinegar
2	tablespoons fresh lemon juice
1/4	cup olive oil
2	tablespoons bottled white horseradish
1/2	teaspoon coarse salt, or to taste
1/4	teaspoon freshly ground black pepper, or to taste
1	bunch watercress, stems removed

Bring a large pot of water to a boil. Add the shrimp. When the water returns to a boil, cook the shrimp for 2 minutes, or just until they are tender. Do not overcook them, or they'll be tough.

Drain the shrimp in a colander and rinse them with cold water until they are no longer hot. Peel the shrimp, devein them, and transfer them to a large plastic container.

In a food processor, pulse the parsley, shallot, garlic, ginger, and sugar until smooth. Add the vinegar and lemon juice and pulse just until thoroughly blended. With the machine running, add the oil in a steady stream, followed by the horseradish, salt, and pepper.

Spoon the marinade over the shrimp and turn the shrimp so they are coated all over. Cover the container and refrigerate for at least several hours or for as long as 1 day. Turn the shrimp in the marinade several times.

To serve, arrange the watercress on a platter. Remove the shrimp from the marinade and set them in concentric circles on the greens.

summer tomato soup in teacups

When tomatoes are so ripe that they barely need anything besides salt, we cook them in a pot with a few herbs and work them through a food mill. What results is the most glorious summer soup. Ladle it into teacups for guests to sip hot. We often make this soup in large quantities and freeze it for winter.

    1   tablespoon vegetable oil
3½–4   pounds (6 large) ripe tomatoes, cored and cut into 2-inch
           pieces
    1   teaspoon coarse salt, or to taste
    ½   teaspoon freshly ground black pepper, or to taste
         Large handful fresh herbs on their sprigs (thyme, basil,
           rosemary)
         Pinch of crushed red pepper
         Pinch of sugar

In a large, flameproof casserole, heat the oil and add the tomatoes, salt, and pepper. Cook over medium-high heat, stirring often, for 2 minutes, or until the tomatoes begin to release their juices.

Add the herbs and red pepper. Bring to a boil. (If the tomatoes are not very ripe, add ½ cup water and a pinch of sugar to the pan.) Turn the heat to low and cook the tomatoes for 15 minutes, or until they collapse completely.

Transfer the mixture, a little at a time, to a food mill set over a large bowl. Puree the tomatoes. Return the puree to the pan and heat it just until boiling. Taste for seasoning and add more salt and black pepper, if you like. Ladle it into teacups and serve at once.

creamy carrot soup
with just a little cream

For this creamy soup, carrots are simmered in water with a few tablespoons of short-grain rice (the kind you use for risotto). The rice adds enough body to the broth so the mixture needs only a little cream. Serve it in mugs with Turkey Salad with Green Beans and Dried Cranberries (page 73).

- 2 **tablespoons butter**
- 1 **large Spanish onion, coarsely chopped**
- 1/2 **teaspoon coarse salt, or to taste**
- 1/4 **teaspoon freshly ground black pepper, or to taste**
- 2 **garlic cloves, finely chopped**
- 1 **teaspoon ground cumin**
  Pinch of cayenne pepper
- 2 **pounds carrots, coarsely chopped**
- 2 1/2 **quarts water**
- 3 **tablespoons short-grain white rice**
- 2 **tablespoons fresh lemon juice**
- 3 **cups fresh or frozen (not thawed) green peas**
- 4 **tablespoons heavy cream**
- 1/4 **teaspoon ground nutmeg**
- 2 **tablespoons chopped fresh mint**

Melt the butter in a large, flameproof casserole. Add the onion, salt, and pepper. Cook over low heat, stirring occasionally, for 10 minutes, or until the onion softens.

Add the garlic, cumin, and cayenne and cook for 1 minute, stirring. Add the carrots, water, and rice. Bring the liquid to a boil. Reduce the heat to medium, and cook for 50 minutes, or until the carrots are very soft.

Lift out the solids with a slotted spoon, and puree them in a food processor; return them to the soup.

Add the lemon juice and peas. Simmer the soup, stirring occasionally, for 2 to 5 minutes, or until the peas are tender. Add the cream, nutmeg and mint, and warm through.

Taste the soup for seasoning, and add more salt or lemon juice, if you like. To serve, ladle the soup into mugs.

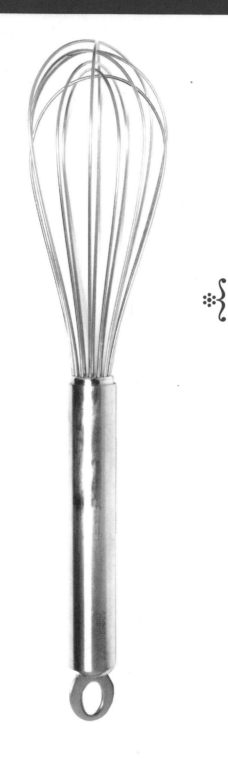

If we were to make a file of recipes for a cook who is harried and couldn't care less about the kitchen, we would include a simple roast chicken, a stew, a pasta dish, and several salads. Salads require very little fuss. You combine a few greens in one bowl and whisk some dressing together in another one, and especially if there is an unusual flavor or something particularly crunchy or a taste that's familiar but unexpected tossed with the greens, you look brilliant.

Generally, salads are eaten when people are hungry — at the beginning of the meal — so they're always well received. You're flooded with compliments for combining six ingredients together.

Both of us think that a meal isn't complete without a salad. We usually like a few greens that are lightly dressed with a good vinegar and a fine oil. Every week we wash lettuces as soon as we get home from the market, layer the leaves with paper towels, and slip them into a plastic zipper bag to store in the vegetable drawer of the fridge. The greens stay crisp all week, and making a salad is a breeze. On busy nights, after tearing up the lettuce, we drizzle it with oil from a bottle with a spout on top (we save empty wine bottles for this), add vinegar, also directly from the bottle, some coarse salt, and a few grinds of black pepper. Taste, adjust, and serve.

We tend to offer an array of salads at buffet dinners. One might be something green, such as Watercress and Endive Salad with Dried Cranberry Dressing. With that we'll make a potato salad in the warm weather. Russian Beet and Potato Salad tossed with golden beets and a half-sour pickle is a favorite. Grain salads such as Curried Brown Rice Salad with Cashews can be nourishing in the cold weather, but they're also fine potluck contributions for outdoor parties. Montreal Slaw means a long bout with your favorite hand-held slicing machine, but the slaw is so popular in Julie's house (and now in Sheryl's) that most of the people who try it go home and make it themselves. Some markets carry ready-shredded slaw, which saves lots of time.

Every once in a while, we walk slowly past the salad bar in the natural foods market where we shop and look over the array to see exactly what it is that other customers are drawn to. The lettuces are beautiful: cut-up romaine in one bin, mesclun greens in another. All the expected vegetables are there, along with hard-cooked eggs, beets, nuts, and chickpeas. The dressings are prepared in-house; there's coarse salt, and even a pepper mill.

Sheryl, who has made a salad to take work every day for the past eight years, stopped by the market to get something else one day and bought a salad from the bar. She called Julie from her desk at the *Boston Globe* to confess.

"Don't feel bad," Julie said. "I buy them all the time."

salads

iceberg lettuce with blue cheese dressing

Julie loves iceberg lettuce, particularly served in a wedge with tomatoes, red onion, and blue cheese dressing. The lettuce acts as a superb scoop for a rich dressing, the taste of which depends upon the cheese. Maytag is excellent, Roquefort is another good choice, Danish blue is milder. The dressing will stay in the refrigerator for several days. Stir before using.

- 1 head iceberg lettuce, cored and quartered
- 2 medium tomatoes, cored and sliced
- 1/2 medium red onion, thinly sliced
- 1/4 medium yellow onion
- 1 garlic clove
- 1/4 cup mayonnaise
- 1/4 cup sour cream
- 2 ounces blue cheese, coarsely crumbled
- 1 1/2 teaspoons white wine vinegar
- 1/2 teaspoon Worcestershire sauce

  Dash of hot sauce

  Coarse salt and freshly ground black pepper, to taste

Place a quarter of the lettuce on each of four salad plates. Surround them with the tomatoes and red onion.

In a food processor, pulse the yellow onion until it is finely chopped. With the machine running, drop the garlic through the feed tube and process until it is finely chopped.

Remove the top from the processor. Add the mayonnaise, sour cream, blue cheese, vinegar, Worcestershire sauce, hot sauce, salt, and pepper. Pulse just until the ingredients are combined but a few small chunks remain. Taste for seasoning and add more salt and pepper, if you like.

Spoon the dressing over each salad and serve.

wilted spinach salad
with eggs and walnuts

Raw spinach has a slightly gritty texture that doesn't suit us, so we wilt the greens with hot oil and dress them with honey-mustard vinegar, toasted walnuts, and chopped hard-cooked eggs. Serve with broiled fish or Steak Marchand de Vin with Caramelized Onions (page 152).

  2 tablespoons balsamic vinegar
  1 tablespoon honey
  1 teaspoon Dijon mustard
  1 pound fresh baby spinach, stems removed if large
  1/4 cup olive oil
  1 garlic clove, finely chopped
  2 hard-cooked eggs, coarsely chopped (see page 293)
  1/4 cup walnuts, toasted and coarsely chopped (see page 149)
     Coarse salt and freshly ground black pepper, to taste

In a small bowl, whisk together the vinegar, honey, and mustard. Set aside.

Place the spinach in a salad bowl. In a small skillet, heat the oil and cook the garlic for 15 seconds, or until you begin to notice its aroma. Remove from the heat and drizzle the oil over the spinach. Toss the leaves to coat and wilt them.

Add the eggs, walnuts, vinegar mixture, salt, and pepper. Toss again before serving.

arugula salad with orange dressing

In this salad, peppery, aniselike arugula leaves are mixed with mild red or green leaf lettuce and tossed with a dressing sweetened by orange juice and balsamic vinegar. Serve this as a first course before Roast Cornish Game Hens with Tomato-Caper Sauce (page 190) or Roast Rack of Pork (page 168), or use it as an accompaniment to Roast Pork Tenderloins with Caramelized Onions (page 86).

 1 **large bunch arugula, thick stems removed (about 4 cups)**
 1/2 **head red or green leaf lettuce, torn into pieces**
 1/4 **cup orange juice**
 2 **tablespoons balsamic vinegar**
 1/2 **teaspoon coarse salt, or to taste**
 1/2 **teaspoon freshly ground black pepper, or to taste**
 1/4 **cup olive oil**

Toss the arugula and lettuce in a large bowl.

In a small bowl, whisk together the orange juice, balsamic vinegar, salt, and pepper, just until the salt dissolves. Add the oil in a thin stream, whisking constantly.

Pour the dressing over the salad, toss thoroughly, and serve.

eggless caesar salad

This Caesar dressing omits the raw egg and has a high proportion of both Dijon mustard and Parmesan cheese, which sufficiently thickens it. Whole romaine lettuce hearts make a beautiful presentation, or use the outer leaves, cut up and arranged on a platter. Then sprinkle them with dressing, homemade croutons, and anchovy fillets, if you like. White anchovies are plumper and less salty.

FOR THE DRESSING

- 1 large garlic clove
- 2 anchovy fillets, coarsely chopped
- Juice of 1/2 lemon
- 2 teaspoons Dijon mustard
- 1 teaspoon Worcestershire sauce
- 1/2 teaspoon coarse salt, or to taste
- 1/2 teaspoon freshly ground black pepper, or to taste
- 1/4 cup freshly ground Parmesan cheese
- 1/3 cup olive oil

Turn on a food processor, and with the machine running, drop the garlic through the feed tube, processing until the garlic is chopped.

Add the anchovies, lemon juice, mustard, and Worcestershire sauce. Pulse until thoroughly mixed. Add salt, pepper, and cheese and mix until smooth.

With the machine running, gradually add the oil through the feed tube, 1 teaspoon at a time, until the dressing emulsifies. Taste for seasoning, add more salt and pepper, if you like, and set aside while you make the salad.

To Make Homemade Croutons

Use an unsliced white sandwich loaf, challah, or hearty country bread. Set the oven at 350 degrees. Slice the bread 1 inch thick, then cut the slices into ½-inch pieces. Spread them out on a rimmed baking sheet, sprinkle them lightly with vegetable oil, then toss them with your hands. Add only enough oil to moisten them lightly.

Toast the croutons, turning them often, for 20 minutes or until they are lightly golden. As the bread toasts, remove any pieces from the pan that are brown.

❋⸳ FOR THE SALAD

2 heads romaine hearts
Homemade croutons, made
with ¹/₄ loaf of bread
(see above)
¹/₂ cup freshly grated Parmesan
cheese, for sprinkling
8 anchovy fillets (optional)
Freshly ground black pepper,
to taste

Core the inner lettuce leaves, and arrange them on a platter so the tips of the leaves are all facing the same way.

❋⸳ TO ASSEMBLE

Sprinkle the leaves with croutons, dressing, and the Parmesan cheese. Place the anchovies, if using, on the lettuce leaves, sprinkle the croutons over them, and season with pepper. Serve.

montreal slaw

Vinegary and crunchy without a trace of mayonnaise and with just a little oil, this slaw is standard fare in Montreal. Everyone we know who tastes it never goes back to the old-fashioned mayonnaise version. It's wonderful on the Thanksgiving table and to accompany ordinary stews, such as Yankee Pot Roast with Caramelized Vegetables (page 128), and Herb-Roasted Flattened Chicken (page 192). It needs to sit for several hours before serving, until the cabbage begins releasing its liquid. The following day, however, the slaw is still very crunchy, but mellow. We grate the cabbage on a Feemster's Famous Vegetable Slicer (right) or a mandoline. The shredding blade on a food processor will turn the cabbage to mush, but it's fine for the carrots.

> 1 **large green cabbage, quartered and cored**
> 2 **tablespoons coarse salt**
> 4 **carrots, grated (see page 49)**
> 1 **green bell pepper, cored, seeded, and cut into 2-inch strips**
> 1 **bunch scallions, thinly sliced**
> 3–6 **tablespoons sugar**
> 1/2 **cup distilled white vinegar**
> 3 **tablespoons canola oil**

Shred the cabbage and transfer it to a large colander, sprinkling the layers with salt.

Set the colander in a large bowl, cover loosely with plastic wrap, and set aside for 30 minutes.

With your hands, press the cabbage to remove the excess moisture and transfer to a large bowl. Add the carrots, green pepper, and scallions and toss thoroughly.

Sprinkle the vegetables with 3 tablespoons of the sugar, the vinegar, and the oil. Toss again. Taste for seasoning and add more salt, sugar, or vinegar, if you like. Cover the bowl with plastic wrap and refrigerate the slaw for at least 2 hours or for as long as overnight. Toss again just before serving.

To Grate Vegetables

Root vegetables such as radishes and carrots make fine grated salads, but you have to be careful to grate the vegetables rather than shred them into mush. Doing that successfully depends upon the grater. Some very good models are available in Asian specialty markets; well-stocked kitchen shops also carry Asian implements. The best are hand-held stainless steel grating and slicing machines made in China or Japan ($10 to $30). Look for graters with small, sharp openings, which will produce long, slender pieces of vegetables.

The grating blade on a food processor works well if the feed tube is full and if the vegetables about to be grated, such as carrots, are cut into pieces and are lying on their sides as they hit the grater. Standing vegetables in the food processor feed tube results in short, unattractive pieces.

We've had the least success with the standard box grater, in which the largest openings don't seem to be sharp enough to work well.

grated radish salad with parsley

Treat this salad like a relish and spoon it alongside grilled fish or chicken. Use the grating blade on the food processor, a box grater, or one of the new hand-held Microplane brand graters, available at most cookware shops.

   2 **bunches radishes, trimmed**
   1 **bunch scallions (white part only), thinly sliced**
 1/2 **cup chopped fresh parsley**
2 1/2 **tablespoons red wine vinegar**
 1/2 **teaspoon coarse salt, or to taste**
 1/4 **teaspoon freshly ground black pepper, or to taste**
 1/4 **cup olive oil**

Coarsely grate the radishes. Transfer them to a salad bowl. Add the scallions and parsley and toss thoroughly.

In a small bowl, whisk together the vinegar, salt, and pepper. Drizzle in the oil, adding 1 teaspoon at a time and whisking constantly, until the dressing emulsifies.

Pour enough of the dressing over the salad to moisten it and toss to mix. Taste for seasoning and add more salt and pepper, if you like, before serving.

cucumber and sweet onion salad

Made without oil, this salad of cucumbers, onion, and rice vinegar can be served beside rich fish, such as Roast Side of Salmon (page 200), or rich meat, such as Braised Beef in Balsamic Vinegar (page 236). We slice the cucumbers on a Feemster's Famous Vegetable Slicer (page 263) or on a mandoline. Lacking either one, use a knife. If you grow the cucumbers yourself or get them from a farmers' market, don't bother peeling them. Seasoned rice vinegar, which contains salt and sugar, is available at Asian and specialty markets.

8 pickling cucumbers or 2 English cucumbers
1 large sweet onion (Oso Sweet, Walla Walla, Vidalia, or
       another super-sweet variety), halved and thinly sliced
2 tablespoons seasoned rice vinegar
1/2 teaspoon coarse salt, or to taste
1/2 teaspoon freshly ground black pepper, or to taste
1/4 cup chopped fresh dill

Peel the cucumbers and slice them as thinly as possible. Layer the cucumbers, onion slices, vinegar, salt, pepper, and dill in a medium bowl.

Cover the bowl with plastic wrap and refrigerate the salad for at least 2 hours or for up to 1 day. Toss before serving.

roasted pear, walnut, and goat cheese on greens

Composed salads are ideal first courses. You set the ingredients out on the counter and simply arrange them on a plate, then serve the salad without tossing. Here, the pears are sliced lengthwise — each slice has the classic shape — and roasted in a low oven until they caramelize at the edges. You can use very ripe pears and omit the roasting, if you prefer.

Serve this as an appetizer before a roast pork dinner or alongside broiled fish or chicken breasts.

> 2 **firm Bosc or Bartlett pears**
> 1/2 **head red or green leaf lettuce, cored and pulled apart into leaves**
> 2 **ounces firm fresh goat cheese, cut into thick slices**
> 1/2 **cup walnut halves, toasted (see page 149)**
> 2 **tablespoons balsamic vinegar**
> 1/2 **teaspoon coarse salt, or to taste**
> 1/4 **teaspoon freshly ground black pepper, or to taste**
> 1/3 **cup olive oil**

Set the oven at 250 degrees, and oil a rimmed baking sheet.

Without peeling the pears, halve them lengthwise. With the tip of a paring knife, remove the cores and stems. Cut the pears lengthwise into 1/8-inch-thick slices. Set the slices on the baking sheet.

Roast the pears for 40 to 50 minutes, or until they begin to turn golden at the edges.

Divide the greens among 4 salad plates. Arrange the pear slices, cheese, and walnuts over the greens.

In a small bowl, whisk together the vinegar, salt, and pepper just until the salt dissolves. Drizzle in the oil 1 teaspoon at a time. When half the oil is added, pour in the remaining oil in a thin, steady stream, whisking constantly until the dressing emulsifies.

Drizzle the dressing over the salads. Sprinkle with a little more salt and pepper, if you like. Serve at once without tossing.

french market salad with bacon and eggs

This salad is on many café menus in France. The greens — usually curly frisée — and thick unsmoked pieces of bacon are topped with a poached egg. When you break the egg, it spills into the dressing and enriches the sauce. Everything about it seems lavish. This version contains smoky bacon (use slab bacon, if you can find it, since the quality is better) and soft-cooked eggs because they're easier to make. Serve with crusty bread.

- 4   thick slices bacon
- 1   head (about 8 cups) frisée, chicory, escarole, arugula, or other bitter greens (or a mixture), torn up
- 3   tablespoons red wine vinegar
- 1   teaspoon Dijon mustard
- 1/2   teaspoon coarse salt, or to taste
- 1/4   teaspoon freshly ground black pepper, or to taste
- 1/3   cup olive oil
- 4   soft-cooked eggs (see page 55)

In a skillet, render the bacon over medium-high heat, turning it often, until it is crisp. Transfer to a plate lined with paper towels. When the bacon is cool, place the greens and bacon in a salad bowl.

In a small bowl, whisk together the vinegar, mustard, salt, and pepper. Drizzle in the oil a few drops at a time. When half the oil is added, pour in the remaining oil in a thin, steady stream, whisking constantly until the dressing emulsifies. Pour the dressing over the salad a little at a time, tossing the leaves to coat them.

Arrange the salad on each of four dinner plates. Scoop the soft-cooked eggs out of the shells and add to each salad. Sprinkle with more black pepper and serve at once.

To Soft-Cook Eggs

Bring a large pot of water to a boil. The pot should be large enough to hold the eggs in one layer. With a straight pin, prick a hole in the rounded end of each egg. Using a slotted spoon, lower the eggs into the boiling water. Return the water to a low boil and cook the eggs for exactly 5 minutes.

Drain the eggs and run them under cold water just until they are cool enough to handle. Choose a spoon that is the same size as the eggs. With the back of it, crack only the pointed end of the egg. Peel the pointed end of the egg (or the entire egg if you can do it without tearing the white). Insert the spoon into the egg between the shell and the white (top left) and gently scoop the egg out of the shell (top right). Peel the remaining eggs in the same way.

watercress and endive salad with dried cranberry dressing

The peppery leaves of watercress, mixed with sliced endive and leaf lettuce, are tossed with dried cranberries, scallions, and toasted pecans. Use this salad as a bed for leftover turkey or roast chicken or serve it as a first course.

2 Belgian endives, sliced thickly on the diagonal
1 bunch watercress, stems removed
1/2 head red or green leaf lettuce, torn up
4 scallions, trimmed and cut into 1-inch pieces
2 tablespoons white wine vinegar
1 teaspoon Dijon mustard
1/2 teaspoon coarse salt, or to taste
1/2 teaspoon freshly ground black pepper, or to taste
1 garlic clove, finely chopped
1/4 cup olive oil
1/4 cup dried cranberries

1/2 cup pecans, toasted and coarsely chopped (see page 149)

In a large bowl, combine the endives, watercress, lettuce, and scallions. Toss gently and set aside.

In a small bowl, whisk together the vinegar, mustard, salt, pepper, and garlic. Drizzle in the oil 1 teaspoon at a time. When half the oil is added, pour in the remaining oil in a thin, steady stream, whisking constantly until the dressing emulsifies. Use a spoon to stir in the dried cranberries.

Just before serving, drizzle enough dressing on the greens to coat them thoroughly and sprinkle with pecans. Lift the berries from the dressing and toss them with the salad before serving.

note: Leftover dressing can be stored in the refrigerator and used on any other lettuce salad.

greek cypriot village salad

Real Greek salads are made from romaine lettuce, tomatoes, pickling cucumbers, and bell peppers, all chopped finely and tossed with a lemony dressing, olives, and feta cheese. In the Greek villages of Cyprus, where this version comes from, the salad also includes a sprinkling of sumac (a spicy red powder ground from sumac berries, sold in Middle Eastern markets) and a deeply aromatic dried oregano that grows wild in the hills. Agni Charalambous Thurner, who was raised in Kakopepria in Greek Cyprus and now lives in Belmont, Massachusetts, still makes this salad often. She suggests using either dried basil or mint in place of the wild oregano. Romaine lettuce, she says, is chewier and has more flavor than iceberg lettuce, which is so often used in this country to make Greek salad.

$1/2$ head romaine lettuce, cored and chopped

1 bunch scallions, thinly sliced

4 pickling cucumbers, peeled, seeded, and chopped

3 medium tomatoes, seeded and chopped

1 green bell pepper, cored, seeded, and chopped

$1/4$ cup pitted Kalamata olives, chopped

4 ounces feta cheese, crumbled

1 teaspoon sumac (optional)

3 tablespoons fresh lemon juice

2 teaspoons dried basil or mint

$1/2$ teaspoon coarse salt, or to taste

$1/2$ teaspoon freshly ground black pepper, or to taste

$1/4$ cup olive oil

In a medium bowl, combine the lettuce, scallions, cucumbers, tomatoes, and green pepper. Add the olives and feta cheese. Sprinkle with the sumac, if using. Set aside.

In a small bowl, whisk together the lemon juice, basil or mint, salt, and pepper. Drizzle in the oil 1 teaspoon at a time. When half the oil is added, pour in the remaining oil in a thin, steady stream, whisking constantly until the dressing emulsifies. Taste for seasoning and add more salt, pepper, or herbs, if you like.

Before serving, sprinkle the salad with a few spoonfuls of the dressing, toss gently but thoroughly, and add enough of the remaining dressing to moisten the greens lightly. Serve at once.

creamy potato salad with bacon and scallions

This salad uses red potatoes, which hold their shape during cooking and look nice with their skins on. One of the tricks to a good salad is to sprinkle the hot potatoes with cider vinegar. They absorb it as they cool and the salad tastes better later. Try to use potatoes that are slightly larger than eggs.

16 small red potatoes (3–3 1/2 pounds)
2 tablespoons cider vinegar, plus more for sprinkling
1/2 teaspoon coarse salt, or to taste
1/2 teaspoon freshly ground black pepper, or to taste
5 strips bacon, rendered until golden brown, broken up into pieces
4 celery stalks, halved lengthwise and thinly sliced
1/2 red onion, finely chopped
1/4 cup chopped fresh parsley
3/4 cup mayonnaise
2 tablespoons warm water, or more if needed
1/2 teaspoon sugar

1 bunch scallions, trimmed and thinly sliced on an extreme diagonal

In a saucepan fitted with a steamer insert, steam the potatoes over several inches of boiling water, covered, over high heat, for 15 to 20 minutes, or until they are tender when pierced with a skewer. (If your pan is too small for a steamer insert, you can boil the potatoes for 15 to 20 minutes.) Use a slotted spoon to remove the potatoes from the pan and put them in a large shallow bowl.

When they are still quite hot, slice the potatoes 1/4 inch thick. Sprinkle them with the vinegar, salt, and pepper. Cool, stirring occasionally. Gently but thoroughly stir in the bacon, celery, onion, and parsley.

In a small bowl, whisk together the mayonnaise, 1 tablespoon of the water, sugar, and a pinch each of salt and pepper. The dressing should be of pouring consistency. If it's too thick, add more water, 1 teaspoon at a time.

Pour the dressing over the potatoes, and toss gently. Taste for seasoning and add more vinegar, salt, and pepper, if you like. Garnish with scallions and serve or cover tightly with plastic wrap and refrigerate for several hours.

wheat berry salad
with sugar snap peas and almonds

Wheat berries, whole kernels of wheat, are tiny round beads that need soaking and simmering. We get them at the local health food store. When cooked, they are delightfully chewy, and they're delicious mixed with crisp vegetables in a salad. This is nice beside Herb-Roasted Flattened Chicken (page 192) or Roast Pork Tenderloins with Caramelized Onions (page 86).

1 **cup wheat berries, soaked overnight and drained**
1 **quart water**
1/4 **pound sugar snap peas, strings removed, thinly sliced**
1 **yellow bell pepper, cored, seeded, and cut into thin strips**
1 **sweet onion (Vidalia, Maui, or Walla Walla), cut into thin strips**
1/4 **cup slivered almonds, toasted (see page 149)**
1/4 **cup golden raisins**
1/4 **cup chopped fresh cilantro**
1/2 **teaspoon coarse salt, or to taste**
1/2 **teaspoon freshly ground black pepper, or to taste**
1/4 **cup olive oil**
1 **tablespoon honey**

Put the wheat berries and water in a medium saucepan and bring the water to a boil. Turn the heat to medium-low, and cook for 50 to 55 minutes, or until the berries are tender but still have some bite.

Drain the berries and transfer them to a medium bowl to cool. Fluff the berries with a fork, cover with plastic wrap, and refrigerate them for 1 hour, or until they are cold.

Fluff the berries again. With the fork, gently stir in the sugar snap peas, bell pepper, onion, almonds, raisins, cilantro, salt, and pepper. Toss gently but thoroughly.

Pour the oil into a small bowl. Dip a 1-tablespoon measure into the oil to coat it. Then measure the honey (it will roll right off the spoon). Stir the honey into the oil.

Pour the dressing over the wheat berries. Toss gently again. Taste for seasoning and add more salt and pepper, if you like. Cover the salad with plastic wrap and refrigerate for at least 1 hour or for as long as overnight before serving.

russian beet and potato salad

The classic Russian beet salad was created in the czarist court in the nineteenth century, when French chefs were cooking in Russia. That salad combined the country's plentiful beets with French mayonnaise and half-sour pickles, which added a little bite to the rich dressing. Instead of the traditional crimson beets, which turn the salad pink, we like to use the beautiful golden beets now available. When they're combined with potatoes and carrots — the other classic ingredients — the whole salad becomes golden. Other versions of this salad include peas, cucumbers, and onions. You can also make this with red beets, of course, in the usual manner. Serve with rye bread and butter.

4 large golden beets, trimmed
1/4 cup canola oil, plus more for sprinkling
1/4 teaspoon coarse salt, or to taste
1/4 teaspoon freshly ground black pepper, or to taste
2 russet potatoes, peeled and quartered
2 large carrots, cut into thirds
1 bunch scallions (white part only), thinly sliced
1 sour or half-sour pickle, cut into 1-inch strips
2 tablespoons cider vinegar
2 tablespoons mayonnaise
1/2 teaspoon sugar
1/4 cup chopped fresh parsley
2 tablespoons chopped fresh dill

6 leaves Boston or leaf lettuce, for serving

Set the oven at 400 degrees.

Place the beets in a small baking dish and sprinkle them with a little oil, salt, and pepper. Pour 1/2 inch of water into the dish, cover it with foil, shiny side down, and roast the beets for 50 minutes, or until they are tender when pierced with a skewer.

Remove the beets from the oven, uncover them, and set them aside until they are cool enough to handle.

Meanwhile, in a saucepan fitted with a steamer insert, steam the potatoes and carrots over several inches of boiling water, covered, over high heat for 20 minutes, or until tender. Check the vegetables after 15 minutes and remove any that are tender when pierced with a skewer. Set aside to cool.

Cut the potatoes and carrots into ½-inch cubes and place in a medium bowl. Add the scallions and pickle.

Using your hands or a paring knife, slip the skins off the beets. Cut the beets into ½-inch cubes and transfer them to the bowl.

In a small bowl, whisk together the vinegar, mayonnaise, a pinch each of salt and pepper, and the sugar. Whisk in the ¼ cup oil a few drops at a time.

Pour the dressing over the vegetables and toss them gently to coat them all over.

Stir in the parsley and dill. Taste for seasoning and add more salt and pepper, if you like. Cover the salad and refrigerate it for at least several hours and for up to 1 day before serving. To serve, spoon the salad onto the lettuce leaves.

curried brown rice salad with cashews

Sheryl has been making this salad — or a version of it — since the 1970s. It has grated carrots, red bell pepper, toasted cashews, and lots of ginger. The curry powder you use is important. A good imported one from an Indian market will give you depth and some heat. That flavor will mellow if you store the salad overnight.

⁂} FOR THE RICE
- 1¹/₂ **cups long-grain brown rice**
- 3 **cups water**
- ¹/₈ **teaspoon coarse salt**

Rinse the rice thoroughly in a fine-mesh strainer.

Put the rice, water, and salt in a large saucepan, and bring to a boil, stirring often. Reduce the heat to low, cover the pan, and simmer for 40 minutes. Remove from the heat and set aside for 15 minutes.

Transfer the rice to a large bowl and stir it often until it cools.

Meanwhile, make the salad.

note: To serve the rice hot on its own, fluff it with a fork after it has rested for 15 minutes.

❊⟩ FOR THE SALAD
2 tablespoons peanut oil
2 tablespoons finely chopped fresh ginger
1/4 cup golden raisins
1/4 cup dark raisins
1 tablespoon curry powder
1 1/2 cups grated carrots
1 bunch scallions, cut into 1/2-inch pieces
1/2 red onion, cut into thin strips
1 red bell pepper, cored, seeded, and cut into thin strips
1/4 cup chopped fresh parsley
1/2 cup cashews, toasted (see page 149)
1/2 teaspoon coarse salt, or to taste
1/2 teaspoon freshly ground black pepper, or to taste
3 tablespoons rice vinegar

Heat the oil in a small skillet, and cook the ginger, the raisins, and the curry powder for 1 minute, stirring constantly.

Spoon the curry mixture over the cooled rice. Add the carrots, scallions, onion, red pepper, parsley, cashews, salt, and pepper. Toss gently but thoroughly. Drizzle the rice with the vinegar and toss again.

Taste for seasoning, add more salt and pepper, if you like, and transfer to a plastic container. Cover and refrigerate for at least 2 hours or for as long as overnight for the flavors to mellow before serving.

lebanese bread salad (fattoush)

Stale-bread salads and soups are popular in all cultures in which bread is important to the diet. This Lebanese bread salad is made with toasted stale pita, which is tossed with tomatoes, cucumbers, scallions, bell pepper, mint, and parsley. There is a lot of chopping here, but you get a big, impressive-looking salad. Seta Keshishian, an Armenian cook who was born in Beirut, makes hers with sumac, a red spice ground from the sumac berry, and Aleppo pepper, which gives a warm heat. You can omit both of them if you don't live near a Middle Eastern grocery, but add some ground black pepper instead.

- 2 bunches flat-leaf parsley (about 3 cups leaves), coarsely chopped
- 1 bunch scallions, thinly sliced
- 1/2 bunch fresh mint (about 1 cup leaves), coarsely chopped
- 4 medium tomatoes, quartered, seeded, and cut into strips
- 2 cucumbers, peeled, seeded, and finely chopped
- 1 red bell pepper, cored, seeded, and cut into thin strips
- 1/3 cup olive oil
- 1/4 cup fresh lemon juice
- 2 tablespoons sumac (see above; optional)
- 2 teaspoons ground Aleppo pepper (see above; optional)
- 1 teaspoon coarse salt, or to taste
- 3 medium pitas, torn into small pieces and toasted (see page 13)

In a medium bowl, combine the parsley, scallions, mint, tomatoes, cucumbers, bell pepper, oil, lemon juice, sumac and Aleppo pepper (if using), and salt. Stir gently but thoroughly.

Just before serving, add the toasted pita and toss well.

spanish roasted vegetable salad (escalivada)

This roasted vegetable salad sprinkled with a sherry vinaigrette is the sort of dish you can add to a buffet (the vegetarians will be pleased). This version is served as part of the tapas table at Taberna de Haro, a restaurant in Brookline, Massachusetts.

❊} FOR THE SALAD

- 2 **large eggplants (2–2^1/2 pounds)**
- 4 **red bell peppers**
- 4 **green bell peppers**
- 3 **Spanish onions, cut into 8 wedges**
   Olive oil, for drizzling
- 1 **teaspoon coarse salt, or to taste**

Set the oven at 350 degrees.

In a roasting pan large enough to hold all the vegetables, arrange the whole eggplants, whole red and green peppers, and onion wedges. Drizzle the vegetables with olive oil. Roast the vegetables for 2 hours or until tender, turning them every 30 minutes.

When the eggplants are cool enough to handle, slit them down the center and peel off the skin. Cut them into long 1-inch-wide strips and arrange them on a platter.

Peel the peppers, discarding the skin and seeds. Slice the peppers into 1-inch strips. Arrange them on the platter. Add the onions to the platter. Salt the vegetables lightly and set them aside until they are cool. Meanwhile, make the dressing.

❊} FOR THE DRESSING

- 2 **tablespoons Spanish sherry vinegar**
- 1 **teaspoon coarse salt, or to taste**
- ^{1}/2 **teaspoon freshly ground black pepper, or to taste**
- ^{1}/4 **cup olive oil**
- 3 **tablespoons chopped fresh parsley**

In a bowl, whisk together the vinegar, salt, and pepper. Whisk in the olive oil 1 teaspoon at a time, until the dressing is emulsified.

Spoon enough of the dressing over the vegetables to moisten them.
Sprinkle with parsley and serve.

Cooking for company is satisfying, and the gesture is certainly generous. Cooking for your family is both of those and, we think, is one of the most important things you can do for them. It's not the nutrition that matters, though well-balanced meals are nourishing. It's providing a warm setting where good conversation can take place, where the kids can tell you what they're up to, where you can laugh together over the silliest thing.

In most households, family supper is given short shrift. The cook is always in a rush, and few people are willing to devote much energy to this meal at the most exhausted time of day. That's one of the reasons pizza carryout statistics are so high. We're not entirely against calling up for pizza. But we don't think it should be the steady diet in any household.

We're often asked what to do about the nightly meal and how to remove the drudgery from it. We always suggest having a plan, rather than deciding what to do at 5 p.m. That doesn't mean you need to know the week's menus in advance (though this is a great system for large families), but you should know several nights' meals.

To begin, think of these dishes as one-pot meals, the modern version of a casserole. Once you give up the notion of preparing a supper that Mrs. Cleaver might have fed Beaver and Wally — a piece of meat with a vegetable and potato — you'll be happier. When you assemble Chicken Roasted on a Bed of Apples, for instance, you have apples and onions as the accompaniment and succulent chicken on top. As for the timing, there's virtually nothing to do but cut the fruit and vegetables and sea-son the breasts. Lentil and Smoked Turkey Soup is another meal-in-a-pot, morsels of smoked turkey in a hearty broth. The soup will take 45 minutes to simmer, but it will cook unattended, with an occasional stir when you happen by.

When you have a dish that seems to work well, make it several more times. Make it once a week, so it becomes yours. When you tire of it (your family will probably speak up before you're ready to hear them), start making another dish. Then you have two meals, and you can rotate them. Eventually you'll have a decent weeknight repertoire.

Everyone cooks well when the dish is familiar. You should be able to dash into the grocery store without a list for some of the dishes you make. It's comforting for the cook to be able to produce something so easily, and it's also reassuring to the family to sit down to a favorite meal. To give just one example, Ten-Minute Bolognese doesn't require much time, and the pickiest kids seem to like it. Someday, in fact, you might find that it edges out pizza.

when you're in a rush

lentil and smoked turkey soup

Use whatever kind of brown or green lentils you can find. We like Beluga lentils, which are smaller and plumper than the regular kind and firmer than the green French Le Puy variety. We find both at our local natural foods market; they're also at specialty stores. Here, they're simmered with smoked turkey breast, onion, and carrots.

1	**Spanish onion, finely chopped**
4	**carrots, finely chopped**
1/2	**teaspoon coarse salt, or to taste**
1/2	**teaspoon freshly ground black pepper, or to taste**
1	**teaspoon ground cumin**
3/4	**pound (three 1/8-inch-thick slices) smoked turkey breast, coarsely chopped**
1	**pound (2 cups) Beluga lentils (see above)**
	Pinch of crushed red pepper
6 1/2	**cups chicken stock**
1	**tablespoon chopped fresh thyme**

In a large, flameproof casserole, combine the onion, carrots, salt, pepper, cumin, turkey, lentils, crushed pepper, 6 cups of the chicken stock, and thyme. Bring the mixture to a boil, lower the heat, and simmer the soup, stirring occasionally, for 30 minutes.

Remove 2 cups of the solids from the pot and transfer to a large soup bowl. With a fork, mash the solids. Return the mashed solids to the pot. Add the remaining 1/2 cup chicken stock.

Continue to cook for 15 minutes more, or until the lentils are tender. Taste for seasoning and add more salt, crushed red pepper, or black pepper, if you like. Ladle into bowls and serve.

hot and sour soup

Massachusetts restaurateur Alice Hui scaled down her hot and sour soup so we could make it at home. It's a good family supper dish. Like all Chinese dishes, you need to assemble everything and have all the ingredients ready beside the stove: pork loin, tofu, bamboo shoots, straw mushrooms, eggs, and seasonings. Then the soup cooks in minutes. In a pinch, we've made it with delicatessen turkey cut into strips (substitute it ounce for ounce for the pork). In that case, skip the initial cooking and add the turkey to the soup with the tofu and bamboo shoots. This soup also can be made for vegetarians: just omit the meat and use vegetable stock. Serve with bowls of steamed rice and fresh pineapple for dessert.

1   boneless pork loin chop (8 ounces), trimmed of all fat
1   package (15–16 ounces) soft tofu
2   quarts chicken stock
1   can (8 ounces) sliced bamboo shoots, drained and coarsely
      chopped
1   can (15 ounces) straw mushrooms, drained and sliced
3   tablespoons soy sauce
1   teaspoon coarse salt
1   teaspoon freshly ground black pepper, or to taste
2½ tablespoons cornstarch, mixed with 6 tablespoons cold
      water
2   large eggs, lightly beaten
2   tablespoons rice wine vinegar, or to taste

4   scallions, finely chopped
    Dark sesame oil, for sprinkling

Cut the pork and tofu into strips that are 2 inches long and ½ inch wide (top right). Set aside.

Heat the stock in a large flame-proof casserole. Add the pork, tofu, bamboo shoots, mushrooms, soy sauce, salt, and pepper. Bring the mixture to a boil and lower the heat to simmer.

Stir the cornstarch and water in a small bowl until the mixture is smooth. Add it to the soup and return the soup to a boil.

Pour the eggs on top of the soup in a circle (bottom right). Turn off the heat and pour the vinegar over the eggs.

Taste for seasoning, and add more pepper if the soup is not hot enough, or more vinegar, if you like.

To serve, ladle the soup into bowls. Garnish with scallions and sprinkle a few drops of sesame oil into each bowl.

fried rice with ham and eggs

Exceptional fried rice is very different from the kind you get in restaurants. This one is Japanese and very lightly seasoned. The rice should be freshly made. The recipe comes from Junko Hirano, who lives in Fukuoka in the south of Japan. She lived with Sheryl for a year and made this several times a week. Children adore it.

*} FOR THE COOKED RICE
 1 1/2 cups long-grain white rice
 2 3/4 cups water
   1 teaspoon coarse salt

In a fine-mesh strainer, rinse the rice under cold water and set it aside to drain for a few minutes. Transfer the rice to a saucepan with a tight-fitting lid. Pour in the water, add the salt, and bring to a boil. Cover, reduce the heat to low, and cook for exactly 20 minutes. Without opening the pan, remove it from the heat. Let the rice stand for 10 minutes. Fluff with a fork and set aside.

*} FOR THE FRIED RICE
   2 tablespoons vegetable oil
 1/4 pound baked ham, finely chopped
 1/2 medium onion, finely chopped
   2 large eggs, lightly beaten
 1 1/2 cups frozen peas, thawed
   2 tablespoons soy sauce

Heat the oil in a large, deep skillet, and cook the ham and onion over low heat, stirring occasionally, for 8 minutes, or until the onion is tender.

Add the hot rice to the pan and cook, stirring, for 2 minutes, or until the rice and ham are thoroughly combined.

Add the eggs and continue cooking, stirring constantly, until you can see pieces of scrambled egg in the rice. Add the peas, then the soy sauce, a few drops at a time, still stirring, to distribute it evenly. Cook the rice until it is evenly coated with the soy sauce. Serve.

turkey salad with green beans and dried cranberries

We make this main-dish salad with leftover roast turkey, but when the weather gets hot and we don't feel like cooking, we buy turkey from the deli. Ask for it thickly sliced, so you can cut the meat into strips. The dressing has a mild sweet-and-sour taste from lots of vinegar and dried cranberries, and there's plenty of crunch from celery and green beans. If you're in a mad rush, omit the step that makes this salad a little more refined — don't bother trimming the strings from the celery.

4   ¹/4-inch-thick slices (1 pound) roast turkey
3   celery stalks
1   pound green beans, trimmed and blanched (see page 74)
³/4   cup dried cranberries
3   tablespoons chopped fresh parsley
1   tablespoon balsamic vinegar
3   tablespoons red wine vinegar
¹/2   teaspoon coarse salt, or to taste
¹/2   teaspoon freshly ground black pepper, or to taste
1   teaspoon Dijon mustard
3   tablespoons olive oil

8   leaves red- or green-leaf lettuce, for garnish
1   crusty French bread, for serving

Slice the turkey into 2-inch-long strips and transfer them to a large bowl. With a paring knife, remove the strings on the surface of the celery stalks. Halve them lengthwise and cut them thinly on an extreme diagonal. Add the celery to the turkey with the green beans, cranberries, and parsley. Toss well.

In a small bowl, whisk together the vinegars, salt, pepper, and mustard. Gradually whisk in the oil in a thin, steady stream.

Pour the dressing over the turkey and vegetables, toss again, and taste for seasoning. Add more salt and pepper, if you like.

To serve, arrange the salad on the lettuce on dinner plates and serve with crusty bread or spoon the salad and lettuce inside the bread.

To Blanch Green Beans

Trim the stem ends of the beans and leave the pointed ends intact. Bring a large saucepan of water to a boil and drop in the beans. When the water returns to a boil, let the beans bubble steadily for 3 to 4 minutes, or until they are very green and still crisp. Drain them and transfer them to a bowl of ice water. When they are cold, spread them out on paper towels to dry. If necessary, store the beans in a plastic container lined with paper towels for up to 1 day.

chickpea salad with tuna

When the fridge is bare, we grab tuna and chickpeas from the cupboard and mix them with tomatoes and green beans to dress them up. The salad is quick and portable and can go to the beach or ski house if you need to carry a dish with you. Use tuna in olive oil, which has a lot of flavor (we buy it in Italian markets); if you find only tuna in water, add an extra tablespoon or two of oil to the salad.

1/2	pound green beans, trimmed and halved
2	cans (15 ounces each) chickpeas
1/2	cup pitted black olives
1/4	cup chopped fresh parsley
2	tablespoons olive oil
1/2	teaspoon coarse salt, or to taste
1/2	teaspoon freshly ground black pepper, or to taste
1/2	bunch scallions, finely chopped
1/2	green bell pepper, finely chopped
2	cans or jars (6–8 ounces each) tuna in olive oil or water, drained and flaked
2	ripe tomatoes, cored and finely chopped
	Juice of 1 lemon, to taste
3	medium pita breads, cut in half
6	leaves red- or green-leaf lettuce

In a saucepan fitted with a steamer insert, steam the green beans over several inches of boiling water, covered, over high heat for 3 minutes, or until they are tender but still have some bite. Rinse them with very cold water until they are no longer hot. Set them on paper towels to dry.

Drain the chickpeas into a colander, then rinse them, shaking the colander to remove the excess water.

In a large bowl, combine the chickpeas, olives, parsley, oil, salt, and pepper. Stir thoroughly. Stir in the scallions, bell pepper, tuna, tomatoes, and green beans. Add the lemon juice, 1 tablespoon at a time, tasting as you go. Mix gently to combine. Taste for seasoning and add more salt and pepper, if you like.

Spoon the salad into pita pockets, add lettuce, and serve.

spaghettini with tuna sauce

This thin spaghetti is intensely flavored — hot, salty, and a little sweet — from crushed peppers, capers, anchovies, and raisins. The pasta is cooked until it's not quite tender, then tipped into the fresh and canned tomato sauce. As it cools, the strands continue to cook and soak up all the juices. The dish is served at room temperature. That's the way Daniele Baliani's Aunt Adriana taught him to make it. Daniele, a talented chef who lived in Italy as a boy, trained at Le Cirque in New York City and was chef of Pignoli in Boston. He is now a caterer.

1 tablespoon coarse salt
1/4 cup olive oil
2 tablespoons pine nuts
2 garlic cloves, finely chopped
3–4 anchovy fillets (preferably white)
1 teaspoon capers, coarsely chopped
1 teaspoon crushed red pepper
1 can (28 ounces) whole peeled tomatoes, crushed in a bowl with their juices
4 summer vine-ripened tomatoes, cored, peeled, and finely chopped
1 can or jar (6–8 ounces) Italian tuna in olive oil, partially drained
1/4 cup golden raisins
1 pound spaghettini
Freshly ground black pepper, to taste
1/4 cup chopped fresh parsley

Bring a large pot of water to a boil. Add the salt to the water.

Meanwhile, in a large flame-proof casserole, heat the oil and cook the pine nuts over medium heat, stirring often, for 2 minutes, or until they begin to turn lightly golden.

Add the garlic, anchovies, capers, and crushed pepper. Cook, stirring often, for 2 minutes, breaking up the anchovies as you stir.

Add the canned and fresh tomatoes, and bring to a boil, stirring occasionally. Reduce the heat to low and simmer, stirring occasionally, for 30 minutes, or until the sauce thickens.

Stir in the tuna and the raisins, breaking up the tuna into small pieces as you stir. Return the sauce to a simmer, then remove it from the heat and set aside.

When the pasta water is boiling, plunge the spaghettini into the water and let the water return to a full boil,

stirring constantly. Cook the spaghettini for 8 minutes, or until it is not quite cooked through.

Drain the pasta into a colander and immediately transfer it to the sauce. Add the black pepper and parsley, and toss well to coat the spaghettini. Set aside to cool. Serve at room temperature.

ten-minute bolognese

Thirty years ago, every university student had a version of this sauce. This is our ten-minute streamlined recipe. It's a light, fresh-tasting sauce. Make it in quantity and freeze it in plastic zipper bags. Dip the bag into a bowl of cold water, and the sauce should defrost in a few minutes.

1 **pound lean ground beef**
$1/2$ **teaspoon coarse salt, or to taste**
$1/2$ **teaspoon freshly ground black pepper, or to taste**
1 **can (28 ounces) whole tomatoes, with their juices**
1 **cup water**
1 **garlic clove, finely chopped**
2 **tablespoons tomato paste**
$1/8$ **teaspoon sugar**
$1/8$ **teaspoon crushed red pepper**
  Pinch of freshly grated nutmeg
3 **tablespoons chopped fresh oregano**
2 **tablespoons heavy cream (optional)**

Brown the beef in a large dry skillet over medium-high heat with the salt and pepper, stirring, for 3 to 4 minutes.

Meanwhile, tip the tomatoes and their juices into a bowl. Using kitchen shears, snip the tomatoes into small pieces. Add the water to the tomato can. Set both aside.

Tip the skillet of meat and use a spoon to move the meat to the high end. Remove and discard all of the excess liquid in the pan.

Add the garlic and tomato paste, the tomatoes and their liquid, the water in the can, the sugar, red pepper, and nutmeg. Bring to a boil.

Reduce the heat to low and simmer, stirring occasionally, for 10 minutes. Add the oregano and cream, if using. Taste for seasoning and add more salt and pepper, if you like. Heat until hot and serve over pasta.

VARIATION
Ten-Minute Meatless Tomato Sauce

Omit the meat. Begin by cooking the garlic in 1 tablespoon of olive oil. Then add the tomato paste, tomatoes and their liquid, and the remaining ingredients, including the salt and pepper.

eggplant "lasagna"

Long slices of grilled eggplant replace the usual noodles in this easy "lasagna," which makes a nice vegetarian main course or a side dish for grilled leg of lamb. As the tomatoes bake, they release their juices, which makes this dish a little messier than a pasta-based lasagna. But it means that there's plenty to soak up when you pass crusty bread. Or, serve on large slices of Stovetop Toasts (page 12).

2	large eggplants, cut lengthwise into $1/2$-inch-thick slices
1	tablespoon coarse salt, or to taste
	Olive oil, for sprinkling
$1/2$	teaspoon freshly ground black pepper, or to taste
$1/2$	cup basil leaves, cut into thin strips
8	plum tomatoes, peeled (see page 9) and thickly sliced
1	pound fresh mozzarella cheese, sliced
1	cup freshly grated Parmesan cheese

Oil a 9-by-13-inch baking dish or another dish with a $3^{1}/_{2}$-quart capacity.

Layer the eggplant in a colander set over a large plate, sprinkling each layer with salt. Set it aside for 20 minutes. Rinse the eggplant slices and pat them dry with paper towels.

Turn on the broiler. Sprinkle the eggplant on both sides with oil. Set the slices on a large rimmed baking sheet and broil them for 8 minutes, watching them carefully, until they are lightly charred and cooked through. They may stick to the pan, but that's OK.

Set the oven at 350 degrees.

Place several slices of eggplant in the baking dish. Add some of the black pepper, half of the basil, half of the tomatoes, one third of the mozzarella, and one third of the Parmesan. Continue layering in this fashion until you have 3 layers of eggplant and 2 of basil and tomatoes. Sprinkle the top layer of eggplant with the remaining cheeses.

Bake for 40 to 45 minutes, or until the cheese browns and the slices are bubbling at the edges, then serve.

chicken paillards
with tomato-orange sauce

A paillard, which is a skinless, boneless breast of chicken that has been pounded thin, cooks just like a veal cutlet and is similarly versatile. We once wrote a column that offered four different ways to treat chicken paillards, and years later, we still get requests for the recipes. This is the one we like best.

8 skinless, boneless chicken breast halves (about 3$^1/_2$ pounds)
3 tablespoons olive oil
$^1/_2$ teaspoon coarse salt, or to taste
$^1/_2$ teaspoon freshly ground black pepper, or to taste
1 garlic clove, finely chopped
1 can (15 ounces) whole tomatoes, crushed in a bowl with their juices
1 cup chicken stock
$^1/_2$ cup chopped pitted black olives, such as Niçoise
   Grated rind of $^1/_2$ orange
1 tablespoon chopped fresh thyme

Remove any pieces of fat along the edges of the chicken breasts. Put one breast between two sheets of strong plastic wrap. With a meat pounder or the bottom of a heavy skillet, pound the meat several times. Pound the remaining breasts in the same way, using fresh plastic wrap when it tears.

Rub the chicken all over with 1 tablespoon of the oil. Sprinkle with the salt and pepper. In a 12-inch nonstick skillet, heat 1 tablespoon oil. When it is hot, add several of the paillards and cook them for 1 minute per side over high heat. Remove the chicken from the pan, heat the remaining 1 tablespoon oil, and cook the remaining pieces in the same way. Set them aside.

Add the garlic, tomatoes, stock, olives, orange rind, and thyme to the pan. Bring the mixture to a boil, reduce the heat to low, and simmer, stirring occasionally, for 5 minutes.

Return the chicken to the pan, overlapping the pieces, and cook over medium-low heat for 10 minutes, or until they are all cooked through, moving the paillards on the bottom to the top halfway through cooking. Taste for seasoning, add more salt and pepper, if you like, and serve.

chicken roasted on a bed of apples

You can put practically anything under a roasting chicken, and that bed — of vegetables or pasta or potatoes, or, in this case, apples and onion — will taste fabulous. Choose an apple that will hold its shape during cooking (see page 256). Serve with steamed red potatoes.

- 3 **apples, peeled, cored, and thinly sliced**
- 1 **Spanish onion, thinly sliced**
- 1/2 **teaspoon coarse salt, or to taste**
- 1/2 **teaspoon freshly ground black pepper, or to taste**
- 2 **tablespoons vegetable oil**
- 4 **chicken breast halves (about 3 pounds)**
- 2 **tablespoons chopped fresh thyme**
- 1 **tablespoon chopped fresh rosemary**

Set the oven at 400 degrees.

In a large bowl, toss the apples and onion with salt, pepper, and 1 tablespoon of the oil. Transfer the mixture to a 12-inch baking dish or another dish that will hold the chicken breasts in one layer. Roast for 25 minutes, stirring once.

Add the chicken to the pan, skin side up. Sprinkle it with the remaining 1 tablespoon of oil, some salt and pepper, and the thyme and rosemary. Roast for 35 minutes, or until tender. Spoon some of the apples and onion onto each plate, top with a chicken breast half, and serve.

maple-glazed chicken breasts with pears

Glazed with mustard and maple syrup, the chicken breasts roast on a bed of sautéed onions and pears. If you like, cook the pear mixture and brown the breasts in advance, then roast them together just before serving. Serve with steamed potatoes sprinkled with parsley.

- 2 tablespoons butter
- 1 Spanish onion, coarsely chopped
- 1/2 teaspoon coarse salt, or to taste
- 1/2 teaspoon freshly ground black pepper, or to taste
- 2 Bartlett pears (or other firm pears), peeled, cored, and thickly sliced
- 2 tablespoons chopped fresh sage
- 4 chicken breast halves (about 3 pounds)
- 2 tablespoons grainy mustard
- 2 tablespoons pure maple syrup

Set the oven at 450 degrees.

In a large skillet with an oven-proof handle (cast-iron works well), heat 1 tablespoon of the butter. Cook the onion with a pinch of salt and pepper over medium heat, stirring often, for 10 minutes, or until softened. Add the pears and cook for 5 minutes more. Sprinkle with the sage.

Meanwhile, sprinkle the chicken breasts with the salt and pepper. Remove the onion and pears from the pan and set aside. Add the remaining 1 tablespoon butter and set the breasts in the pan, skin side down. Cook over medium heat for 5 minutes, or until the skin side is browned.

In a small bowl, combine the mustard and maple syrup. Turn the breasts skin side up. With the back of a spoon, spread the mustard mixture onto the skin of the chicken. Return the onion and pears to the pan, tucking them under the breasts.

Place the skillet in the oven and roast for 15 minutes, or until the chicken breasts are cooked through and glazed on top. Place a chicken breast half on each plate, add roasted pears and onion, and serve.

chicken paprikás

This old-fashioned dish is made with chicken thighs — because they're the most fla-vorful part of the bird. For a simple pan sauce, sour cream is whisked into the paprika-seasoned cooking juices. A real Hungarian paprika will make a big difference. Serve with buttered noodles.

2	tablespoons canola oil
1	large Spanish onion, finely chopped
3	pounds chicken thighs
2	tablespoons sweet Hungarian paprika
1/2	teaspoon coarse salt, or to taste
1/4	teaspoon freshly ground black pepper, or to taste
2	green bell peppers, cored, seeded, and cut into strips
3	cups chicken stock
4	plum tomatoes, peeled and finely chopped
1	tablespoon caraway seeds (optional)
1/2	cup sour cream
	Chopped fresh parsley

In a large flameproof casserole, heat the oil and cook the onion over medium heat for 10 minutes, stirring often, or until the onion softens.

Meanwhile, pull the skin off the chicken thighs and trim any pockets of fat along the edges. Add the chicken to the pan with the paprika, salt, and pepper. Cook the chicken, turning it often in the seasonings, for 5 minutes.

Add the peppers and cook for 5 minutes more, turning the peppers often. Pour in the stock, and add the tomatoes and caraway seeds, if using. Bring the mixture to a boil.

Reduce the heat to low, partially cover the pan, and cook the chicken for 35 minutes, or until tender.

In a small bowl, whisk the sour cream with a few spoons of the sauce. Add a few more spoons of sauce and whisk well. Set the heat under the chicken to its lowest setting. Pour the sour cream mixture into the chicken and stir thoroughly. Cook the sauce just until it is warmed through, but do not let it boil. Taste the sauce for seasoning and add more salt and pepper, if you like.

Sprinkle with parsley before serving.

turkey scallopini
smothered with mushrooms

Turkey cutlets come two ways. One kind is simply sliced off the breast, while the other is the cylindrical-shaped tenderloin that runs along the breast. If you buy the slices, use them as is. If you buy tenderloins, butterfly them, cutting them lengthwise but not all the way through. Open them, then pound them with a meat pounder or with the bottom of a skillet to make them thinner.

6 turkey cutlets (1$\frac{1}{2}$ pounds)
$\frac{1}{2}$ teaspoon coarse salt, or to taste
$\frac{1}{2}$ teaspoon freshly ground black pepper, or to taste
2 tablespoons butter
1 shallot, finely chopped
1 pound small white mushrooms, thinly sliced
$\frac{3}{4}$ cup chicken stock

2 tablespoons chopped fresh parsley

Sprinkle the turkey with salt and pepper. In a large skillet, melt 1 tablespoon of the butter. Add the turkey to the skillet without crowding the pan. Cook over high heat for 3 minutes on each side, or until golden brown. Transfer to a plate and set aside. Cook any remaining turkey in the same way.

In the same skillet, melt the remaining 1 tablespoon butter. Add the shallot, mushrooms, salt, and pepper.

Cook over medium heat for 5 minutes, or until the mushrooms give up their juices, stirring constantly to keep them from burning.

Add the chicken stock to the pan and bring it to a boil. Return the cutlets to the pan. Let them bubble in the sauce for 2 minutes, turning once. Taste the sauce for seasoning, add more salt and pepper, if you like, and sprinkle the mixture with parsley before serving.

pork chops with apples and onion

Buy the thick center-cut loin chops for this dish because they can be browned first, which caramelizes them a little. Then, in a hot oven, they become moist and tender. Use any apples you have on hand. If they fall apart, they'll add an appealing softness; if the slices stay firm, they'll provide texture. Serve the chops with Crusty Smashed Potatoes (page 260).

4 **thick center-cut pork loin chops (about 2 pounds)**
1/2 **teaspoon coarse salt, or to taste**
1/2 **teaspoon freshly ground black pepper, or to taste**
1 **tablespoon vegetable oil**
1 **tablespoon butter**
1 **Spanish onion, thinly sliced**
2 **medium apples, peeled, halved, and thinly sliced**
1 **tablespoon all-purpose flour**
1 1/2 **cups chicken stock**
2 **tablespoons chopped fresh thyme**

Set the oven at 400 degrees.

Sprinkle the pork chops all over with salt and pepper. In a large skillet with an ovenproof handle (cast-iron works well), heat the oil, and when it is hot, add the butter. Brown the pork chops over high heat on both sides, turning, for 2 minutes per side. Remove from the pan.

Add the onion and apples to the skillet and cook over medium heat, stirring often, for 10 minutes, or until the onion softens. Add the flour and cook, stirring constantly, for 2 minutes.

Pour the stock into the pan. Stir until the mixture comes to a boil and thickens slightly. Add the salt, pepper, and half of the thyme.

Return the pork chops to the pan, and spoon some of the onion mixture over them. Place the skillet in the oven and roast the pork for 10 minutes, or until the chops are cooked through.

Taste the sauce for seasoning. Add more salt and pepper, if you like. Sprinkle with the remaining 1 tablespoon thyme before serving.

roast pork tenderloins with caramelized onions

Rub two skinny pork tenderloins with oil and dry mustard, then brown them on top of the stove and finish them quickly in a hot oven. Pork is safe — and quite good — cooked until it is pink, not grayish white like everyone did years ago. You can rub the meat and let it sit overnight, if you like, but you can also put the dish together at the last minute. Serve with Arugula Salad with Orange Dressing (page 45) or Watercress and Endive Salad with Dried Cranberry Dressing (page 56).

3	tablespoons olive oil
1	tablespoon dry mustard
1/2	teaspoon coarse salt, or to taste
1/2	teaspoon freshly ground black pepper, or to taste
2	pork tenderloins (1 1/2 pounds total)
3	red onions, halved and thinly sliced
1/8	teaspoon sugar
2	tablespoons chopped fresh sage

Set the oven at 450 degrees.

In a small bowl, combine 1 tablespoon of the oil and the mustard, salt, and pepper. Rub over the pork so it is well coated.

In a large skillet with an oven-proof handle (cast-iron works well), heat 1 tablespoon of the remaining oil and cook the onions with a pinch of salt and pepper over medium heat, stirring often, for 5 minutes. Add the sugar and sage, turn the heat to medium-high, and continue to cook, stirring often, for 20 minutes, or until the onions begin to caramelize.

Remove the onions from the pan and set them aside. Add the remaining 1 tablespoon oil to the skillet and set the pan over medium-high heat. Brown the pork tenderloins, turning them often, for 3 minutes.

Place the skillet in the oven and roast the pork for 10 minutes, or until a meat thermometer inserted in the center registers 150 degrees. The meat will be pink. If you prefer meat that is not pink in the center, cook the pork to 160 degrees, about 5 minutes more.

Set the pork on a cutting board and let rest in a warm place for 5 minutes. While the pork is resting, return the onions to the pan and stir them over medium heat just until they are hot. Slice the pork on an extreme diagonal, tip any juices on the cutting board into the onions, and taste the onions for seasoning. Add more salt and pepper, if you like. Arrange the pork slices on the onions and serve.

smothered steak sandwiches

Julie grew up with these steak sandwiches, made with "minute" steak and very good sub rolls. We use flank steak and French bread, but the idea is the same. The meat is cooked first (broil it, as we do here, or grill it), then it's sliced and tucked inside crusty bread with onions cooked in a tomato sauce seasoned with brown sugar and Worcestershire. We'd say that it's a kid's dish, except that it has a wider appeal.

1 flank steak (1^1/$_2$ pounds), or one 1^1/$_2$–2 pound skirt steak
  Olive oil, for sprinkling
^{1}/$_2$ teaspoon coarse salt, or to taste
^{1}/$_2$ teaspoon freshly ground black pepper, or to taste
1 tablespoon olive oil
2 large Spanish onions, thinly sliced
1 cup (8 ounces) canned tomato sauce
^{1}/$_4$ cup dark brown sugar
2 tablespoons Worcestershire sauce
2 long French baguettes

Turn on the broiler. Place the flank steak in a broiling pan. With the tip of a paring knife, score the steak in a very shallow crosshatch pattern on both sides. Sprinkle the steak with oil, salt, and pepper.

Broil the meat about 8 inches from the element for 5 to 8 minutes, turning it and seasoning the other side with oil, salt, and pepper halfway through cooking. The meat should be quite pink — or rare, if you prefer that — when it's done.

Meanwhile, in a large skillet, heat the oil and cook the onions over medium heat, stirring often, for 10 minutes, or until they soften. Then stir in the tomato sauce, brown sugar, Worcestershire sauce, salt, and pepper. Cook the mixture over medium heat, stirring occasionally, for 5 minutes.

Slice the baguettes into thirds and open each one to make a sandwich.

When the meat is cooked, transfer it to a cutting board and slice it on an extreme diagonal. Tip all the juices on the board into the tomato sauce and stir.

Set a bottom piece of bread on each of six dinner plates, add some steak slices, then some of the tomato sauce. Set the sandwich tops on the sauce and serve.

quick fish stew with ginger and thyme

There is so little liquid in this dish, so few ingredients, and so little cooking that it's hard to picture a splendid stew emerging from the pot, but the results will surprise you. Use the full amount of ginger and only enough liquid to submerge the fish. The potatoes are steamed first, so they don't absorb any of the cooking juices.

    3   medium red potatoes, sliced $^1/_2$ inch thick
    2   cans (28 ounces each) imported whole tomatoes
 1$^1/_2$ cups bottled clam broth
  $^1/_2$ cup finely chopped fresh ginger
  $^1/_4$ cup chopped fresh thyme
  $^1/_2$ teaspoon coarse salt, or to taste
  $^1/_2$ teaspoon freshly ground black pepper, or to taste
    2   pounds skinless boneless haddock, cut into 2-inch pieces
        (or use any firm-fleshed white fish fillets)

In a large saucepan fitted with a steamer insert, steam the potatoes over several inches of boiling water, covered, over high heat for 10 minutes, or until tender.

Meanwhile, drain the tomatoes. Tip them into a bowl and use kitchen shears to chop them coarsely.

In a large flameproof casserole, combine the tomatoes, clam broth, ginger, thyme, salt, and pepper. Bring to a boil, reduce the heat to low, and simmer for 5 minutes.

Add the potatoes and return to a boil, stirring occasionally. Add the fish, pressing it down lightly to submerge it in the liquid. Cover the casserole and cook the fish for 4 minutes, or until it is cooked through and the potatoes are hot.

Taste for seasoning, add more salt and pepper, if you like, and ladle into bowls. Serve at once.

salmon cooked in its own juices

There is no liquid in this dish, just finely chopped tomatoes. Their liquid mixes with the juices in the salmon to make a quick sauce. You begin by cutting "scallops" from a thick salmon fillet, layering them in a buttered skillet, then covering the salmon with the tomatoes. A circle of buttered parchment paper, pressed directly onto the salmon before covering the skillet, keeps the fish very moist. Serve with angel hair pasta tossed with olive oil.

   2   **pounds center-cut salmon fillet (skinned or skin on)**
  1/2 **teaspoon coarse salt, or to taste**
  1/2 **teaspoon freshly ground black pepper, or to taste**
   2   **tablespoons butter, at room temperature**
   2   **medium tomatoes, peeled, seeded, and coarsely chopped**
       (see page 9)
   1   **shallot, finely chopped**

       Handful fresh dill sprigs, finely chopped
       Handful fresh parsley sprigs, finely chopped

Set the salmon on a cutting board, skin or skinned side down. Hold onto one end and use a long knife to cut the salmon on an extreme diagonal into 6 thick pieces (right).

Sprinkle the salmon pieces on both sides with salt and pepper. Rub the bottom of a 12-inch skillet with 1 tablespoon of the butter. Cut a circle of parchment paper the same size as the skillet and rub one side with the remaining 1 tablespoon butter.

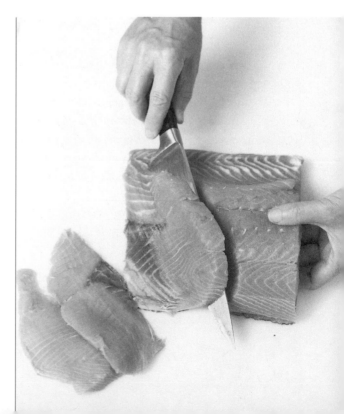

Set the salmon scallops in the skillet, overlapping them tightly. Sprinkle them with the tomatoes, shallot, salt, and pepper. Press the parchment paper, buttered side down, onto the salmon, cover with a lid, and set the skillet over medium-high heat. Cook the fish for 5 minutes, or until it turns opaque on the outside and is just cooked through.

Remove the parchment paper (right), sprinkle the fish with dill and parsley, and serve at once. If the pieces were very crowded in the pan, they will stick together. Separate them or cut into the layers to serve.

seared scallops
with wild mushrooms and potatoes

The local scallops that we get in the waters off Cape Cod are so incredibly sweet that you have to do hardly anything to them. They're the ultimate fast food. You can broil them if you have a strong broiling element, and they also do well seared in a hot skillet. This dish is adapted from Michael Leviton of Lumière restaurant in Newton, Massachusetts. The cooking is quick, and the results are dressy.

2	**Yukon Gold or Yellow Finn potatoes, cut into $^1/_4$-inch pieces**
1	**pound sea scallops**
$^1/_2$	**teaspoon coarse salt, or to taste**
$^1/_2$	**teaspoon freshly ground black pepper, or to taste**
3	**tablespoons olive oil**
2	**tablespoons butter**
$^3/_4$	**pound mushrooms (shiitake, oyster, black trumpet, or chanterelle), trimmed and cut into $^1/_4$-inch pieces**
2	**tablespoons chopped mixed fresh herbs (chives, tarragon, parsley, or just parsley)**
1	**small shallot, finely chopped**
$^1/_4$	**cup dry vermouth or white wine**
1	**cup chicken stock**

In a saucepan fitted with a steamer insert, steam the potatoes over several inches of boiling water, covered, over high heat for 10 minutes, or until they are tender but not falling apart. Remove from the steamer and set aside.

Sprinkle the scallops with the salt and pepper. Heat a large skillet over high heat. Add 1 tablespoon of the oil, and when it is hot, sear the scallops for 1 minute, or until they are golden on one side. Turn them and sear the other side. Transfer the scallops to a plate.

In the same skillet, heat the remaining 2 tablespoons oil. Add the butter, and when it melts, cook the mushrooms over medium-high heat, stirring occasionally, for 3 to 5 minutes, or until crisp at the edges. Add the potatoes and cook, stirring, for 2 minutes.

Stir in the chopped herbs, taste for seasoning, and add salt and pepper, if you like. Transfer the mushrooms and potatoes to a plate.

In the same skillet, cook the shallot over medium heat, stirring, for 1 minute. Add the vermouth or wine, bring to a boil, and reduce the liquid to 1 tablespoon.

Add the chicken stock, bring to a boil, and reduce to ½ cup. Return the scallops, mushrooms, and potatoes to the pan and warm them through.

Divide the scallops among four dinner plates, top with the vegetables, and serve at once.

shrimp in coconut milk with red curry paste

These shrimp cook quickly in a sweet, spicy coconut milk broth. We find red curry paste in the international section of our local supermarket, along with coconut milk and fish sauce. The recipe comes from Thai cooking teacher Wichian Rojanawon of Somerville, Massachusetts. Serve it with Jasmine Rice (page 274) and steamed broccoli.

1	**can (14 ounces) unsweetened light coconut milk**
1	**tablespoon canned red curry paste**
1	**tablespoon dark brown sugar**
2	**teaspoons bottled Asian fish sauce**
1¹/₂	**pounds large shrimp, shelled**

Shake the can of coconut milk vigorously. In a large skillet or wok, bring 1 cup of the coconut milk to a boil (watch carefully because it may splatter a little). Stir in the curry paste and brown sugar. Turn the heat to low and simmer the mixture for 2 minutes. Add the remaining coconut milk and fish sauce, and stir to combine.

Add the shrimp and cook over medium-high heat, stirring often, for 3 minutes, or just until the shrimp turn pink.

Spoon the shrimp into bowls and serve.

striped bass on a bed of squash, zucchini, and tomatoes

This is a favorite summertime dish that Sheryl has been making for thirty years. She first had it when cookbook author and cooking teacher Anne Willan and her husband, Mark Cherniavsky, made it at their summer house in Maryland. Anne used a whole fish, but Sheryl uses fillets. Because the pieces of fish cook quickly, you have to give the vegetables a head start. Serve with steamed red potatoes.

- 2 summer squash, halved lengthwise and thinly sliced
- 4 zucchini, halved lengthwise and thinly sliced
- 3 large ripe tomatoes, cored and thinly sliced
  Olive oil, for sprinkling
  Handful fresh oregano leaves, finely chopped
- 1/2 teaspoon coarse salt, or to taste
- 1/2 teaspoon freshly ground black pepper, or to taste
- 2 pounds skinless striped bass fillets (or use any firm-fleshed white fish fillets that are 3/4 to 1 inch thick)

Set the oven at 400 degrees. Lightly oil a 9-by-13-inch baking dish.

Arrange the summer squash, zucchini, and tomatoes in overlapping rows in the baking dish. Sprinkle with oil, then with the oregano, salt, and pepper. Cover with foil, shiny side down.

Bake for 30 minutes, or until the vegetables are tender when pierced with a fork.

Cut the fish into 6 even pieces. Set them, skinned side down, on the vegetables. Cover with the foil and return the baking dish to the oven.

Cook the fish for 15 minutes, or until it flakes easily when pierced with a fork. With a large spoon, scoop some of the vegetables onto each plate, top with a fillet, and serve at once.

lobster rolls

This is lunch at the beach or dinner on a hot night in New England, served on paper plates with plastic forks (in case a morsel of lobster pops out of the roll). Take succulent lobster meat, mix it with commercial mayonnaise, and tuck it inside buttered, toasted hot dog rolls. The roll is important if you want it to be authentic: you *must* use ordinary hot dog rolls. We mix the mayonnaise with yogurt and lemon juice, which makes it slightly less sweet. There is only enough dressing to hold the lobster together. You can certainly add more mayonnaise if you like.

- 1 **pound cooked lobster meat, cut into 1/2-inch pieces**
- 2 **celery stalks, finely chopped**
- 4 **scallions, finely chopped**
- 1/4 **cup chopped fresh parsley**
- 1/2 **cup commercial mayonnaise**
- 1/4 **cup plain whole-milk yogurt**
- 2 **tablespoons lemon juice**
- 1/8 **teaspoon cayenne pepper**
- 1/2 **teaspoon coarse salt, or to taste**
- 1/2 **teaspoon freshly ground black pepper, or to taste**
- 4 **hot dog rolls**
- 2 **tablespoons butter, at room temperature**

In a medium bowl, combine the lobster meat, celery, scallions, and parsley.

In a small bowl, whisk together the mayonnaise, yogurt, lemon juice, cayenne pepper, salt, and black pepper. Pour the dressing over the lobster and mix thoroughly. Taste for seasoning and add more salt and pepper, if you like.

Spread both sides of the hot dog rolls with a faint coating of butter. Heat a cast-iron skillet over medium heat and place the rolls, cut side down, in the pan. (You may have to do this in batches.) Cook the rolls until the undersides are golden brown, pressing them down gently with a long metal spatula as they brown.

Turn the rolls and brown the other sides. To serve, remove the rolls from the pan, open them at the slit, and fill each roll with lobster salad, heaping it onto the roll.

dishes we make all the time

We're good examples of the national statistics that describe families eating the same dozen meals year in and year out. Most of the cooks we've interviewed tell us this is true for them as well: they have their repertoire and they drop a dish and add a new one about every six months — every year even — so the lineup changes very slowly.

Their standard fare often includes something their mothers or grandmothers made, something clipped from a newspaper or magazine years ago, and something they ate at a friend's house and ran home to re-create.

These cooks also tell us that their weekday meal preparations tend to be very simple. They have to be able to assemble this food without thinking. When they have time to cook and experiment, it's on the weekends.

We're the same way. We cook a lot on Saturdays and Sundays. We try new things, and yes, they get served to company. But weeknights are different. Everyday food has to be predictable, especially when we're tired or it's dreary out. We want to make what we know, we want to smell the aromas from our childhoods, and we don't want any surprises.

Those are the days that Julie makes Bow Ties with Pot Cheese and Peas, which she ate on Sunday nights as a girl, or her Chicken and Corn Chili, which serves a crowd watching football or basketball. She might make Meat Loaf with Roast Potato Topping when one of her sons is about to appear on the doorstep or Turkey Meat Loaf with Golden Raisins and Apples. Baked Meatballs with Tomato Sauce go into the oven

when her nieces and nephews are coming. At her beach house, she makes Mussels in Spicy Tomato Sauce, and, on lazy nights, Grilled Chicken in Lettuce Leaves with Asian Vinaigrette. Sheryl prepares Pressure-Cooker Chicken Soup once a week from the time the weather first turns chilly straight through to lilac season. Yankee Pot Roast with Caramelized Vegetables goes onto the stove when her parents are coming. Spicy Lamb Stew with Chickpeas is on the menu when old friends are expected and she's told them to come in jeans. Summers she makes Zucchini and Tomato Stew with Soft-Cooked Eggs several times a week and Salade Niçoise for guests, who eat on the back porch.

Dishes that become regulars in our households aren't delicate or hard to handle, and the food isn't fussy. Some meals seem ordinary, such as Orb Weaver Farm's Macaroni and Cheese. But when it's made with a farmhouse cheese and topped with buttery crumbs, the word ordinary never comes to mind.

We love learning about new dishes and ingredients and discovering professional techniques. But when the doors are closed — and when the table is filled with family and close friends — this is how we really eat.

dishes we make all the time

beetless borscht with cabbage

This is a hearty borscht made with chuck roast and tomatoes — but no beets — in a mildly sweet-and-sour broth. The cabbage is added during the last hour. Make this a day in advance, since it's best to let it sit. To serve, add steamed potatoes sprinkled with parsley to each bowl. When Julie's father, who was a family doctor in Montreal, would come home late, her mother would serve him this soup and a big chunk of pumpernickel bread to go with it.

- 2 tablespoons vegetable oil
- 2 medium onions, coarsely chopped
- 2 pounds chuck roast, fat removed and cut into 1^1/$_2$-inch pieces
- 3 quarts water
- 1 can (28 ounces) crushed peeled tomatoes
  Juice of ^{1}/$_2$ lemon, or to taste
- 4 tablespoons sugar, or to taste
- 1 head white cabbage, coarsely chopped
- ^{1}/$_2$ teaspoon coarse salt, or to taste
- ^{1}/$_2$ teaspoon freshly ground black pepper, or to taste

Heat the oil in a large flameproof casserole, and cook the onions with a pinch of salt over medium-high heat, stirring often, for 10 minutes, or until they soften. Add the meat and cook, stirring often, until it no longer looks raw on the outside.

Add the water and tomatoes and bring to a boil. Reduce the heat to low and simmer, partially covered, stirring occasionally, for 1½ to 2 hours, or until the meat offers no resistance when pierced with a fork.

Stir in the lemon juice, 4 tablespoons of the sugar, and the cabbage. Cook for 1 hour more, or until the cabbage is very soft. Add salt and pepper to taste. Adjust the sweet-sour flavors with more lemon juice or sugar, if you like. Ladle the soup into deep bowls and serve.

old-fashioned vegetable soup

Sometimes we go out and buy all the ingredients for this recipe, but more often we make a variation that we like to call Bottom-of-the-Fridge Soup. It's more or less this version, depending upon what needs using up that week. Ham or bacon always lends its smokiness, a cup of tomatoes adds flavor but doesn't cook to a thick sauciness, and green beans and zucchini (or peas and yellow squash) are added, along with yellow potatoes and a handful of tiny pasta shells. The soup may thicken a lot as you reheat it, so just keep adding spoonfuls of water. You can even reheat it with leftover cooked vegetables from another meal. Consider this a vague outline for your own pot. If you want to make a vegetarian version, omit the ham and chicken stock and use vegetable stock or water.

2 tablespoons canola oil

1 thick slice ($^1/_8$ pound) flavorful ham, such as Black Forest or Westphalian, finely chopped

4 medium carrots, chopped

2 celery stalks, chopped

1 large Spanish onion, chopped

$^1/_2$ teaspoon coarse salt, or to taste

$^1/_2$ teaspoon freshly ground black pepper, or to taste

2 medium zucchini, quartered lengthwise and thinly sliced

2 garlic cloves, finely chopped

3 quarts chicken stock, or more

1 cup canned whole tomatoes, crushed in a bowl

$^1/_2$ pound green beans, cut into $^1/_4$-inch pieces

2 medium Yukon Gold or Yellow Finn potatoes, cut into $^1/_2$-inch dice

$^1/_4$ cup tiny pasta shells

1 rind (about 3 inches) Parmesan cheese (see page 103)

$^1/_2$ cup finely chopped fresh basil

1 cup freshly grated Parmesan cheese, for serving

To Flavor a Soup with Parmesan Rind

If you have a Parmesan rind left over from a fresh chunk of cheese or if you can purchase one in the supermarket (it won't cost very much), add it to a pot of vegetable soup to infuse it with flavor. As the broth cooks, the rind will melt and, along with the starchier vegetables, help to thicken it. Sometimes the rind melts completely, but more often there's a tender piece remaining. Dice it and return it to the pot.

Heat the oil in a large flameproof casserole, and when it is hot, add the ham, carrots, celery, onion, salt, and pepper. Cook the vegetables over medium heat, stirring often, for 10 minutes, or until they soften.

Add the zucchini and garlic and continue cooking for 10 minutes.

Pour in the chicken stock and tomatoes. Bring to a boil and add the green beans, potatoes, and pasta shells, and cook, stirring often, until the mixture returns to a boil.

Lower the heat, add the Parmesan rind, cover the pan, and simmer the soup for 2 hours, stirring occasionally.

Add the basil and more salt and pepper, if you like. If the soup seems thick, add water ¼ cup at a time, until it is the consistency you like. Fish out the Parmesan rind and dice it. Ladle the soup into bowls, sprinkle with cheese, and serve.

french onion soup with roasted onions

We roast the onions for this soup inside a steamy tent of foil, then turn the oven way up and uncover the onions to caramelize the cut sides. The best part is their dark tips. You can use the onions as a side dish with meat or poultry. They form the basis of this soup, which is served with a cheese croûte (made separately) on top, something like the classic French version. But unlike the traditional soup, this one uses commercial beef stock.

FOR THE ONIONS
- 4 **large Spanish onions, peeled and cut into sixths**
- 4 **garlic cloves, unpeeled**
- 1/2 **cup beef stock**
- **Olive oil, for drizzling**
- 1/2 **teaspoon coarse salt, or to taste**
- 1/2 **teaspoon freshly ground black pepper, or to taste**

Set the oven at 375 degrees.

Arrange the onions as tightly as possible in a 9-by-13-inch (3½-quart) baking dish (they will shrink as they cook and release their liquid). Scatter them with the garlic cloves. Add the beef stock at the sides of the dish. Drizzle the onions with oil and sprinkle them with the salt and pepper.

Cover the dish with foil, shiny side down, and transfer it to the oven. Roast the onions for 1 hour.

Increase the oven temperature to 425 degrees. Lift off the foil, remove the garlic, and continue roasting the onions for 45 minutes, or until they are tender. As soon as the garlic is cool enough to handle, pop the cloves out of their skins.

note: The onions and garlic can be made up to this point 2 days in advance.

Coarsely chop the onions, reserving the cooking juices, and chop the garlic, then make the soup.

❄⟩ FOR THE SOUP

  2 tablespoons butter

  1 teaspoon sugar

  $^1/_2$ teaspoon coarse salt, or to taste

  $^1/_2$ teaspoon freshly ground black pepper, or to taste

  $^1/_2$ cup port

  2 cups dry red wine

  $3^1/_2$ cups beef stock

  1 cup water

  2 tablespoons chopped fresh thyme

  6 slices day-old French bread, toasted

  $^3/4$ cup grated Gruyère cheese

Melt the butter in a large flameproof casserole. Add the roasted onions and the garlic and their juices. Cook over medium heat, stirring often, for 2 minutes. Sprinkle with sugar, salt, and pepper. Stir well.

Pour in the port, wine, stock, and water. Increase the heat to high, and bring to a boil. Reduce the heat to low and simmer the soup, covered, for 1 hour. Stir in the thyme.

Arrange the French bread on a rimmed baking sheet and sprinkle the slices with cheese. Broil the toasts (or use a toaster oven) until the cheese melts. Watch them carefully, because they burn easily. Ladle the soup into bowls. Top each with a cheese toast and serve at once.

pressure-cooker chicken soup

Sarah (Sally) Shapiro of Providence, Rhode Island, has been making this chicken soup in an old jiggle-top pressure cooker for nearly sixty years. What would ordinarily take a couple of hours takes her 20 minutes. Though neither of us owns much cooking equipment beyond good pots and pans, we both own modern, spring-valve, burst-proof pressure cookers. As Sally says, "The pressure cooker was the greatest gift to women of our age, who had to stay home for hours to cook chicken soup." This is an especially good broth, which you can make in an ordinary pot (see page 107). One of the secrets is the ratio of chicken to water. Follow the pressure cooker's manual for bringing the pressure up to high.

1 kosher chicken (about 3^1/$_2$ pounds), cut into quarters
2 split chicken breasts
6 carrots, halved crosswise
3 celery stalks (including leaves), cut into 1^1/$_2$-inch pieces
3 medium onions, cut into quarters
2 parsnips, halved crosswise
6 stalks fresh dill
8–10 stalks parsley
1 bay leaf
1 tablespoon kosher or coarse salt
8 cups water

4 ounces fine egg noodles, for serving

Remove any pinfeathers and pockets of fat from the chicken. Place the chicken neck, gizzard, and all of the chicken pieces in a heatproof bowl. Pour a tea kettle of boiling water over them. Let them sit for 10 minutes. Rinse the chicken.

Place the carrots, celery, onions, parsnips, dill, parsley, and bay leaf in the bottom of the pressure cooker. Add the chicken (including the neck and gizzard), salt, and 8 cups of water.

Lock the lid of the pressure cooker in place and set it over high heat to bring the pressure to high. Adjust the heat to maintain high pressure. Cook for 15 minutes.

Turn off the heat. Carefully carry the pressure cooker to the sink. Run very cold water onto the top to bring the pressure down. When it is safe, remove the lid, tilting it away from you.

Let the soup cool for 10 minutes. Use a slotted spoon to lift out the chicken and vegetables and transfer them to a large plastic container. Discard the bay leaf, parsley, dill, chicken neck, and gizzard when you find them. Tip the soup into another container. Let cool completely, then cover and refrigerate.

Remove the fat from the soup, and transfer the soup to a large pot. Cut up some of the chicken and return it to the soup (or serve the chicken cold, separately). Cut up the vegetables and add them to the soup. Bring the soup to a boil.

In a large saucepan of boiling salted water, cook the noodles for 6 minutes, or until they are tender but still have some bite. Drain.

Add the noodles to each of six soup plates, ladle the soup over the noodles, and serve.

VARIATION
Pressure-Cooker Chicken Soup with Tomatoes and Mushrooms

Prepare the ingredients for Pressure-Cooker Chicken Soup and place them in the pot. Add the following ingredients before covering with the lid:

- 1/2 **pound green beans, cut into 1-inch lengths**
- 1/2 **pound portobello mushrooms, cut into 1-inch pieces**
- 1 **cup canned whole tomatoes, crushed in a bowl**

Cook the soup as directed.

VARIATION
Chicken Soup in a Pot

Prepare the ingredients for Pressure-Cooker Chicken Soup, but add the ingredients, omitting the dill, parsley, and bay leaf, to a large soup pot. Bring the water to a boil, skim the surface thoroughly, and lower the heat. Skim again, then add the dill, parsley, and bay leaf. Cover the pot and simmer the chicken for 1½ hours, or until very tender.

Cool and store as directed.

andalusian gazpacho

We understand why field-workers in Andalusia eat this soup every day: the base is smooth and faintly cumin-scented, mildly flavored with sherry vinegar, and garnished with chopped bell peppers and onions, which add crunch. Make the tomato puree up to several days in advance for subtler flavors. At Taberna de Haro in Brookline, Massachusetts, this soup has become a signature summer dish.

❊} FOR THE GAZPACHO

20 ripe plum tomatoes, cored and peeled
1 pale green Italian sweet pepper, cored and seeded
1 pickling cucumber, peeled and seeded
1/2 large Spanish onion, halved
2 garlic cloves, peeled
1 tablespoon coarse salt
1 tablespoon sugar
1/2 teaspoon ground cumin
1 cup olive oil
1/2 cup Spanish sherry vinegar
1 tablespoon tomato paste (optional)

In a food processor, finely chop the tomatoes, sweet pepper, cucumber, onion, garlic, salt, sugar, and cumin. Add the olive oil and vinegar and mix just until combined. Add the tomato paste if the mixture doesn't look red enough and process just to mix it in. Prepare the garnish.

❊} FOR THE GARNISH

1 green bell pepper, cored, seeded, and finely chopped
1 red bell pepper, cored, seeded, and finely chopped
1/2 Spanish onion, finely chopped
Olive oil, for sprinkling

Mix together the bell peppers and onion. To serve, ladle the gazpacho into large bowls, garnish with some of the chopped vegetables, and sprinkle each portion with a little oil.

zucchini and tomato stew with soft-cooked eggs

This stewy vegetable dish is enriched by the addition of a soft egg that is cooked in the shell, peeled, and placed on top of the stew like a poached egg. At the table, guests cut open the eggs, and the yolks spill into the sauce.

2 tablespoons olive oil

1 large Spanish onion, coarsely chopped

1/2 teaspoon coarse salt, or to taste

6 medium zucchini, trimmed, quartered, and thickly sliced

4 medium plum tomatoes, peeled (see page 9) and cut into strips

1/2 cup chicken stock or water

1/2 teaspoon freshly ground pepper, or to taste

1/4 cup chopped fresh parsley

3/4 cup freshly grated Parmesan cheese

4 soft-cooked eggs (see page 55)

Heat the oil in a large flameproof casserole. Add the onion and salt and cook over medium-low heat, stirring often, for 10 minutes, or until the onion softens.

Add the zucchini, and cook, stirring, for 5 minutes. Add the tomatoes, stock or water, and pepper. Reduce the heat to low and cook the vegetables for 30 to 40 minutes, or until they are very tender and soupy. If at any point they dry out, add a little more stock or water.

Ladle the zucchini stew into four large deep bowls. Sprinkle each one with parsley and cheese. Add a cooked egg to each bowl, sprinkle with more pepper, and serve at once.

grilled chicken in lettuce leaves with asian vinaigrette

If you've ever sat in a Vietnamese or Chinese restaurant and eaten meat or chicken wrapped in lettuce, then you know that wonderful combination of hot, crunchy, and soothing in one packet. Invariably the filling leaks and drips down your chin and your hand, and this is part of the fun. Sometimes we do this with Thanksgiving leftovers, wrapping roast turkey, hot mustard, a little stuffing, and cranberry sauce in lettuce leaves. You can do the same thing with roast chicken, roast potatoes, and coleslaw.

FOR THE VINAIGRETTE

- 1/4 **cup rice wine vinegar**
- 1/2 **teaspoon coarse salt, or to taste**
- 1/2 **teaspoon freshly ground black pepper, or to taste**
- 1/2 **teaspoon sugar**
- 2 **teaspoons prepared Chinese mustard**
- 1/4 **cup canola oil**
- 1 **tablespoon toasted sesame oil**
- 1 **garlic clove, finely chopped**
- 1 **teaspoon finely chopped fresh ginger**
- 1 **scallion, finely chopped**

In a small bowl, whisk together the vinegar, salt, and pepper just until the salt dissolves. Whisk in the sugar and mustard. Gradually add the canola and sesame oils, whisking constantly. Using a fork, stir in the garlic, ginger, and scallion. Cover and refrigerate the dressing while you prepare the chicken.

❋} FOR THE CHICKEN

4 chicken breast halves (about 3 pounds)
Canola oil, for drizzling
1/2 teaspoon coarse salt, or to taste
1/2 teaspoon freshly ground black pepper, or to taste

1 head Boston lettuce
2 tablespoons chopped fresh cilantro
1/4 cup finely chopped roasted peanuts

Light a grill or turn on the broiler.

Rub the breasts on both sides with oil. Sprinkle with salt and pepper. Grill the chicken, turning often, 10 inches from the coals, or broil, turning several times, for 15 to 20 minutes, or until it is cooked through but still moist.

Remove the chicken from the grill or broiler and transfer it to a plate to cool.

When the chicken is cool enough to handle, pull the meat off the bones and slice it thinly into diagonal strips. Pull off any meat that still clings to the bones and add it to the strips.

❋} TO ASSEMBLE

Place several lettuce leaves on each of four dinner plates, stacking them on one side. Add some chicken strips to each plate and sprinkle them with cilantro and peanuts (or put the cilantro and peanuts in little dishes and pass them separately).

Use a fork to stir the dressing again. Divide it among four small ramekins or cups and set one on each of the plates. Serve at once. Instruct your guests to use the lettuce leaves as wrappers, fill them with chicken and dressing, and roll them up.

corn and pasta salad

For years this has been Sheryl's potluck offering. Fresh corn and tiny pasta shells are tossed with red bell pepper and red onion, lots of fresh herbs, and a cider vinaigrette. Make it with the smallest pasta shells you can find because as you stir the salad, something miraculous happens: the corn kernels manage to tuck themselves inside the shells. People will think that you've placed each one there yourself.

- 1 tablespoon plus $^1/_2$ teaspoon coarse salt, or to taste
- 2 cups tiny pasta shells
- 8 ears fresh corn, kernels removed from the cobs (see page 113)
- $^1/_4$ cup cider vinegar, plus more to taste
- 1 tablespoon Dijon mustard
- $^1/_2$ teaspoon freshly ground black pepper, or to taste
- $^1/_2$ cup canola oil
- 1 red bell pepper, cored, seeded, and finely chopped
- $^1/_2$ red onion, finely chopped
- 4 scallions, finely chopped
- 3 tablespoons chopped fresh parsley
- 3 tablespoons chopped fresh oregano

To Remove Corn Kernels from the Cob

Bring a large saucepan of water to a boil, and add 1 tablespoon of the salt. Add the pasta shells, and when the water returns to a boil, reduce the heat to medium-high and simmer for 6 minutes. Add the corn and cook for 2 minutes more, or until the pasta is tender but still has some bite.

Drain in a colander, shaking it to remove the excess moisture. Transfer the shells and corn to a large bowl.

In a small bowl, whisk together the vinegar, mustard, remaining ½ teaspoon salt, and pepper. Gradually whisk in the oil in a slow, steady stream, until the dressing emulsifies. Pour the dressing over the warm pasta and stir gently to coat the shells.

Add the bell pepper, onion, scallions, parsley, and oregano. Add more salt and pepper and another splash of vinegar, if you like.

Cover tightly with plastic wrap and refrigerate for 1 hour for the flavors to mellow before serving.

Shuck the corn and lay an ear on a cutting board. Hold it firmly in place with one hand. Using a small, sharp knife, cut off several rows of kernels, pulling the knife from the pointed end of the corn to the stalk end. Keep turning the cob until all the kernels have been cut from it. Use the cut kernels within several hours.

salade niçoise

Sheryl makes this salad often for back-porch suppers on summer evenings. She cooks everything the night before and assembles individual plates in the kitchen. One year in the south of France, she ordered it every day at lunch for ten days to see if she should be doing something different, or better. In the end, she didn't change a thing. It's very traditional — hard-cooked eggs, green beans, potatoes, tomatoes, and olives. To arrange the plates, remember the rule of gardening: everything will look better if you find it in several places on the plate, rather than in one large cluster. Green beans, for instance, should be placed in two mounds on the plates, potatoes in two places, and so on.

8 medium red potatoes, unpeeled
2 tablespoons cider vinegar
Olive oil, for sprinkling
1 bunch scallions (white part only)
3 tablespoons chopped fresh parsley
1/2 teaspoon coarse salt, or to taste
1/2 teaspoon freshly ground black pepper, or to taste
3 tablespoons white wine vinegar
1 tablespoon Dijon mustard
1/3 cup olive oil
1 pint cherry tomatoes
1 pound slender green beans, blanched (see page 74)
1 can or jar (6–8 ounces) tuna in oil (reserve oil)
Juice of 1 lemon
4 eggs, hard-cooked (see page 293)
1/4 cup Niçoise or other small black olives
3 tablespoons capers, drained

In a saucepan fitted with a steamer insert, steam the potatoes over several inches of boiling water, covered, over high heat for 20 minutes, or until tender. Remove from the steamer and transfer to a large shallow bowl.

When the potatoes are cool enough to handle, cut them into thick slices.

Sprinkle the potatoes with cider vinegar and enough oil to coat them lightly. Add the scallions, parsley, and half of the salt and pepper. Stir gently with a rubber spatula.

In a small bowl, whisk together the white wine vinegar, mustard, and remaining salt and pepper. Add the oil a little at a time, whisking constantly.

Halve some of the smaller cherry tomatoes and cut the larger ones into quarters. Transfer them to a small bowl and add 2 tablespoons of the dressing and some salt and pepper.

On each of four dinner plates, arrange the green beans, tomatoes, and potatoes in clusters. Spoon some of the dressing over them.

Flake the tuna into a bowl and pour the oil from the can or jar over it. Add the lemon juice.

Scatter the tuna on the plates and sprinkle it with the lemon dressing left in the bowl. Quarter the eggs lengthwise and garnish each plate with 4 quarters. Add olives, capers, and more black pepper, if you like. Serve.

orb weaver farm's macaroni and cheese

A good mac and cheese has to include a classic white sauce to keep the pasta moist, grated cheese with a distinctive taste, and a thick crust of crumbs with more cheese on top. We first tried this dish at Orb Weaver Farm in New Haven, Vermont, where owners Marjorie Susman and Marian Pollock use their own Vermont Farmhouse Cheese (a Colby-style, which is like a mild cheddar).

FOR THE CHEESE SAUCE

- 4 **tablespoons (1/2 stick) butter**
- 4 **tablespoons all-purpose flour**
- 4 **cups milk, heated to scalding**
- 1/2 **teaspoon coarse salt, or to taste**
- 1/2 **teaspoon freshly ground black pepper, or to taste**
- 2 **cups grated firm Colby or mild cheddar cheese**
  Pinch of cayenne pepper

Melt the butter in a medium saucepan, stir in the flour, and cook, stirring constantly, for 2 minutes. Add the hot milk gradually, stirring all the while, until the sauce thickens.

Bring to a boil, reduce the heat to low, add the salt and pepper, and simmer for 2 minutes, stirring often.

Stir in the cheese and cayenne pepper. When the cheese melts, remove the sauce from the heat and set aside while you prepare the pasta and topping.

FOR THE PASTA AND TOPPING

1/4 **cup fresh white bread crumbs (see page 29)**

1 **teaspoon olive oil**

1 **tablespoon coarse salt**

1 **pound dried penne pasta**

2 **cups grated firm Colby or cheddar cheese**

Set the oven at 300 degrees. Butter a 9-by-13-inch baking dish or another dish with a 3½-quart capacity. Bring a large pot of water to a boil.

Meanwhile, toss the bread crumbs and oil together. Spread the crumbs on a rimmed baking sheet and toast them in the hot oven for 30 minutes, turning several times. Set them aside.

Turn the oven temperature up to 375 degrees.

Add the salt and penne to the boiling water and stir once or twice,

until the water comes back to a boil. Cook, stirring occasionally, for 5 minutes, or until the penne is tender but still has some bite.

Drain the pasta and transfer it to the baking dish, layering it with half the cheese. Add the cheese sauce and stir gently. Sprinkle the remaining cheese on top, then scatter the bread crumbs over the cheese.

Bake the macaroni and cheese for 30 minutes, or until the top is golden brown and the sauce is bubbling at the edges. Serve.

bow ties with pot cheese and peas

Julie's mother, Ghita Riven, used to make this quick dish for Sunday supper. It's a satisfying one-pot meal, in which bow tie pasta is tossed with pot or farmer cheese. Julie adds some of the pasta cooking water to the cooked pasta, then adds Parmesan cheese with the pot cheese, fresh oregano, and peas. When fresh peas are in season, use them in this dish.

1 **pound dried bow tie (farfalle) pasta**

1 **package (10 ounces) frozen (not thawed) peas**

2 **tablespoons olive oil, plus more for drizzling**

1 **cup crumbled pot or farmer cheese**

3/4 **cup freshly grated Parmesan cheese, plus more for sprinkling**

3 **tablespoons chopped fresh oregano**

1 **teaspoon coarse salt, or to taste**

1/2 **teaspoon freshly ground black pepper, or to taste**

1/4 **cup fresh bread crumbs, lightly toasted (see page 29)**

Set the oven at 400 degrees. Generously butter or coat with oil an 11-by-7-inch baking dish or another dish with a 2½-quart capacity.

Bring a large pot of salted water to a boil. Add the pasta and bring the water back to a boil, stirring constantly. Cook the pasta for 6 minutes, add the peas, and cook for 2 minutes more, or until the pasta is almost tender.

Before draining the pasta, dip a glass measuring cup into the pasta water and remove ½ cup. Set aside.

Drain the pasta and peas in a colander and, without shaking the colander, return the mixture to the pan. Drizzle the mixture with the 2 tablespoons oil and toss gently. Add ¼ cup of the reserved pasta-cooking water, the pot or farmer cheese, ½ cup of the Parmesan cheese, oregano, salt, and pepper. Toss again to combine the ingredients. If the dish seems too dry, add a little more pasta water.

Transfer the pasta to the prepared dish. In a small bowl, mix together the bread crumbs and the remaining ¼ cup Parmesan cheese. Sprinkle the mixture on top of the pasta. Drizzle with a little extra olive oil. Bake the pasta for 15 minutes, or until the cheese has softened and the top is lightly golden.

Remove the dish from the oven, spoon into deep plates, and serve at once. Pass extra Parmesan cheese at the table.

turkey meat loaf with golden raisins and apples

You can use ground turkey in place of ground beef in some meat loaf recipes — but it dries out too quickly and it never turns golden and crisp, as do loaves made with beef, pork, and veal. This is our solution for those shortcomings: raisins and applesauce moisten the ground turkey mixture, then slices of apples, fanned out on the loaf, protect the top. This loaf makes fine sandwiches the following day. Slice it and sandwich it between whole wheat bread spread with cranberry sauce or mango chutney.

2	pounds ground turkey
1/2	medium onion, grated
3/4	cup applesauce
1/2	cup fresh white bread crumbs (see page 29)
1	large egg, lightly beaten
1/4	cup golden raisins
2	tablespoons pine nuts, toasted (optional; see page 149)
1/2	teaspoon dried thyme
1/4	teaspoon ground cinnamon
	Pinch of ground nutmeg
	Pinch of ground allspice
1/2	teaspoon coarse salt, or to taste
1/2	teaspoon freshly ground black pepper, or to taste
1	large green apple, such as Granny Smith, cored, seeded, and very thinly sliced

Vegetable oil, for brushing

Set the oven at 400 degrees. Rub a 9-by-5-inch Pyrex loaf pan with oil.

In a large bowl, combine the ground turkey, onion, applesauce, bread crumbs, egg, raisins, pine nuts (if using), thyme, cinnamon, nutmeg, allspice, salt, and pepper.

Place the meat-loaf mixture in the prepared pan, patting it down to flatten it. Overlap the apple slices on the meat. Brush the apples with the oil and set the dish on a rimmed baking sheet to catch any spills.

Bake the meat loaf for 55 minutes, or until the juices are bubbling at the edges. Remove the meat loaf from the oven and let it settle for 5 minutes. Cut into thick slices and serve.

meat loaf with roast potato topping

Meat loaf and potatoes always go together on the plate, and in this version, instead of being made separately, they're cooked in one dish. The meat is on the bottom, and thickly sliced potatoes tossed in tomato sauce are on top. The potatoes act as a blanket for the ground beef and keep it moist. Use canned tomato sauce or pasta sauce.

- 2 russet (baking) potatoes, peeled and cut into $1/2$-inch-thick slices
- 1 cup canned tomato or pasta sauce
- 2 tablespoons dark brown sugar
- 2 tablespoons distilled white vinegar
- 2 tablespoons Dijon mustard
- 1 pound lean ground beef
- 1 small onion, grated
- 1 large egg, lightly beaten
- $1/2$ cup fresh white bread crumbs (see page 29)
- 1 teaspoon coarse salt, or to taste
- $1/2$ teaspoon freshly ground black pepper, or to taste

Set the oven at 375 degrees. Rub a 9-by-5-inch Pyrex loaf pan with oil.

In a saucepan fitted with a steamer insert, steam the potatoes over several inches of boiling water, covered, over high heat for 12 to 15 minutes, or until tender but not falling apart. Remove from the pan and let them cool slightly.

Meanwhile, in a bowl, combine the tomato sauce, sugar, vinegar, and mustard.

In a large bowl, combine the beef, onion, egg, bread crumbs, salt, and pepper. Add half of the tomato mixture and stir well.

Place the meat loaf in the prepared pan, patting it down to flatten the surface.

Carefully toss the potatoes and the remaining tomato mixture in a bowl. Arrange the potatoes so they overlap on the meat loaf. Pour any remaining sauce from the bowl on top. Set the meat loaf on a rimmed baking sheet to catch any spills.

Bake for $1\frac{1}{4}$ hours, or until the juices are bubbling and the potatoes are crusty at the edges. Remove the meat loaf from the oven, let it settle for 5 minutes, then cut it into thick slices, and serve.

chicken and corn chili

Dark meat maintains its texture and juiciness and gives this chili much more flavor than white meat. If your market doesn't carry boneless chicken thighs, buy them bone-in and remove the meat at home. It doesn't matter if you're not skilled at this; all you have to do is cut the chicken into small morsels for this dish. Serve it with Corn Bread Baked in a Skillet (page 161) or Rosemary Biscuits (page 16).

- 2 tablespoons olive oil
- 1 large Spanish onion, coarsely chopped
- 1 green bell pepper, cored, seeded, and chopped
- 6 plum tomatoes, peeled, cored, and chopped
- 2 garlic cloves, finely chopped
- 2 teaspoons chili powder
- 2 teaspoons ground cumin
- 1 teaspoon dried oregano
- 1/2 teaspoon crushed red pepper, or to taste
- 1/2 teaspoon coarse salt, or to taste
- 1/2 teaspoon freshly ground black pepper, or to taste
- 12 boneless chicken thighs, skin removed, cut into 1/2-inch pieces
- 3 cups chicken stock
- 4 ears fresh corn (kernels removed from cobs — see page 113) or 3 cups frozen corn

Heat the oil in a large flameproof casserole, and cook the onion and bell pepper over medium heat, stirring often, for 10 minutes, or until softened. Add the tomatoes and garlic and cook for 2 minutes more. Stir in the chili powder, cumin, oregano, crushed red pepper, salt, and black pepper.

Add the chicken and cook, stirring, for 5 minutes.

Pour in the stock, bring to a boil, reduce the heat to low, cover, and simmer for 30 minutes, or until the chicken is tender and cooked through. Add water if the mixture seems dry.

Add the corn and simmer for 10 minutes more. Taste for seasoning, add more salt, black pepper, and crushed red pepper, if you like, and serve.

mussels in spicy tomato sauce

This saucy dish is tomato-based, a little spicy, and served in big bowls with crusty bread. You can also serve it over linguine (see the variation that follows).

❊}   FOR THE MUSSELS

- 1 **cup white wine**
- 1/2 **cup water**
- 1 **small onion, root intact and scored**
- 1 **bunch parsley stems**
- 3 **thyme sprigs**
- 4 **peppercorns**
- 4 **pounds mussels, rinsed, beards removed**

Bring the wine and water to a boil in a large flameproof casserole. Tie the onion, parsley, thyme, and peppercorns in cheesecloth and drop the bundle into the pot. Add the mussels, cover, and steam for 5 minutes, or until they open.

Use a slotted spoon to lift out and discard any unopened mussels.

Strain the broth through cheesecloth and reserve 2 cups of the liquid. Set the mussels aside while you make the sauce.

❊}   FOR THE SAUCE

- 1 **tablespoon olive oil**
- 1 **medium onion, finely chopped**
- 1 **can (15 ounces) imported whole tomatoes, crushed**
- 2 **garlic cloves, finely chopped**
- 1/2 **teaspoon crushed red pepper**
- 1/2 **teaspoon coarse salt, or to taste**
- 1/2 **teaspoon freshly ground black pepper, or to taste**

- 4 **thick slices crusty bread, toasted**
- 3 **tablespoons chopped fresh parsley**
- 3 **tablespoons chopped fresh basil**

Heat the oil in a large flameproof casserole. Add the onion and cook over medium heat, stirring often, for 10 minutes, or until soft but not brown.

Stir in the tomatoes, garlic, and crushed red pepper, and cook, stirring often, for 5 minutes. Add the reserved mussel-cooking liquid and bring to a boil. Reduce the heat to low and simmer for 10 minutes. Taste for seasoning and add salt and pepper.

Place a piece of toasted bread in the bottom of 4 shallow bowls. Ladle the mussels and sauce on top. Sprinkle with parsley and basil and serve.

VARIATION
Mussels in Spicy Tomato Sauce over Linguine

Make the Mussels in Spicy Tomato Sauce using 2 pounds mussels. Bring a large pan of salted water to a boil, add 1 pound linguine, and cook, stirring occasionally, for 8 to 10 minutes, or until it is tender but still has some bite.

Drain the linguine and divide it among four bowls. Top with mussels and tomato sauce, then sprinkle with parsley and basil. Serve.

shrimp with spanish rice

A dressed-up version of the 1950s classic, this pepper-flecked rice is made with shrimp and shrimp stock. You can also use bottled clam broth instead of making a broth from shrimp shells. Use 3 cups of clam broth mixed with 3 cups water instead of the 6 cups water called for in the stock recipe. The rice is cooked pilaf-style. This is not a dry mixture; it should be soupy on the plate.

FOR THE STOCK

- 1 **tablespoon vegetable oil**
- 2 **medium onions, quartered**
- 2 **medium carrots, cut into 4 pieces**
- 1 **celery stalk, cut into 4 pieces**
- 2 **plum tomatoes, quartered**
  Shells from 1 pound shrimp
- 1 **cup dry white wine**
- 6 **cups water**
- 1 **bunch parsley stems, tied**
- 3 **whole peppercorns**
- 1 **bay leaf**

Heat the oil in a large flameproof casserole, and cook the onions, carrots, and celery over medium heat, stirring often, for 10 minutes.

Stir in the tomatoes and shrimp shells, increase the heat to medium-high. Cook, stirring, for 2 minutes.

Pour in the wine and water. Add the parsley, peppercorns, and bay leaf, bring to a boil, reduce the heat to low, and simmer for 20 minutes. Strain the stock into a bowl. Measure the stock; add enough water to make 6 cups. Set aside to cool while you make the rice.

❧ FOR THE RICE

- 1 tablespoon olive oil
- 1 Spanish onion, finely chopped
- 1/2 teaspoon coarse salt, or to taste
- 1/2 teaspoon freshly ground black pepper, or to taste
- 1 red bell pepper, cored, seeded, and finely chopped
- 1 green bell pepper, cored, seeded, and finely chopped
- 1 garlic clove, finely chopped
- 1 cup long-grain white rice
- 1/4 teaspoon crushed red pepper, or to taste
  Pinch of saffron threads
- 1 pound large shrimp, shelled
- 1/4 cup pitted green Spanish olives, quartered
- 1 package (10 ounces) frozen (not thawed) peas
- 1/4 cup chopped fresh parsley

Heat the oil in a large flameproof casserole, and cook the onion with the salt and pepper over medium heat, stirring often, for 10 minutes.

Add the bell peppers and garlic to the pan. Cook, stirring often, for 10 minutes more. Stir in the rice and cook for 1 minute.

Add the shrimp stock, red pepper, and saffron to the rice. Bring to a boil, reduce the heat to low, cover, and simmer for 15 minutes, or until the rice is tender but still has some bite. There will be some liquid left in the pan.

Add the shrimp and olives to the rice. Increase the heat so the liquid boils again, then quickly reduce the heat to low and simmer the mixture for 2 minutes, or until the shrimp are firm. Add the peas and parsley and cook for 2 minutes, or just until the peas are hot. The mixture should be soupy.

Taste for seasoning, add more salt, black pepper, and crushed red pepper, if you like. Stir thoroughly and serve.

chicken curry

Because we love curries, we were looking for a chicken curry that we could make with supermarket ingredients. On tired nights on the way home from work, we didn't want to make a detour to the Indian market for garam masala and other hard-to-find seasonings. Arthi Subramaniam of the *Boston Globe* staff, who comes from the south of India, near Madras, came to the rescue with this "regal" curry, an elegant dish appropriate for entertaining. The big morsels of chicken turn rust-colored, and you can taste the aromatic layering of spices, nuts, ginger, and garlic. Serve with Basmati Rice (page 275).

4 skinless, boneless chicken breast halves (about 2^{1}/2 pounds)

3 garlic cloves

1 ^{1}/2-inch piece fresh ginger

^{1}/4 cup dry-roasted cashews

^{1}/4 cup dry-roasted almonds

2 medium tomatoes, cored and quartered

2 teaspoons vegetable oil

1 large onion, finely chopped

2 cinnamon sticks

2 whole cloves

1^{1}/4 cups water

2 teaspoons red chili powder

1 teaspoon ground coriander

^{1}/4 teaspoon ground turmeric

^{1}/2 teaspoon coarse salt, or to taste

^{1}/4 teaspoon saffron threads

3 tablespoons chopped fresh cilantro, for garnish

Trim any fat from the chicken breasts. Cut into 3-inch pieces. Set aside.

In a food processor, puree the garlic and ginger until they form a paste. Transfer to a bowl.

Without rinsing the food processor container, pulse the cashews and almonds until they are smooth and pasty. Transfer to another bowl.

Without rinsing the work bowl, puree the tomatoes in the food processor until the mixture is smooth. Transfer to the bowl of nuts.

In a deep skillet, heat the oil and cook the onion, stirring often, for 8 minutes, or until it softens. Add the cinnamon sticks and cloves and cook for 2 minutes more. Add the ginger mixture with ¼ cup of the water. Cook, stirring, for 1 minute. Stir in the chili powder, coriander, turmeric, and salt.

Add the nut and tomato mixture and the water. Bring to a boil and add the chicken pieces, turning them in the sauce until the sauce returns to a boil.

Reduce the heat to low and simmer the chicken gently, turning several times, for 10 minutes, or until cooked through. Add more water if the mixture seems dry.

Add the saffron and simmer the sauce for 1 minute. Taste for seasoning, add more salt, if you like, and remove the cloves and cinnamon stick from the sauce. Sprinkle with cilantro and serve.

yankee pot roast
with caramelized vegetables

Usually made in a big pot (hence the name), pot roast and root vegetables usually spend 3 hours together in cooking liquid and meld into one taste. We cook a big piece of boneless chuck roast in red wine for 3 hours, and roast the vegetables separately. Then we combine the vegetables and meat and cook them together. If you don't have room in the oven to roast them both at once, make one the day before or simmer the meat gently on top of the stove, or make it in one pot. This dish is infinitely better if prepared the day before serving. Serve with mashed potatoes.

❊⦚ FOR THE MEAT

- 1 5-pound boneless chuck roast, tied with string
- 3 tablespoons vegetable oil, plus more for sprinkling
- 1/2 teaspoon coarse salt, or to taste
- 1/2 teaspoon freshly ground black pepper, or to taste
- 1 Spanish onion, chopped
- 1 bunch parsley
- 6 sprigs fresh thyme
- 4 allspice berries
- 2 whole cloves
- 1 bay leaf
- 1 bottle (750 ml) dry red wine
- 2 cups chicken stock
- 3 tablespoons prepared white horseradish
- 2 tablespoons tomato paste
- 2 tablespoons light brown sugar

Set the oven at 500 degrees.

Place the meat in a roasting pan. Sprinkle it lightly all over with oil, salt, and pepper, and rub them in with your hands. Transfer the meat to the oven and roast for 30 minutes, turning once halfway through cooking. Remove from the oven and set aside.

Reduce the oven temperature to 350 degrees.

In a large flameproof casserole, heat the 3 tablespoons oil. Add the onion and cook over medium heat, stirring often, for 10 minutes, or until softened.

Tie the parsley, thyme, allspice berries, cloves, and bay leaf in a piece of cheesecloth.

Pour the wine over the onion. Stir in the cheesecloth bag, stock, horseradish, tomato paste, and brown sugar and bring to a boil. Add the meat to the liquid, together with any juices in the pan. Cover, transfer the pot roast to the oven, and cook for 3 hours, or until the meat is very tender and a fork inserted into the center slides out without any resistance. Meanwhile, prepare the vegetables.

*⟩ FOR THE VEGETABLES

- 10 carrots, halved lengthwise
- 4 parsnips, halved lengthwise
- 3 red onions, quartered
- 2 purple-topped turnips, quartered
- 1 large butternut squash, peeled, seeded, and cut into 3-inch pieces
- 1 cup water, plus more if needed
  Vegetable oil, for sprinkling
  Coarse salt and freshly ground black pepper, to taste

- 1/4 cup chopped fresh parsley

Arrange the carrots, parsnips, onions, turnips, and squash in a roasting pan. Add enough water to the bottom of the pan to make a thin layer. Sprinkle the vegetables with oil, salt, and pepper. Cover the pan with foil, shiny side down, and transfer to the oven (it can sit beside the meat or on a rack under it).

Roast the vegetables for 1 hour, then remove the foil and continue roasting for 30 minutes, or until very tender.

When the meat has cooked for 3 hours, remove the cheesecloth bag. Transfer the vegetables and any liquid in the pan to the meat.

Return the pan to the oven and continue cooking the vegetables and meat, uncovered, for 30 minutes, basting the meat and vegetables with the cooking juices once or twice. Add more water if the juices are too thick.

Remove the meat from the pan, discard any strings, then cut off as much fat as you can. Cut the meat where it breaks naturally. The pieces should be about 4 inches thick.

Arrange the meat and vegetables on a large platter, spoon the cooking juices over the meat and vegetables, sprinkle with parsley, and serve.

sausages in homemade blankets

If you ever want to get children interested in cooking, this is a good dish to start them off. You can make the dough together — or buy it (1 pound prepared pizza dough will wrap 4 sausages). The sausages are cooked first, so the dough takes only half an hour to bake, and the results are delightful: they look like completely encased hot dogs. Make the dough, and while it's rising, cook and cool the sausages. Then wrap them together with provolone cheese before baking. If you're serving teenagers, you'll make them happy.

❊⟩ FOR THE DOUGH

3/4	cup lukewarm water
1	teaspoon sugar
1	package (2¼ teaspoons) active dry yeast
2	tablespoons olive oil
1/4	cup whole milk, heated to lukewarm
2	teaspoons coarse salt
2¼–2½	cups all-purpose flour, plus more for sprinkling

Combine the water and sugar in a large bowl. Sprinkle the yeast over the water and let it sit for 5 minutes, or until bubbly.

Stir in the oil, milk, and salt. With a wooden spoon, stir in the flour ½ cup at a time, mixing well between each addition. When the mixture comes together to form a dough, turn it out of the bowl and set it on a lightly floured counter.

Knead the dough, adding more flour, if necessary, until it is smooth. Oil a bowl and add the dough. Turn it over in the oil to coat it on all sides.

Cover the bowl with plastic wrap and set in a warm place to rise for 1¼ to 1½ hours, or until it doubles in bulk. Meanwhile, prepare the sausages.

note: If you're not ready to bake the sausages, punch down the dough, shape it into a small ball, cover, and refrigerate for up to 1 hour.

※} FOR THE SAUSAGES

4 **sweet Italian chicken or turkey sausages (14–16 ounces total)**

Olive oil, for drizzling

4 **ounces (4 thick slices) provolone cheese**

Mustard, for serving

Set the oven at 400 degrees. Lightly grease a rimmed baking sheet.

Put the sausages in a baking dish and prick them well all over. Drizzle them with oil. Roast them for 35 to 40 minutes, turning them halfway through cooking, or until they are cooked through. Leave the oven on. Set the sausages aside to cool.

※} TO ASSEMBLE

On a lightly floured counter, punch down the dough and divide it into 4 even pieces. Shape each piece into a ball and flatten with the heel of your hand. Set them aside, loosely covered with a cloth, while you roll one out.

Roll one piece of dough into a 6-by-8-inch oval. Place a slice of provolone in the center of the oval and set a sausage on top, lengthwise on the oval.

Fold the short edges of dough up onto the sausage. Then roll the sausage in the dough like a jelly roll until you have a bundle. Pinch the seam closed. Place the dough on the baking sheet, seamed side down.

Continue rolling until all the sausages and pieces of dough are used.

Bake for 30 to 35 minutes, or until the crust is firm and golden brown. Serve with mustard.

baked meatballs with tomato sauce

A few years ago, we asked several professional chefs who are also parents what they feed their children after a long day at work. Of the recipes we received, these baked meatballs became favorites. They're made in quantity (the recipe begins with 4 pounds of ground sirloin and veal and a whole challah), then frozen 4 at a time with tomato sauce in plastic zipper bags. When you want to serve them, you can pull out as many bags as you need and defrost them overnight in the refrigerator, or put them in a bowl of cold water for several hours. Linda Marino, co-owner of La Bonne Cuisine Caterers outside Boston, serves them over spaghetti.

FOR THE MEATBALLS

- 1 whole day-old (1-pound) challah or white sandwich loaf, torn into 1-inch pieces
- 1 cup whole milk
- 2 pounds ground sirloin
- 2 pounds ground veal
- 4 large eggs
- 1 cup grated Parmesan cheese
- 2 garlic cloves, finely chopped
- 1/4 cup chopped fresh oregano
- 1/4 cup chopped fresh basil
- 1/4 cup chopped fresh Italian parsley
- 1/2 teaspoon crushed red pepper
- 1 teaspoon coarse salt, or to taste
- 1/2 teaspoon freshly ground black pepper, or to taste

Set the oven at 400 degrees.

In a bowl, combine the bread and milk. Set aside for 30 minutes.

In another large bowl, combine the ground meats, eggs, Parmesan, garlic, oregano, basil, parsley, crushed red pepper, salt, and pepper. Add the bread mixture. With your hands, knead the meat and seasonings.

Fill a mixing bowl with cold water. Dip your hands into the water and then pick up enough meat to make a 2-inch meatball. Place the meatball in a large roasting pan (you may need to use two pans so the meatballs aren't crowded and cook properly) and continue shaping until all the meat is used. Bake for 30 to 40 minutes, turning several times, or until the meatballs are browned.

Meanwhile, make the tomato sauce.

note: The meatballs can be made ahead and stored in plastic zipper bags in the freezer for up to 3 months.

⁂{ FOR THE TOMATO SAUCE
  2 **tablespoons olive oil**
  2 **large Spanish onions, coarsely chopped**
  2 **carrots, finely chopped**
  2 **garlic cloves, finely chopped**
  1/4 **cup chopped fresh Italian parsley**
  1 **can (28 ounces) whole tomatoes, crushed**
  1 **can (28 ounces) tomato puree**
  2 **tablespoons tomato paste**
  8 **ripe plum tomatoes, cored and chopped (optional)**
  8 **cups water**
  3 **tablespoons chopped fresh oregano**
  3 **tablespoons chopped fresh basil**
  1/2 **teaspoon coarse salt, or to taste**
  1/2 **teaspoon freshly ground black pepper, or to taste**

Heat the oil in a large flameproof casserole. Add the onions and carrots and cook over medium heat, stirring occasionally, for 10 minutes, or until softened. Add the garlic and parsley and cook for 1 minute. Stir in the crushed tomatoes, tomato puree, tomato paste, plum tomatoes (if using), and water and bring to a boil. Reduce the heat to low and simmer for 1 hour, stirring occasionally.

Stir in the oregano, basil, salt, and pepper. Taste for seasoning and add more salt and pepper, if you like.

Warm the meatballs in the hot tomato sauce and serve.

spicy lamb stew with chickpeas

Instead of shoulder of lamb, which takes time to trim, we use the tender pieces of leg of lamb for this stew. They cook in a dark, spicy sauce with tomatoes and raisins for 1½ hours, which makes the dish rich and aromatic. Serve it with Quick Couscous (page 276).

1	2-pound boneless leg of lamb (in one piece)
1	tablespoon vegetable oil, plus more for sprinkling
½	teaspoon coarse salt, or to taste
½	teaspoon freshly ground black pepper, or to taste
1	large Spanish onion, coarsely chopped
2	garlic cloves, finely chopped
1	teaspoon ground cinnamon
½	teaspoon ground cumin
¼	teaspoon ground allspice
¼	teaspoon cayenne pepper
¼	teaspoon ground nutmeg
1	cup chopped canned tomatoes
2	cups chicken stock
½	cup raisins
1	can (15 ounces) chickpeas, drained and rinsed
¼	cup chopped fresh parsley
2	tablespoons chopped fresh cilantro

Set the oven at 500 degrees.

Remove as much fat as possible from the lamb. Cut it along its natural lines into 4-inch pieces.

Arrange the meat in a roasting pan, sprinkle it very lightly with oil and with the salt and pepper. Roast for 25 minutes, turning once or twice, until it is browned all over.

Heat the 1 tablespoon oil in a large flameproof casserole. Add the onion and cook over medium heat, stirring often, for 10 minutes, or until it softens. Add the garlic and cook for 1 minute. Stir in the cinnamon, cumin, allspice, cayenne pepper, and nutmeg. Cook for 30 seconds, stirring. Add the tomatoes and cook for 2 minutes. Add salt and pepper to taste.

Pour in the stock and transfer the meat to the casserole dish. Tip the juices from the lamb into the dish. Bring to a boil, reduce the heat to low, cover, and simmer for 1 hour.

Stir in the raisins and chickpeas. Cover the pan and simmer for 30 minutes more, or until the lamb is very tender.

Add the parsley and cilantro to the lamb and taste for seasoning, adding more salt and pepper, if necessary, and serve.

new classics

It's hard to fiddle with a classic. It seems so presumptuous. Who are we to change a dish that has been firmly established for several generations — sometimes for hundreds of years?

And yet that's what all cooks do. That's what cooking is, in fact. You take a recipe into your kitchen, and the only way to make it yours is to change it.

You're not trying to prove that you know more than the recipe's author. It may be that you're using a technique that feels more comfortable. Or perhaps years ago you realized that you like your stews loose and saucy, not as thick as they often are. Or maybe your doctor said that fried foods and your heart are not compatible.

Recipes change for all those reasons, and then they evolve because ingredients don't stay the same. Meat is leaner than it once was. Poultry doesn't have as much flavor. We don't mean to sound like the people who prattle on about how dreadful everything is now and how wonderful it used to be. But as the way foods are raised changes over time, so, too, do their texture and taste. They're bound to be affected. And with that, you have to adjust cooking methods.

There are other things to take into account: we — all of us — like thinner sauces, food with more seasoning, fanciful presentations. We want to keep the integrity of the old recipes but make them brighter somehow. Give them some excitement.

With that in mind, we have adjusted some dishes that were around before our grandparents were born, and we've reinterpreted others. Our Fish and Chips is oven-fried, for instance. Our Boston Baked Beans are soupier than traditional versions, and we've replaced some of the heavy molasses with maple syrup. The sauce inside our Chicken Pot Pie with Rich Pastry is really a sauce — quite a beautiful velouté sauce, in fact — and the crust is decorated with cutouts of tiny stars, instead of steam vents. Our Roasted Coq au Vin is served with sugar snap peas, and our Steak Marchand de Vin is accompanied by rings of caramelized onions.

We grind the corn for Smoky Corn Chowder so it bursts with corn flavor, mix our own fish cakes with fresh salmon, and make stuffing for the holiday turkey from croutons made of challah bread, then bake it separately from the bird so the top turns crusty and golden.

When you take these recipes into the kitchen, add your own whims to ours. We once heard from a friend who told us that she loved one of the dishes we had printed in the previous Sunday's column, but she had changed it a little. It was a traditional Italian dish of spaghetti tossed with a hot tomato sauce. She used penne because she had no spaghetti and a few fresh uncooked tomatoes, not enough to make a sauce. And so on. But she was delighted with the dish she had prepared — and she intended to make it again.

There are all kinds of ways to adapt a classic.

new classics

smoky corn chowder

To get the most flavor from the corn, we grind half of the kernels in a food processor so the corn "milk" flavors the pot and turns the chowder creamy.

- 4 **thick slices bacon, chopped**
- 1 **Spanish onion, chopped**
- 4 **cups fresh raw corn kernels (removed from about 6 ears fresh corn — see page 113)**
- 5 **cups chicken stock**
- 1/2 **teaspoon coarse salt, or to taste**
- 1/2 **teaspoon freshly ground black pepper, or to taste**
- 1 **cup heavy cream**
- 1 **yellow bell pepper, cored, seeded, and very finely chopped**
- 2 **pickling cucumbers, peeled, seeded, and very finely chopped**
- 2 **tablespoons chopped fresh parsley**
- 1 **tablespoon chopped fresh chives**

Render the bacon in a large flameproof casserole over medium-high heat until it is golden brown. Remove from the pan. Discard all but 1 tablespoon fat.

Add the onion and cook, stirring often, for 10 minutes, or until softened.

In a food processor, process 2 cups of the corn kernels until they are coarsely ground. Add the ground and whole corn kernels to the onion. Return the bacon to the pan. Pour in the stock, salt, and pepper. Bring to a boil, reduce the heat to low, and simmer for 20 minutes.

Stir in the cream and return the soup to a boil. Simmer for 3 minutes.

Ladle the soup into bowls. Sprinkle each one with yellow pepper, cucumber, parsley, and chives. Serve.

new england oyster stew

When oysters were so cheap that New Englanders fed them to their servants, this stew — nothing but a few plump oysters in a creamy broth — became popular. Today, we maintain the original simplicity of the dish, but we use more oysters. Cook them briefly: when their edges curl, they're done. Their briny liquor will flavor the cream. If you can't buy fresh oysters, look for pints in the supermarket. Serve this as an informal supper for friends with lots of crusty bread and Asparagus Cooked for Two Minutes (page 247). We also love to serve the stew with common crackers. Very good ones, packaged in bright green tins and shipped all over the nation, have been made since 1828 by the Vermont Country Store, Route 100, Weston, VT 05161.

2   tablespoons butter
1   Spanish onion, finely chopped
1/2 teaspoon coarse salt, or to taste
4   dozen oysters, shucked, with their liquor reserved,
        or 2 pints shucked oysters
2   cups milk
2   cups heavy cream
1/4 teaspoon freshly ground black pepper, or to taste

2   tablespoons chopped fresh parsley, for garnish
     Common crackers (see above), for serving (optional)

Melt the butter in a large flameproof casserole and cook the onion with a pinch of salt over medium heat, stirring often, for 15 minutes, or until softened.

Add the oysters and their liquor. Continue cooking for 3 minutes, or just until the oysters begin to curl at the edges; do not overcook. With a slotted spoon, remove the oysters from the liquid and transfer them to a small bowl. Set aside.

Bring the liquid in the pan to a rolling boil. Add the milk and cream and return to a boil, reduce the heat to low, and simmer for 5 minutes. Return the oysters to the pan. Cook for 1 minute, just to heat them through. Add salt and pepper and ladle the stew into bowls.

Garnish each one with parsley and serve with the crackers, if using.

succotash with seared scallops

This is instant cooking at its most luxurious. During the weeks in the summer when corn is plentiful and you can find young zucchini, we make this succotash and use it as a bed for scallops. These tender shellfish have a small muscle flap attached to them, a tiny piece that never gets tender. With your fingers, pull it off each scallop before frying.

      4 **small zucchini**
      3 **tablespoons butter**
    1¹/₂ **pounds sea scallops, small muscle flap removed**
     ¹/₂ **teaspoon coarse salt, or to taste**
     ¹/₂ **teaspoon freshly ground black pepper, or to taste**
      6 **ears corn, kernels removed (4 cups); (see page 113)**
     ¹/₄ **cup heavy cream**
      3 **tablespoons chopped fresh basil**
      2 **tablespoons chopped fresh parsley**
         Pinch of cayenne pepper

Trim the zucchini and quarter them lengthwise. With a paring knife, remove the seeds from each long strip. Cut the strips crosswise into ¹/₈-inch-thick slices.

Melt 2 tablespoons of the butter in a large skillet and, when it foams, add the scallops. Sprinkle them with ¹/₄ teaspoon of the salt and ¹/₄ teaspoon of the black pepper. Cook them over high heat for 2 minutes on a side, or until golden at the edges, barely cooked through, tender, and only slightly resistant to the touch; do not overcook. Transfer the scallops to a plate and set aside in a warm place.

Without wiping out the skillet, melt the remaining 1 tablespoon butter, and cook the zucchini with the remaining ¹/₄ teaspoon salt and ¹/₄ teaspoon pepper over medium-high heat, stirring often, for 3 minutes. Add the corn to the pan, cover, and cook over medium heat, stirring occasionally, for 3 to 5 minutes, or until the zucchini and corn are tender but still have some bite. Do not let the vegetables get mushy.

Add the cream, basil, parsley, and cayenne to the pan, stirring, and heat just until the cream is hot. Taste for seasoning and add more salt and pepper, if you like. Spoon the succotash onto four plates, top with the scallops, and serve at once.

chicken pot pie with rich pastry

A grand pot pie looks pretty spectacular on the buffet table for company, and it's also a homey, charming supper for friends. In one dish, you can offer pastry, poultry, and vegetables. Begin with roasted chicken breasts, which lend the dish their unmistakable caramelized flavor. You can add water to the juices in the roasting pan for a stock and make up the difference with canned (or use all canned stock).

   The rich pastry is practically foolproof and very flaky. Cream cheese, an egg, and a teaspoon of vinegar all help to keep it tender during a long stay in the oven. (You can also use the pastry for deep-dish pies or as the base of a large, freestanding tart. Or, roll it out, sprinkle it with cinnamon sugar and some chopped walnuts, and roll it up jelly-roll fashion, then slice and bake as cookies.) The sauce, a classic French velouté, is thin, so the finished pie doesn't have the starchy quality of the old versions. For whimsy, cut vent holes in the pastry with a tiny five-point cutter.

6 **chicken breast halves (about 4 pounds)**
   Vegetable oil, for drizzling
1 **teaspoon coarse salt, or to taste**
$^1\!/_2$ **teaspoon freshly ground black pepper, or to taste**
4 **tablespoons ($^1\!/_2$ stick) butter, plus more for greasing**
1 **large Spanish onion, coarsely chopped**
4 **tablespoons all-purpose flour, plus more for rolling**
$3^1\!/_2$ **cups chicken stock, warmed**
1 **package (10 ounces) frozen (not thawed) peas**
3 **tablespoons chopped fresh thyme**
3 **tablespoons chopped fresh parsley**
6 **medium carrots, thinly sliced and steamed until tender**

Set the oven at 450 degrees. Butter a 9-by-13-inch baking dish or a deep $3^1\!/_2$-quart dish.

Arrange the chicken breasts skin side up in a roasting pan large enough to hold them in one layer. Drizzle them with oil and sprinkle them with $^1\!/_4$ teaspoon of salt and $^1\!/_4$ teaspoon of pepper. Roast them for 40 to 45 minutes, or until they are golden brown and cooked through. Let the breasts cool until you can handle them.

Melt the butter in a flameproof casserole and cook the onion with the remaining $^1\!/_2$ teaspoon salt and $^1\!/_4$ teaspoon pepper over medium heat, stirring often, for 10 minutes, or until softened. Add the flour and cook for 2 minutes over low heat, stirring constantly, or until the flour just begins to brown.

Gradually whisk in the warm stock in a steady stream, whisking constantly to prevent lumps from forming, until all of it has been added. Bring to a boil, reduce the heat to low, and simmer gently for 2 minutes.

Stir in the peas, thyme, and parsley.

Remove and discard the skin and bones from the chicken. Cut the meat into 2-inch pieces. Scatter the chicken and carrots in the baking dish and pour the sauce over them. Cool completely while you make the pastry.

❈} FOR THE RICH PASTRY

2 cups all-purpose flour, plus more for rolling

1/4 teaspoon baking powder

1/2 teaspoon salt

4 tablespoons (1/2 stick) unsalted butter, cut into pieces

1 small package (3 ounces) cream cheese, cut into pieces

1 tablespoon sugar

1 large egg, lightly beaten with 1 teaspoon white vinegar

1/4 cup ice water

3 tablespoons whole milk or heavy cream, for brushing

In a food processor, combine the flour, baking powder, and salt. Pulse twice. Scatter the butter and cream cheese on top and pulse just until the mixture resembles sand with some large pieces mixed in. Add the sugar and pulse twice.

Stir together the egg mixture and ice water in a small bowl. Sprinkle onto the flour and butter. Pulse just until you see large clumps of dough — do not let the dough come together to form a ball.

Turn the clumps out onto a lightly floured counter. Bring them together gently to form an 8-inch disk. Shape the disk into a rectangle or round, depending on the dish you're using, wrap in foil, and refrigerate for 1 hour.

❈} TO ROLL AND ASSEMBLE

Set the oven at 375 degrees.

On a lightly floured counter, roll the dough slightly larger than the dish. With a 2-inch 5-pointed star cutter, stamp out 8 pastry stars (bake these separately as a little treat for the cook).

Lift the dough onto the rolling pin and ease it onto the filling. Fold under the edges to make a hem. Brush the dough lightly with milk or cream.

Using the tines of a fork, press the edges of the pastry into the rim of the dish all around.

VARIATION
Salmon and Mushroom Pot Pie

To use this pastry for Salmon and Mushroom Pot Pie (page 202), halve the recipe, using 1 cup flour, $\frac{1}{8}$ teaspoon baking powder, $\frac{1}{4}$ teaspoon salt, 2 tablespoons butter, $\frac{1}{2}$ small package cream cheese, $\frac{1}{2}$ tablespoon sugar, 1 egg, lightly beaten with 1 teaspoon vinegar, and 2 tablespoons ice water.

Set the dish on a rimmed baking sheet to catch any drips, and bake for 50 to 60 minutes, or until the pastry is golden and the filling is bubbling at the edges. Remove from the oven and set aside for a few minutes so the juices can settle.

Use a small knife to cut the top of the pie into large squares. Place a piece of crust on each of six large plates. Spoon some filling beside the crust and serve.

roasted coq au vin with sugar snap peas

Coq au vin used to be made with an old bird that simmered a long time, which produced a flavorful sauce. Our challenge was to get the same rich taste with today's young and tender chicken, without overcooking it and with convenient store-bought stock. Our solution: we roast the chicken in pieces, along with onion. Then we let a bottle of white wine bubble until it reduces by half, add the canned chicken stock, and reduce the mixture again. When the chicken, deglazed juices, sautéed sugar snap peas, and shiitake mushrooms have been added, the sauce tastes as though it has been simmering on the back burner all afternoon. This dish is more involved than almost anything else we make, but we think the results are worth it.

4 chicken breast halves (about 3 pounds)
4 whole chicken legs, with thighs (about 2 pounds)
2 medium red onions, quartered
2 medium yellow onions, quartered
  Olive oil, for sprinkling
1 teaspoon coarse salt, or to taste
1/2 teaspoon freshly ground black pepper, or to taste
2 tablespoons olive oil
1 garlic clove, chopped
1/2 pound sugar snap peas, strings removed, peas thickly sliced
  on a diagonal
1/2 pound shiitake mushrooms, stems removed, caps sliced
1 bottle (750 ml) dry white wine
1 quart chicken stock
8 small red potatoes
3 tablespoons chopped fresh thyme

Set the oven at 400 degrees.

In a large roasting pan, arrange the chicken pieces, skin side up, snugly in the pan, tucking the onions around them wherever you can so that everything is in one layer. Sprinkle the chicken and onions with oil, and half of the salt and pepper.

Roast the chicken and onions for 30 minutes, or until the onions are golden brown at the tips (the chicken will not be cooked through). Set aside.

Meanwhile, in a large flame-proof casserole, heat the 2 tablespoons oil and sauté the garlic, sugar snap peas, and shiitake mushrooms for 2 minutes, stirring constantly, or until the peas are tender but still have some bite. Add the remaining salt and pepper. Remove the vegetables from the pan and set aside.

Pour the wine into the pan, bring it to a boil, and let it bubble steadily until it reduces by half. Add the stock and bring it to a boil. Let it bubble steadily until it reduces by half. Remove from the heat and set aside.

Halve the potatoes. In a saucepan fitted with a steamer insert, steam the potatoes over several inches of boiling water, covered, over high heat for 15 to 20 minutes, or until they are tender when pierced with a skewer. Use a slotted spoon to remove the potatoes from the pan.

Cut the chicken breasts horizontally in half. Cut the legs in half to separate the drumstick from the thighs. Add the chicken and onions to the wine mixture with the potatoes. Bring to a boil, reduce the heat to low, and simmer for 15 minutes, or until the chicken is cooked through.

Stir in the garlic, peas, mushrooms, and thyme. Taste for seasoning, add more salt and pepper, if you like, and serve.

VARIATION
Roasted Coq au Vin Tapenade

Tapenade is an olive paste that has an intense taste. It's delightful on crackers as an hors d'oeuvre, but it also gives a sauce an earthy flavor.

Make Roasted Coq au Vin with Sugar Snap Peas, but omit the peas and mushrooms. Sauté the garlic in 1 tablespoon of oil and add the wine. Continue as directed.

When both the wine and stock have reduced, stir ⅓ cup black-olive tapenade into the sauce and taste for seasoning. Add enough tapenade to give the sauce a faint olive taste. Proceed with the recipe as directed.

challah pan stuffing for roast turkey

Everybody has a favorite recipe for roast turkey. The hard part is the stuffing. We found we were rising much too early on holidays to stuff the bird and get it into the oven so it would be ready in time. The solution is a pan stuffing, which can be made ahead (safely, because it's not inside the bird), allowing the turkey to roast more quickly and come out juicy. Challah, the egg bread available at Jewish specialty markets, is the best choice for this, unless you can find rich French brioche. Challah comes in both 1- and 2-pound loaves; use 1½ pounds total. Or use another eggy bread or an unsliced white sandwich loaf. The rest of the stuffing is more traditional: lots of fresh sage, celery, plenty of onions, mushrooms, and a good handful of toasted pecans. This quantity feeds a crowd, and though you can make it in two smaller dishes, the large one is best for keeping the stuffing moist.

1½	unsliced challah breads (1 pound each)
	Canola oil, for sprinkling
1	cup (2 sticks) butter
10	celery stalks, chopped
2	Spanish onions, chopped
1	teaspoon salt, or to taste
½	teaspoon freshly ground pepper, or to taste
4	portobello mushrooms, chopped
2	pounds white button mushrooms, chopped
2	cups pecans, toasted (optional; see page 149)
¼	cup chopped fresh thyme
¼	cup chopped fresh sage
2½	cups chicken stock

Butter a 4-quart dish (14 to 15 inches across) or two 2-quart baking dishes.

Set the oven at 350 degrees.

Cut the challah into 1-inch-thick slices, then cut the slices into 1½-inch pieces. Spread them out on a rimmed baking sheet and sprinkle them with oil. Toast, turning often, for 30 to 50 minutes, or until the pieces are lightly golden. As the bread toasts, remove any pieces from the pan that become brown.

Remove the croutons from the oven. (If you're baking the stuffing the

To Toast Nuts

To toast in the oven: Set the oven at 375 degrees.

Place the nuts on a baking sheet and toast for 10 minutes, turning often and checking for doneness, until they are golden brown. Taste a nut to see if the flavor is heightened: it should be very aromatic and taste quite fresh. Remove the baking sheet from the oven and set aside to cool.

To toast nuts on the stovetop: Heat a cast-iron skillet until it is quite hot but not smoking. Add the nuts and cook, shaking and tossing often, for a few minutes or until you can smell an unmistakable toasty aroma. Remove from the skillet and set aside to cool.

next day, turn the oven off, otherwise leave it on.)

Melt the butter in a large flame-proof casserole, and add the celery, onions, salt, and pepper. Cook over medium heat, stirring occasionally, for 10 minutes, or until the vegetables soften. Add the mushrooms and increase the heat to medium-high. Cook, stirring, until they release their juices.

Transfer the croutons to a large mixing bowl. With a rubber spatula, scrape the vegetables and all the cooking juices into the bowl and stir well. Add the pecans (if using), thyme, sage, and

1½ cups of the stock. Add enough additional stock to make a mixture that is moist but not wet. Pack the mixture into the dish(es), doming it well

The stuffing can be covered with foil and refrigerated overnight at this point. Let it sit at room temperature for 30 minutes before baking.

Bake the stuffing, still covered with the foil, for 30 minutes. Remove the foil, pour the remaining 1 cup stock over the top, and return the stuffing, uncovered, to the oven. Continue baking for 30 minutes, or until crusty on top. Serve.

turkey boulangère

Before French houses had ovens, families carried their Sunday dinner to the local baker on the way to church. After all the loaves had been baked, the casserole dishes were put into the still hot oven. One favorite dish was a leg of lamb roasted on a bed of sliced potatoes, which became known as lamb *boulangère* (French for baker). In this version, turkey thighs replace the lamb. As the pieces roast, their juices drip onto the potatoes and baste them as they cook. Serve with Pickled Red Onions (page 280).

5 **medium russet potatoes, peeled and very thinly sliced**
Olive oil, for sprinkling
2 **tablespoons chopped fresh rosemary**
1 **teaspoon coarse salt, or to taste**
1/2 **teaspoon freshly ground black pepper, or to taste**
2 **turkey thighs (2–2 1/4 pounds each)**

Set the oven at 400 degrees. Oil a 12-by-12-inch baking dish or another dish that will hold the turkey thighs in one layer.

Arrange the potatoes in layers, sprinkling each layer with some of the oil, 1 tablespoon of the rosemary, 1/2 teaspoon of the salt, and 1/4 teaspoon of the pepper.

Cut the turkey thighs in half along the bones to make two pieces that are almost the same size. Set them on the potatoes. Rub the turkey skin with oil and sprinkle with the remaining 1/2 teaspoon salt, 1/4 teaspoon pepper, and the 1 tablespoon rosemary.

Roast the turkey for 1 hour, or until a meat thermometer inserted into the thickest part of the thigh registers 175 degrees. Remove from the oven, and let sit for 5 minutes.

Slice the turkey off the bone and serve with the potatoes.

homemade corned beef hash with thyme

You can't make a decent hash without lots of potatoes, but you'll get quite a nice one with a good mix of vegetables pressed into a cast-iron skillet and turned often so the edges get very brown. The traditional accompaniment is poached or easy-over eggs, which are set directly onto the hash so their yolks form a kind of sauce for the meat and vegetables. Try soft-cooked eggs (see page 55) instead.

- 3   tablespoons vegetable oil
- 1   large onion, finely chopped
- 4   cups chopped leftover cooked corned beef (page 157)
- 6   cups chopped leftover cooked potatoes, carrots, cabbage, and beets (page 157)
- 1   tablespoon chopped fresh thyme
- 1/2   teaspoon crushed red pepper
- 1/2   teaspoon coarse salt, or to taste
- 1/4   teaspoon freshly ground black pepper, or to taste

Heat the oil in a 12-inch nonstick or cast-iron skillet, and cook the onion over low heat for 10 minutes, stirring occasionally, until it softens.

Add the corned beef, vegetables, thyme, red pepper, salt, and black pepper. Stir well to combine. Use a wide metal spatula to press the hash into the pan. Cook it over medium heat for 15 minutes, or until the bottom turns very brown. Use the spatula to turn the hash in big pieces. They'll hold together if there's enough potato. If not, turn the hash with a large metal spoon. Continue pressing the hash on top every few minutes. Cook for 30 minutes more.

Spoon the hash onto plates and serve.

steak marchand de vin with caramelized onions

The French wine merchant (*marchand de vin*) takes home the best bottles for himself, it is said, and makes a little pan sauce to dress up steak. This popular recipe adds caramelized onions, which are very dark and sweet at the end of cooking and quite nice with the red wine sauce and beef. Serve this with Potato Crisps with Fresh Herbs (page 262).

> 3 tablespoons sugar
> 2 Spanish onions, halved
> 5 tablespoons butter
> 4 thick steaks cut from the loin (top loin, strip loin, shell, or Delmonico)
> 1/2 teaspoon coarse salt, or to taste
> 1/2 teaspoon freshly ground black pepper, or to taste
> 1 tablespoon olive oil
> 1 cup dry red wine
> 1 cup chicken stock
> 2 tablespoons chopped fresh parsley
> 1 tablespoon chopped fresh thyme

Sprinkle the sugar on a plate. Dip the cut sides of the onion in the sugar. Add more sugar to the plate if there isn't enough to coat all the cut sides.

Melt 2 tablespoons of the butter in a large skillet. Set the onions in the pan, cut sides down, and cook them over medium heat for 10 minutes, or until they caramelize and turn a deep, golden brown. Remove from the pan.

Sprinkle the steaks on both sides with the salt and pepper.

Rinse and dry the pan and return it to the burner. Add the oil and, when it is hot, add 1 tablespoon of the butter. When the butter melts, add the steaks to the pan. Cook over medium-high heat for 8 to 10 minutes (for medium-rare) or for 10 to 12 minutes (for medium).

Meanwhile, slice the onions thinly.

When the steaks are done, remove them from the pan and keep warm.

Add the wine to the pan along with the onions. Let the wine bubble steadily until it reduces by half. Add the stock and continue boiling until the mixture reduces by half again.

Remove the pan from the heat and swirl the remaining 2 tablespoons butter into the sauce. Add the parsley and thyme. Taste for seasoning and add more salt and pepper, if you like.

Set a steak on each of four dinner plates. Spoon the sauce and onions over each one and serve.

fresh salmon cakes
with homemade tartar sauce

Fresh salmon cakes are memorable. They're made with broiled salmon, mixed with cocktail sauce and dill, and fried in a skillet. The homemade tartar sauce just adds to the luster of the cakes. Begin with commercial mayonnaise, cut it with sour cream, add chopped pickles, capers, and scallions, and you have something wonderful.

FOR THE TARTAR SAUCE
- ½ **cup mayonnaise**
- ½ **cup sour cream**
- ¼ **cup finely chopped bread and butter pickles**
- 2 **scallions, finely chopped**
- 2 **tablespoons capers, drained**
- 1 **tablespoon chopped fresh parsley**
- 1 **tablespoon Dijon mustard**
- 1 **tablespoon fresh lemon juice**
- ½ **teaspoon coarse salt, or to taste**
- ¼ **teaspoon freshly ground black pepper, or to taste**

Combine the mayonnaise and sour cream in a small bowl, blending them thoroughly. Add the pickles, scallions, capers, parsley, mustard, lemon juice, salt, and pepper. Cover tightly and refrigerate for up to 4 hours while you make the salmon cakes.

∗⟩ FOR THE SALMON CAKES

1 1¹/4-pound salmon fillet
   Vegetable oil, for sprinkling and frying
¹/2 teaspoon coarse salt, or to taste
¹/2 teaspoon freshly ground black pepper, or to taste
¹/4 cup fresh dill leaves
1 cup tiny oyster crackers or broken saltines
1 garlic clove, halved
1 large egg, lightly beaten
3 tablespoons bottled cocktail sauce
   Dash of Worcestershire sauce
   All-purpose flour, for shaping

Preheat the broiler.

Set the salmon, skin side down, in an ovenproof baking dish and sprinkle it with oil, ¼ teaspoon of the salt, and ¼ teaspoon of the pepper. Broil for 10 minutes, or until the fish is cooked through. Set aside to cool.

When the salmon is cool enough to handle, remove and discard the skin and any fatty pieces. In a small bowl, flake the fish with a fork.

In a food processor, process the dill, crackers, garlic, the remaining ¼ teaspoon salt, and ¼ teaspoon pepper until they form crumbs. Add the cracker mixture to the fish with the egg, cocktail sauce, and Worcestershire sauce. Mix until thoroughly blended.

Lightly flour the counter. Divide the salmon mixture into 8 pieces. With your hands, form the mixture into patties, coating them with flour.

Set the oven at 250 degrees.

Heat enough oil in a large skillet to make a very thin film on the bottom. When it is hot, add half of the fish cakes. Cook over medium-high heat, turning often, for 10 minutes, or until they are browned and cooked through. Transfer the cakes to a baking sheet and keep warm in the oven.

Use more oil to fry the remaining salmon cakes in the same way. Serve with the tartar sauce.

oven-fried fish and chips

Instead of frying, you can bake coated fish and wedges of potato in a very hot oven until they are quite crisp. The quality of the crumbs is important. Make your own (page 29) or use ordinary unseasoned dry white bread crumbs or, even better, use the very crisp Japanese panko bread crumbs (page 29). The fish never gets the thick coating that batter-fried fish does, but it's kinder to your heart.

> 3 **russet (baking) potatoes**
> 2 **tablespoons vegetable oil, plus more for sprinkling**
> 1 **teaspoon coarse salt, or to taste**
> 1/2 **teaspoon freshly ground black pepper, or to taste**
> 3/4 **cup panko or other dry white bread crumbs**
> 2 **tablespoons freshly grated Parmesan cheese**
> 1 1/2 **pounds firm-fleshed skinless white fish fillets, such as**
> **haddock, cusk, or pollock, cut into 3-inch pieces**

Set the oven at 450 degrees. Lightly oil a rimmed baking sheet for the fish.

Without peeling the potatoes, cut them into long spears that are 1/2 inch thick. If the potatoes are very long, you can halve them horizontally first. In a bowl, toss the potatoes with the 2 tablespoons oil until they are coated. Arrange them on an ungreased baking sheet, cut sides up. Sprinkle them with 1/2 teaspoon of the salt and 1/4 teaspoon of the pepper.

Bake the potatoes for 30 to 40 minutes, or until golden brown. Halfway through cooking, use a wide metal spatula to turn the potatoes so they don't stick to the pan. Meanwhile, prepare the fish.

On a plate, combine the bread crumbs, Parmesan cheese, and the remaining 1/2 teaspoon salt and 1/4 teaspoon pepper. With your fingers, stir the mixture just to combine.

Set the fish on a plate and sprinkle some oil onto it. With your hands, rub the oil all over the fish. Press the fillets into the crumb mixture, turn to coat both sides, and set them on the oiled sheet so they are not touching.

Transfer the fish to the hot oven 15 minutes before the potatoes are done. Bake the fish for 15 minutes, or until golden brown and firm to the touch. Serve at once.

new england boiled dinner with glazed corned beef

A big piece of corned beef is the centerpiece of this meal-in-a-pot, which includes an array of root vegetables. As the vegetables simmer in the cooking water, they absorb some of the spiciness from the meat. Cook the beets separately so the other vegetables don't turn red, then use the leftovers to make Homemade Corned Beef Hash with Thyme (page 151). Start this the day before you serve it, so you can skim the fat from the cooking liquid before you reheat it. An 8-pound corned beef sounds big, but because of shrinkage, you'll have less than 5 pounds after simmering. If you like, serve this with bottled white horseradish or with Horseradish Sauce (page 158).

❊❳ FOR THE MEAT AND VEGETABLES

- 1 **8-pound corned beef brisket**
- 2 **whole peppercorns**
- 2 **whole cloves**
- 2 **pounds carrots (about 14)**
- 2 **pints Brussels sprouts, trimmed, with an "X" cut into the base of each one**
- 1 **Savoy cabbage, cut into thick wedges**
- 20 **small red or white potatoes**
- 2 **bunches (8 medium) beets, peeled and quartered**

Combine the corned beef, peppercorns, and cloves in a large pot. Add water to cover by 2 inches. Bring to a boil, skim the surface thoroughly, reduce the heat to low, cover, and simmer for 3½ hours, turning the meat halfway through cooking.

Remove the corned beef from the water and set it aside to cool.

Add the carrots, Brussels sprouts, cabbage, and potatoes to the water. Return to a boil, reduce the heat to low, and simmer the vegetables for 20 to 30 minutes, or until they are very tender.

Remove the vegetables from the water and transfer them to a baking dish to cool. Add the beets to the cooking liquid, bring to a boil, and simmer for 20 minutes, or until tender. Set aside. Ladle the cooking liquid into a plastic container, cool it, then refrigerate.

Refrigerate the boiled dinner in three containers, separating the meat, vegetables, and beets (they're fine for up to 2 days).

To reheat, set the oven at 325 degrees.

Arrange all the vegetables

(including the beets) around the edges of a large roasting pan, making several layers. Spoon enough cooking liquid onto the vegetables to moisten them. Cover with foil and reheat in the oven for 20 minutes.

Meanwhile, trim all the excess fat from the corned beef. Make the glaze.

※〉 FOR THE GLAZE

2 **tablespoons Dijon mustard**
2 **tablespoons dark brown sugar**
1 **tablespoon Worcestershire sauce**

Combine the mustard, brown sugar, and Worcestershire sauce in a small bowl.

Arrange the corned beef in the middle of the vegetables and spread it with the glaze. Bake, uncovered, for 30 to 40 minutes, or until the top is shiny. Meanwhile, make the Horseradish Sauce, if using.

※〉 FOR THE HORSERADISH SAUCE (OPTIONAL)

1¹/₂ **cups plain yogurt**
³/₄ **cup sour cream**
¹/₃ **cup bottled white horseradish**
2 **teaspoons grated raw onion**
¹/₂ **teaspoon freshly ground black pepper, or to taste**
 Pinch of cayenne pepper or chili powder, or to taste

Whisk the yogurt and sour cream together in a small bowl until they are smooth.

Stir in the horseradish, onion, black pepper, and cayenne or chili powder. Add more horseradish or onion, if you like.

Cover with plastic wrap and refrigerate to mellow the flavors.

note: The Horseradish Sauce can be made up to 2 days ahead, covered, and stored in the refrigerator.

Transfer the meat to a carving board. Carve it on a diagonal against the grain. Serve the meat and vegetables with Horseradish Sauce, if desired.

stefado (greek beef stew)

Once prepared in Greek villages with homemade vinegar, this stew is always made with lots of onions and an inexpensive cut of meat. Add bell pepper, red wine, tomatoes, whole cloves, and a cinnamon stick and the meat turns very dark and the sauce reduces and becomes perfumed at the end of cooking. Crumble a mild feta cheese on top. The late Mary Brown of Cambridge, Massachusetts, made this at a little restaurant she owned. Serve it with boiled potatoes sprinkled with parsley for a quiet Sunday supper, so you have leftovers for a weeknight.

    3   pounds chuck roast
        Olive oil, for sprinkling
    1   teaspoon coarse salt, or to taste
  1/2   teaspoon freshly ground black pepper, or to taste
    2   tablespoons olive oil
    2   large Spanish onions, coarsely chopped
    1   green bell pepper, cored, seeded, and cut into 1-inch pieces
    3   garlic cloves, finely chopped
    2   cups dry red wine
    2   cups chicken stock
    1   can (28 ounces) whole tomatoes, crushed
    2   tablespoons tomato paste
  1/4   cup chopped fresh parsley
    4   whole cloves
    1   cinnamon stick
    1   bay leaf
  1/2   teaspoon ground allspice

    4   ounces feta cheese, crumbled, for garnish
    3   tablespoons chopped fresh parsley, for garnish

Set the oven at 500 degrees.

Remove all the fat from the meat and cut it into 4-inch pieces, making the cuts where the meat falls apart naturally. Put the pieces into a roasting pan and sprinkle them lightly all over with oil, 1/2 teaspoon of the salt, and 1/4 teaspoon of the pepper. Rub them in with your hands to coat them thoroughly.

Roast for 30 minutes, turning the meat once halfway through cooking. Remove from the oven and set aside.

Reduce the oven temperature to 350 degrees.

Heat the oil in a large flame-proof casserole and cook the onions and green pepper over medium heat for 10 minutes, stirring often, or until softened. Add the garlic and cook for 1 minute more.

Add the wine, stock, tomatoes, tomato paste, parsley, cloves, cinnamon, bay leaf, allspice, and the remaining ½ teaspoon salt and ¼ teaspoon pepper. Stir in the meat with any juices in the roasting pan.

Bring to a boil, reduce the heat to low, and cover the pan. Transfer the pan to the oven and cook for 2½ hours. Check the meat several times to make sure there is enough liquid in the pan; add water, ¼ cup at a time, if it seems dry.

Remove from the oven and taste for seasoning. Add more salt and pepper, if you like. Mix the feta cheese and parsley in a small bowl. Ladle the stew into bowls, top each one with the feta mixture, and serve.

corn bread baked in a skillet

Baking corn bread in a cast-iron skillet makes it crusty around the edges but soft inside. You'll need a 10-inch skillet (a nonstick pan will also work).

2 **large eggs**
1/2 **cup sugar**
2/3 **cup canola oil**
1 1/4 **cups buttermilk**
3/4 **cup yellow cornmeal**
1 1/4 **cups all-purpose flour**
1 1/2 **teaspoons baking powder**
1/2 **teaspoon salt**

Set the oven at 325 degrees. Butter a 10-inch cast-iron skillet or another skillet of the same size with a heatproof handle.

Beat the eggs, sugar, and oil in a large bowl with a whisk until thoroughly blended. Add the buttermilk and whisk to combine.

Stir in the cornmeal, flour, baking powder, and salt with a wooden spoon. Pour into the skillet.

Bake for 40 minutes, or until a skewer inserted into the bread comes out clean.

Set the skillet on a rack to cool. Cut the corn bread into wedges and serve warm.

boston baked beans

Baked beans are favorites at potluck suppers and on picnic tables at summer barbe-cues. These thick molasses-and-maple-syrup-infused beans are sweeter than the tra-ditional versions and seasoned with ham instead of the usual salt pork. They spend half a day in the oven and never turn mushy because the molasses protects them. We add more water to the pot than you'll need because the beans just keep soaking up excess liquid. Allow time for the beans to soak overnight.

2¹/₂ cups dried white beans, such as Great Northern or navy
      beans
  1 tablespoon vegetable oil
  2 medium onions, coarsely chopped
  2 thick slices (about ¹/₂ pound total) flavorful baked ham
      (such as Westphalian or Black Forest), cut into ¹/₂-inch
      dice
¹/₄ cup packed dark brown sugar
  3 tablespoons molasses
  3 tablespoons maple syrup
  1 tablespoon tomato paste
  1 tablespoon dry mustard
  1 tablespoon ground ginger
  6 cups water, plus more as needed
¹/₂ teaspoon coarse salt, or to taste
¹/₂ teaspoon freshly ground black pepper, or to taste

Place the beans in a bowl and cover them with cold water. Set them aside to soak overnight, or for at least 8 hours.

Set the oven at 300 degrees.

Heat the oil in a flameproof casserole, and cook the onions over medium heat, stirring often, for 10 minutes, or until they soften.

Drain the beans and add them to the onions. Add the ham, brown sugar, molasses, maple syrup, tomato paste, mustard, ginger, and 6 cups water. Bring to a boil and cover the pan.

Bake for 4 hours, checking the beans every hour, stirring, and adding more water to the pan, ¹/₄ cup at a time, if they seem dry. Add the salt and pepper. Let the beans settle for 15 minutes before serving, or let them cool to room temperature and refrigerate until ready to use.

To store and reheat the beans: Cover the pan and refrigerate the beans for up to 5 days. Set the pan over medium heat and stir the beans. If they have absorbed all their liquid, add water, ¼ cup at a time, until the beans are the consistency you like. Reduce the heat to low and let simmer for 10 minutes, stirring often, until they are very hot.

good enough for company

The most important element for any get-together, of course, is the people. We know lots of hosts and hostesses who aren't fabulous cooks but who throw wonderful dinner parties. The guest list, we think, should be mixed up with people of different ages, some who aren't attached and some who are known characters and will keep the conversation going when you head into the kitchen to bring out another course.

Conversation, after all, is what you're after: lively discussions that make your table seem like *the* place to be and make the evening — especially one with good food — memorable.

When Julia Child lived in her big house in Cambridge, Massachusetts, she always entertained in the kitchen and sat guests very close together. The table was large, but somehow there were always more people than places. It created intimacy, and she didn't miss any of the conversation.

Julia, of course, was the nation's most relaxed hostess, and she wasn't afraid to try something new. We don't necessarily recommend that, unless you're also a proficient cook. In order to be relaxed, we think you need to make a plan that isn't difficult to execute, rather than something you've never done before. It's up to you to entertain the first guests who arrive, so you shouldn't be elbow-deep in the cooking when the doorbell's about to ring. If you are, however, better bring them right into the kitchen.

We believe in making what people are looking for: Tenderloin of Beef with Red Wine Sauce for the meat-and-potato customers; Squash, Zucchini, and White Bean Stew for the vegetarians. Our repertoire includes some dishes that look impressive but don't take much time, like Roast Rack of Pork, which slices into thick, rosy chops, or Orange-Marinated Turkey Breast, moist, almost creamy, poultry. Herb-Roasted Flattened Chicken is often on the table, as is Roast Side of Salmon or Shrimp, Corn, Red Potato, and Green Bean Boil with Dipping Sauces.

But things do go wrong: a roast gets overcooked (dim the lights), something looks a little raw near the bone (make the lights even dimmer), all your guests are dull (turn off the lights).

Once Sheryl served the first course to her guests, sat down, proposed a toast to them, and found them staring at her. She had forgotten the silverware. Julie routinely leaves things in the oven and finds them later when she's cleaning up. Our theory is that if you entertain enough, these make great stories for another day. If things like that upset you, you need to start having more company.

Here are several of our rules: never sit spouses or any two people who came together side by side. Instead of making a boy-girl pattern around the table, seat your guests according to their personalities: boisterous, shy, boisterous, shy, so all the loud people are separated by the soft ones. Dinner parties are not Noah's Ark. Don't just invite people by twos. And finally, plan away. Then, if you feel like serving in the kitchen Julia Child–style, we agree that it's a wonderful way to entertain.

good enough for company

brine for pork or poultry

If you haven't tried this technique, we promise you'll find it a revelation. A brine is good for any dry-roasted bird or cut of pork, helping the meat retain its juiciness and adding flavor. Brines are mixed from kosher salt, granulated sugar, and water. When the meat or poultry goes into the liquid, the brine penetrates the flesh so the muscle fibers swell and absorb moisture. There's nothing difficult about brining, except perhaps finding a container large enough to hold the meat. Brines are much more effective tenderizers than marinades, which are not properly absorbed by meat, though they do add some flavor to the surface.

   1 **gallon water**
 3/4 **cup sugar**
 3/4 **cup kosher salt**
   1 **bay leaf**
  10 **peppercorns**
   4 **dried red chili peppers, crushed**

In a container large enough to hold the meat or poultry, combine the water, sugar, salt, bay leaf, peppercorns, and chilies. Add the meat and turn it in the liquid. Cover the container with plastic wrap and refrigerate overnight. Turn the meat several times while it brines. Just before you're ready to proceed with the recipe, remove the meat from the brine. Pat it dry thoroughly with paper towels. When you use brined meat in a recipe, cut down on the salt because the meat will retain some of the salt from the brine.

roast rack of pork

Rack of pork is another name for a pork loin with the bones intact. Some markets call it simply "bone-in pork loin." Ask the butcher to cut through the backbone (also called the chine bone), so you can carve double-thick chops. Because there's hardly any work to this dish, serve an array of sides: Sautéed Apples (page 257), Crusty Smashed Potatoes (page 260), and Broccolini with Olive Oil and Lemon Juice (page 248).

1   8-rib center-cut rack of pork (about 5 pounds), brined if
      you like (see page 167)

2   garlic cloves, cut into thin slivers

2   tablespoons dry mustard

1   tablespoon dried sage

1/8   teaspoon freshly grated nutmeg, or to taste

1/2   teaspoon coarse salt, or to taste (use only 1/8 teaspoon if the
      meat is brined)

1/2   teaspoon freshly ground black pepper, or to taste

Set the oven at 475 degrees. Insert a baking rack into a roasting pan.

Place the pork, fat side up, on the rack. With the tip of a knife, make shallow slits all over the meat and insert the slivers of garlic.

In a small bowl, combine the mustard, sage, nutmeg, salt, and pepper. Rub the mustard mixture all over the meat.

Roast the meat for 20 minutes.

Turn the oven temperature down to 350 degrees. Continue roasting the pork for 60 minutes, or until an instant-read thermometer inserted into the thickest part of the meat registers 150 degrees. (Once the pork is out of the oven, the temperature will rise to about 155 degrees, which produces perfectly done meat that is faintly pink.)

Remove the pork from the oven and set it on a platter. Cover loosely with foil and set it in a warm place for 20 minutes.

Carve the meat into chops and serve.

roast loin of pork
with macerated dried fruit

Since farmers decided to raise leaner pigs for a health-conscious public forty years ago, pork isn't as marbled as it should be. To compensate for the loss of fat, which gives the meat flavor, we rub the boneless loin with aromatic spices and add prunes, apricots, and dried cranberries macerated in Marsala wine. This center-cut loin is rolled, tied, and cooked just until pink. Pigs are no longer at risk for trichinosis, but if you prefer well-done pork, cook it little longer.

FOR THE PORK

- 1 4-pound boneless center-cut pork loin, rolled and tied
- 2 garlic cloves, cut into thin slivers
- 1 teaspoon coarse salt, or to taste
- $^1/_2$ teaspoon freshly ground black pepper, or to taste
- $^1/_8$ teaspoon ground cinnamon
- $^1/_8$ teaspoon ground allspice
- $^1/_8$ teaspoon ground nutmeg
- 2 tablespoons Dijon mustard
- 2 tablespoons vegetable oil
- 2 Spanish onions, thinly sliced
- 1 bottle (750 ml) dry white wine
- 3 cups water
- 1 bay leaf

Set the oven at 350 degrees. With the tip of a knife, make shallow slits all over the meat and insert the slivers of garlic. Combine the salt, pepper, cinnamon, allspice, and nutmeg in a bowl. Rub the mixture all over the meat.

Heat the oil in a flameproof casserole large enough to hold the meat, and cook the onions over medium heat for 10 minutes, or until they soften. Push the onions to the sides of the pan, add the meat, and brown it, turning occasionally, for 10 minutes. Stir the onions occasionally so they don't get too brown. The meat will only slightly color.

Add the wine, water, and bay leaf to the pan. Bring the mixture to a boil, cover the pan, and transfer it to the oven.

Cook the pork, turning it several times, for 30 minutes. While the meat is cooking, prepare the fruits and vegetables. (The total cooking time will be about $1^1/_2$ hours.)

❋{ FOR THE FRUITS AND VEGETABLES

¹/₂ cup Marsala wine

¹/₂ cup pitted prunes

¹/₂ cup dried apricots

1 cup dried sweet cranberries or cherries

5 carrots, cut thickly on the diagonal

3 medium purple-topped turnips, cut into thick wedges

1 tablespoon dried sage

¹/₄ cup chopped fresh parsley

Combine the Marsala, prunes, apricots, and cranberries or cherries in a large saucepan. Set the mixture over medium heat and bring just to a boil. Remove the pan from the heat, cover it, and set aside for 30 minutes.

After the meat has cooked for 30 minutes, remove the pan from the oven and add the dried fruits and Marsala liquid, and the carrots, turnips, and sage.

Re-cover the pan and return the meat to the oven. Continue cooking for 1 hour, or until an instant-read thermometer registers 150 degrees. (Once the pork is out of the oven, the temperature will rise to about 155 degrees, which produces perfectly done meat that is faintly pink.)

Transfer the meat to a large, warm platter and cover it loosely with foil. Test the vegetables with a skewer to see if they are tender. If not, set the casserole on top of the stove (take care because the handles are very hot). Bring the mixture to a boil and let the vegetables cook for 5 to 8 minutes, or until they are cooked through.

Use a slotted spoon to remove the fruits and vegetables from the cooking juices and spoon them around the pork. Cover the dish loosely with foil.

Discard the bay leaf from the juices, bring them to a boil, then skim off and discard all the fat. Let them bubble steadily, skimming often, for 5 minutes. Taste for seasoning and add more salt and pepper, if you like.

Remove the strings from the pork loin and cut it into thick slices. Spoon some of the cooking juices over the meat. Sprinkle the pork, fruits, and vegetables with the parsley and serve. Pass the remaining juices separately.

tenderloin of beef with red wine sauce

All cooks need an elegant cut of beef in their repertoire. We fought this idea for years on the theory that there are so many more interesting things to make that don't require the careful timing beef demands. Then we decided that there are some people — people we're related to — who are only happy when the meal is meat and potatoes. This is the dish for that occasion, and luckily for you, the beef requires hardly any work. You can make the sauce while the tenderloin rests. In order to roast perfectly cooked meat, you'll need an instant-read thermometer; then relax and let the thermometer be your guide. Serve with Roasted Potato and Red Onion Mélange (page 268) or Potato Crisps with Fresh Herbs (page 262).

FOR THE BEEF

1 3–4-pound beef tenderloin, trimmed of fat
2 tablespoons Dijon mustard
1 tablespoon all-purpose flour
1/2 teaspoon coarse salt, or to taste
1/2 teaspoon freshly ground black pepper, or to taste
1 tablespoon olive oil

Set the oven at 425 degrees.

Place the beef on a work surface. In a small bowl, combine the mustard, flour, salt, and pepper. Rub the mixture all over the meat.

In a large skillet with a heat-proof handle (cast-iron works well), heat the oil over medium-high heat. Brown the beef on all sides, turning often, for 5 minutes, or until golden all over.

Roast for about 25 minutes, or until an instant-read thermometer inserted into the thickest part of the meat registers 125 degrees for rare, or 135 degrees for medium-rare (30 to 35 minutes), or 140 degrees for medium (40 minutes).

Transfer the beef to a cutting board. Cover loosely with foil and let rest in a warm place while you prepare the sauce.

❊⸰ FOR THE SAUCE
4 **tablespoons (¹/₂ stick) butter**
2 **shallots, finely chopped**
1 **cup dry red wine**
1 **cup chicken stock**

1 **bunch watercress, stems removed, for garnish**

Using the same skillet in which you cooked the beef, heat 1 tablespoon of the butter. Add the shallots and cook over medium-low heat, stirring often, for 2 minutes, or until lightly browned. Add the wine and bring to a boil, scraping up any brown bits that cling to the bottom of the pan. Add the stock and return to a boil. Skim the fat from the top of the sauce. Let the sauce bubble steadily until it reduces by half.

Cut the remaining 3 tablespoons of butter into 6 pieces. Slowly whisk in the butter and keep whisking for 1 minute, or until the sauce is smooth. Don't let it boil. Taste for seasoning and add salt and pepper, if you like.

To serve, slice the meat and arrange it on six dinner plates. Garnish with watercress and pour some sauce around the meat. Pass the remaining sauce separately.

flank steak in ginger-soy marinade

For big beef flavor, flank steak is our first choice. It's a chewy piece of lean, boneless meat that sits beneath the loin on the steer. Cook it until it's quite rare and then cut it against the long, coarse grain. The thin meat absorbs enough of the marinade overnight to make it wonderfully tasty on the grill. It's almost as good under the broiler.

2   garlic cloves, finely chopped
1   1-inch piece fresh ginger, peeled and finely chopped
1   teaspoon hot chili paste
2   tablespoons dark brown sugar
2   tablespoons Chinese rice wine
2   tablespoons soy sauce
2   tablespoons sesame oil
1   1½–2-pound flank steak
4   large sweet onions (Oso Sweet, Walla Walla, Vidalia, or
        another of the super-sweet variety), unpeeled
    Peanut oil, for drizzling
½   teaspoon coarse salt, or to taste
½   teaspoon freshly ground black pepper, or to taste

In a dish large enough to hold the steak flat, combine the garlic, ginger, chili paste, brown sugar, wine, soy sauce, and sesame oil.

Use a sharp paring knife to score the meat lightly on both sides, making a shallow crosshatch pattern. Place it in the marinade, turn to coat both sides, cover tightly with plastic wrap, and refrigerate overnight.

About 1½ hours before serving, set the oven at 375 degrees.

Place the onions in a baking dish. Drizzle them with oil and sprinkle them with the salt and pepper. Bake the onions for 1¼ hours, or until they are very tender when pierced with a skewer. When cool enough to handle, remove the skins from the onions.

Prepare a gas or charcoal grill. When the coals turn gray or the gas grill is hot, remove the meat from the marinade and transfer it to the grill. Alternatively, turn on the broiler and set the meat on a rack in a broiler pan.

Cook the meat, turning often, for 6 to 8 minutes, or until it is lightly charred on the outside and rare inside, or cook it a few minutes longer for well-done. Remove the meat from the grill or broiler pan.

      To serve, set the flank steak on a cutting board and hold a long knife at an extreme angle to the meat. Carve the meat very thinly across the grain. Cut the onions into quarters and serve with the meat.

grilled butterflied leg of lamb

Any supermarket butcher will bone and butterfly a leg of lamb for you. Butterflying the meat flattens it so it cooks more quickly on the grill or in a hot oven. We like lamb very pink, bathed in garlic, French mustard, and wine vinegar, as do our butchers, John Dewar and Co. of Boston and Newton, Massachusetts, who gave us this recipe. Serve with Fresh Corn "Risotto" (page 252) or Scalloped Tomatoes (page 254).

- 1 8-pound leg of lamb, boned and trimmed of fat
- 1 garlic clove, cut into slivers
- 1/4 cup red wine vinegar
- 2 tablespoons Dijon mustard
- 1 tablespoon chopped fresh basil
- 1 tablespoon chopped fresh oregano
- 1/2 teaspoon coarse salt, or to taste
- 1/2 teaspoon freshly ground black pepper, or to taste
- 1/4 cup olive oil
- 1 red onion, coarsely chopped
- 1 bay leaf, crushed

Trim as much excess fat from the lamb as you can. Spread out the meat on a cutting board, boned side up. With a small sharp knife, slash the meat across the grain in the thickest places. Use the tip of a paring knife to make slits all over the meat and tuck the slivers of garlic into the slits.

In a small bowl, whisk together the vinegar and mustard. Whisk in the basil, oregano, salt, pepper, and oil.

Place the lamb in a baking dish large enough to hold the meat flat, and pour the mustard mixture over it. Spread it on the meat to coat it all over. Scatter the onion and bay leaf on top. Cover the dish with plastic wrap and refrigerate the meat for at least 2 hours or as long as 1 day, turning it several times.

Let the meat sit at room temperature for 1 hour while you light a charcoal grill or heat a gas grill.

When the coals turn gray or the gas grill is hot, remove the meat from the marinade. Pat it dry with paper towels. Set the meat on the grill and cook it for 20 minutes, turning often, just until the outside is nicely browned. Baste with the marinade while it grills.

Close the vents halfway on the bottom of the grill and on the hood. Close the cover and continue cooking the lamb for 8 minutes more, or until an instant-read thermometer inserted into the thickest part registers 120 degrees, for rare meat.

Transfer the meat to a platter and set it in a warm place for 10 minutes. Slice the meat thinly across the grain and serve.

rack of lamb with fresh mint sauce

Rack of lamb, which is so popular in restaurants, is quite simple to make at home. The cut is the ribs of the lamb; as you carve, you'll see the rib chops come off the rack. Make sure that the coating of fat that covers the back of the rack is completely removed. Then use a small knife to cut away all the fat around the ends of the bones. If you cook this in the summer — a good season for this dish, since the oven is on for such a brief time — serve it with a fresh mint sauce. Simply made with a sugar syrup infused with mint leaves and a little vinegar, the sauce really makes the dish. Accompany with Old-Fashioned Creamy Corn Pudding (page 253), and you have a stunning dinner.

FOR THE MINT SAUCE
- 1/4 **cup water**
- 1/2 **cup sugar**
- 1/2 **cup distilled white vinegar**
- 2 **tablespoons dried mint**
- 1 **bunch fresh mint leaves, finely chopped (about 1 cup)**

In a small saucepan, combine the water, sugar, and vinegar. Cook over very low heat, stirring, until the sugar dissolves. Increase the heat to medium-high and bring to a boil. Reduce the heat again to low, add the dried mint, and simmer for 5 minutes. Remove from the heat and set aside to cool. Stir in the fresh mint. Set aside while you prepare the lamb.

❋{ FOR THE LAMB

- 2 racks of lamb, completely trimmed, with chine bone (back bone) removed
- 1/2 teaspoon coarse salt, or to taste
- 1/2 teaspoon freshly ground black pepper, or to taste
- 1 garlic clove, finely chopped
- 2 tablespoons chopped fresh parsley
- 2 tablespoons Dijon mustard
- 1/4 cup panko bread crumbs (see page 29) or unseasoned dry white bread crumbs
- 2 tablespoons olive oil
- 1/2 cup dry white wine

Set the oven at 450 degrees. Place the lamb in a roasting pan, curved sides up.

In a small bowl, combine the salt, pepper, garlic, parsley, mustard, bread crumbs, and olive oil. Press the coating into the racks of lamb.

Roast the lamb for 10 minutes. Reduce the oven temperature to 400 degrees and sprinkle the lamb with the wine. Continue roasting for 10 minutes, or until an instant-read thermometer inserted into the thickest part of the chops registers 120 degrees for rare. Cook 3 minutes more for medium.

Transfer the lamb to a carving board. Let it rest for 5 minutes in a warm place. Carve the lamb into chops and arrange 4 chops on each of four dinner plates. Serve with the mint sauce.

veal stew with green olives and tomatoes

For a stew, we use a shoulder of veal, which is inexpensive and has lots of flavor. Cut it into 4-inch pieces because they'll shrink during cooking, and if you start with larger pieces, you'll end up with good-sized morsels. Serve with Asparagus Cooked for Two Minutes (page 247) and Crusty Smashed Potatoes (page 260).

- 1/2 cup all-purpose flour
- 1/2 teaspoon coarse salt, or to taste
- 1/2 teaspoon freshly ground black pepper, or to taste
- 2 1/2 pounds veal shoulder, cut into 4-inch pieces
- 3 tablespoons vegetable oil, plus more if needed
- 1 Spanish onion, coarsely chopped
- 2 garlic cloves, finely chopped
- 1 cup canned imported plum tomatoes, crushed in a bowl
- 1/8 teaspoon sugar
- 2 cups dry white wine
- 2 cups chicken stock
- 3 tablespoons chopped fresh thyme
- 1 dried red chili pepper, crushed
- 1 bay leaf
- 1/2 cup green olives, pitted (see page 181)

Place the flour, salt, and pepper on a plate and mix them with your fingers to combine. Turn the veal pieces in the flour to coat them lightly. Pat off any excess flour with your hands.

Heat half of the oil in a large flameproof casserole. Brown half of the veal, turning the pieces often, until they are golden. Transfer to a plate. Use the remaining oil to brown the remaining veal in the same way.

Remove the veal from the pan. If the pan is dry, add 1 tablespoon oil. Add the onion and salt and pepper to taste and cook over medium-low heat, stirring often, for 10 minutes, or until the onion begins to soften.

Add the garlic, tomatoes, sugar, wine, stock, thyme, chili pepper, bay leaf, and olives. Bring the mixture to a boil, scraping up any brown bits that cling to the bottom of the pan.

To Pit Olives

You can pit olives with an olive pitter or simply with your hand. Imagine that you're holding a thumbtack in your hand and that you're pressing it into the counter with your thumb. Stand the olive on the counter, pointed end down, stem end up. Form your hand into a fist and press your thumb into the stem end as hard as you can (top right). This will split the olive open and push the pit out the pointed end. The flesh will peel off the pit easily (bottom right).

Return the veal and any juices on the plate to the pan. Reduce the heat to low, cover the pan, and simmer the veal for 1¼ to 1½ hours, or until very tender. Remove and discard the bay leaf. Taste for seasoning and add more salt and pepper, if you like, and serve.

ossobuco

Perhaps because everyone adores stewy foods, ossobuco (Italian for "bone with a hole") is a popular dinner-party dish. The thickly cut veal shanks have to be tied to the bone so they don't fall off as they cook slowly in white wine with vegetables. The marrow in the center of the bone can be spread onto crusty bread with a demitasse spoon. The dish is garnished with gremolata, a chopped mixture of garlic, lemon rind, and parsley. Serve this with Crusty Smashed Potatoes (see page 260).

FOR THE VEAL SHANKS

- 2 tablespoons olive oil
- 1 tablespoon butter
- 1 Spanish onion, finely chopped
- 2 carrots, finely chopped
- 1 celery stalk, finely chopped
- 8 veal shanks, cut 2 inches thick and tied with string
- 1 teaspoon coarse salt, or to taste
- 1/2 teaspoon freshly ground black pepper, or to taste
- 1 garlic clove, crushed
- 3 tablespoons all-purpose flour
- 1 bottle (750 ml) dry white wine
- 1/2 cup canned imported tomatoes, crushed in a bowl
- 3 tablespoons chopped fresh thyme

Set the oven at 350 degrees.

Heat the oil and butter in a large flameproof casserole, and cook the onion, carrots, and celery, stirring often, for 10 minutes, or until they soften.

Season the veal shanks with 1/2 teaspoon of the salt and 1/4 teaspoon of the pepper.

Add 4 of the shanks to the pan with the vegetables and brown them on both sides, turning often, for 8 minutes. Transfer them to a plate and cook the remaining shanks in the same way. Remove all the veal from the pan.

Add the garlic to the pan and cook for 30 seconds, or until softened. Sprinkle the flour into the pan and cook, stirring, for 2 minutes more. Pour in the wine and bring it to a boil, stirring constantly. Cook for 2 minutes, stirring.

Add the tomatoes, the remaining ½ teaspoon salt and ¼ teaspoon pepper, and the thyme. Stir thoroughly. Return the veal to the pan, bring the liquid to a boil, reduce the heat to low, and cover the pan.

Transfer the pan to the oven and cook for 2 to 2½ hours, turning the meat once or twice, or until it is almost falling off the bone. Meanwhile, make the gremolata.

❋{ FOR THE GREMOLATA
**2 garlic cloves
Pared rind of 1 lemon
Handful fresh Italian parsley
leaves**

Chop the garlic, lemon rind, and parsley together.

❋{ TO ASSEMBLE
Taste the veal cooking liquid for seasoning and add more salt and pepper if necessary.

Sprinkle the gremolata over the veal shanks and serve.

orange-marinated turkey breast

Our friends who cater tell us that most people want to serve something safe and utterly reliable when they entertain. That often means turkey breast. This one is marinated overnight in orange juice, soy sauce, ginger, and honey, which gives the poultry a nice, slightly sweet citrus taste. The recipe comes from Holly Safford of the Catered Affair in Hingham, Massachusetts, who receives loads of compliments when her company makes it for parties. Her staff say it's their favorite dish. She uses a boned and rolled breast (which she buys already rolled and in an elastic mesh sleeve). We prefer it on the bone. If you want to use a boneless breast, see page 185. Serve with Potato Crisps with Fresh Herbs (page 262) or Winter Squashes Roasted in Chunks (page 270).

1	cup canola oil
1/4	cup grated orange rind
5	cups fresh orange juice
1/4	cup fresh lemon juice
2	tablespoons soy sauce
2	tablespoons chopped fresh ginger
2	garlic cloves, finely chopped
1	shallot, finely chopped
1 1/2	tablespoons honey
1	tablespoon Dijon mustard
1	6–7-pound bone-in turkey breast
1/2	teaspoon coarse salt, or to taste
1/2	teaspoon freshly ground black pepper, or to taste

Combine the oil, orange rind and juice, lemon juice, soy sauce, ginger, garlic, shallot, honey, and mustard in a large bowl wide enough to hold all the liquids and the turkey breast. Add the turkey breast and turn it in the marinade to coat it on all sides.

Cover with plastic wrap and refrigerate overnight, turning the turkey in the marinade several times.

Set the oven at 350 degrees.

Remove the turkey from the marinade and set it in a roasting pan. Reserve 2 cups of the marinade. Sprinkle the turkey all over with the salt and pepper. Pour the 2 cups of marinade into the pan.

Roast the turkey for 15 minutes per pound (about 1 1/2 hours), or until an instant-read thermometer inserted into

VARIATION
Boneless Orange-Marinated Turkey Breast

Follow the recipe for Orange-Marinated Turkey Breast but use a 4–5-pound boneless, rolled breast. Cook it for 18 minutes per pound (about 1 hour and 10 minutes), or until an instant-read thermometer inserted into the thickest part of the breast registers 160 degrees. Remove the strings before carving.

the thickest part of the breast (not touching the bone) registers 160 degrees.

Remove the turkey from the oven and let it sit in a warm place for 10 minutes. The temperature will rise about 5 degrees.

Carve the turkey into slices, baste with the pan juices, and serve.

duck breasts
with dried cranberries and madeira wine

Until a few years ago, duck breasts were restaurant food. Faced with a nugget of lean meat covered with an impenetrable coating of skin and fat, home cooks had no idea how to handle the breasts. The secret is to score the skin and cook the breasts in a heavy skillet — then in a hot oven — so that all the fat cooks out of the skin. This is a simple, elegant dish. We make a pan sauce with white wine and chicken stock, then add dried cranberries, which offset the rich meat.

$^1/_2$ **cup dried cranberries**

  1 **cup Madeira wine**

  4 **boneless duck breasts, skin intact**

$^1/_2$ **teaspoon coarse salt, or to taste**

$^1/_2$ **teaspoon freshly ground black pepper, or to taste**

  2 **cups chicken stock**

  2 **tablespoons chopped fresh thyme**

  2 **tablespoons grated lemon rind**

  4 **tablespoons ($^1/_2$ stick) cold butter, cut into pieces**

In a small bowl, combine the cranberries and Madeira and set aside for 1 hour to plump. Drain the cranberries and set aside, reserving the liquid.

Set the oven at 450 degrees.

With a sharp knife, score the duck fat in a crosshatch pattern, taking care not to cut through the flesh. Rub both sides of the breasts with the salt and pepper.

Heat a large, heavy skillet with a heatproof handle over high heat. When it is hot, place the breasts in the pan, fat sides down. Cook them over medium-high heat for 5 minutes, without moving them, or until the skin is golden brown.

Transfer the breasts to a plate. Remove all but 2 tablespoons of the fat from the pan (use it another day to fry potatoes). Return the breasts to the pan, skin side up, and cook for 3 minutes.

Transfer the pan to the oven and cook the breasts for 5 minutes, or until they are golden brown but still pink in the center.

Handle the skillet with a double thickness of potholders. Transfer the skillet to the stovetop. Remove the breasts from the pan and wipe out the excess fat, leaving the sediment. Pour the cranberry soaking liquid into the pan and bring it to a boil, scraping the bottom of the pan thoroughly. Let the liquid bubble steadily until it reduces to ¼ cup, skimming the surface to remove any fat.

Pour in the chicken stock. Bring it to a boil and let the mixture bubble steadily until the sauce reduces again and turns dark and syrupy. Add the thyme, lemon rind, and reserved cran-berries to the sauce. Add the butter, a piece at a time. Without letting the sauce boil, cook it, stirring, for 2 minutes, or until the butter melts and the sauce is shiny. Taste for seasoning and add salt and pepper, if you like. Slice the duck breasts on an extreme diagonal and arrange them on each of four dinner plates. Spoon the sauce over the duck slices and serve.

chicken breasts with ricotta and herbs

Slipped between the skin and flesh, the ricotta-herb mixture keeps the chicken moist and flavors it. The breasts have the drumettes still attached to them, a presentation once called "supreme" because French-trained chefs always served them with a rich white sauce. During roasting, some of the cheese slips out, which you can cut off before you take the chicken to the table (these are nibbles for the hosts during cleanup).

1 cup whole ricotta cheese

1/2 cup freshly grated Parmesan cheese

4 tablespoons chopped fresh herbs (parsley, thyme, marjoram, oregano)

1 garlic clove, finely chopped

1/2 teaspoon coarse salt, or to taste

1/2 teaspoon freshly ground black pepper, or to taste

4 chicken breasts, prepared as directed on page 189
Olive oil, for sprinkling

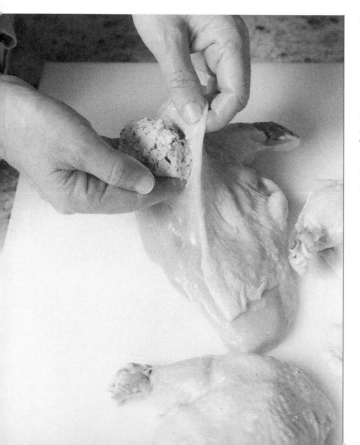

Set the oven at 400 degrees.

In a small bowl, combine the ricotta, Parmesan, herbs, garlic, salt, and pepper. Stir well.

With your fingers, separate the skin from the chicken breasts. With your hand or a spoon, ease the stuffing under the skin, stretching the skin slightly and pushing the stuffing to the tip of the breast (left).

To Prepare Chicken Breasts

Begin with a chicken breast quarter that has the wing intact. With kitchen shears, snip off the 2 smallest wing pieces, leaving the drumette portion attached to the breast. (Use the small pieces to make stock.)

Cut away any backbone still attached to the breast.

Set the breasts, skin side up, in a baking dish large enough to hold them in one layer. Sprinkle them with oil, salt, and pepper.

Roast the breasts for 40 to 45 minutes, or until an instant-read thermometer inserted into the thickest part of the breast registers 160 degrees.

Serve.

roast cornish game hens with tomato-caper sauce

Fresh Cornish hens have been coming into our markets lately, and we cook them often. If you want to serve roasted hens without the tomato-caper sauce, follow the recipe just to the point where the birds come out of the oven. Serve hens without sauce with Cauliflower in Milk with Rosemary (page 258) and lots of crusty bread. Serve hens in sauce with Crusty Smashed Potatoes (page 260).

4	**Cornish hens (about 1¹/₄ pounds each)**
	Olive oil, for rubbing
¹/₂	**teaspoon coarse salt, or to taste**
¹/₂	**teaspoon freshly ground black pepper, or to taste**
	Handful fresh rosemary leaves, finely chopped
¹/₂	**cup dry white wine**
1	**cup chicken stock**
4	**Italian plum tomatoes, peeled and chopped**
	Grated rind of 1 orange
2	**tablespoons capers, drained**
1	**tablespoon honey**
3	**tablespoons chopped fresh parsley**

Set the oven at 400 degrees.

With paper towels, wipe the hens. Remove the innards from the hens, then wipe the insides.

Set the hens in a roasting pan, breast side up. Rub them with oil and sprinkle with the salt, pepper, and rosemary. Tuck the thighs up against the breasts to protect them as they cook and tie the ends of the legs together.

Roast the hens for 50 minutes, or until an instant-read thermometer inserted into the thickest part of the thigh registers 170 degrees. Transfer the hens to a platter; keep warm.

Place the roasting pan over high heat. Add the wine and the stock and bring to a boil. Skim the fat from the liquid. Let the juices bubble steadily, skimming often, until the liquid reduces by half.

When the sauce is free of all fat, add the tomatoes, orange rind, capers, and honey. Simmer for 5 minutes, or until the sauce is well flavored.

Spoon the sauce onto each of four large deep plates. Place a Cornish hen on each one, sprinkle with parsley, and serve.

herb-roasted flattened chicken

A whole bird that has been split and flattened cooks almost as quickly as parts but retains the irresistible juiciness of good roast chicken. Unfortunately, supermarket butchers won't split it for you, but you can do so yourself at home (see page 193). You can brine the chicken (see page 167), if you like. Otherwise, roast it with a mustard and herb paste slipped between the skin and flesh. Serve with Roasted Onion Wedges (page 266), Crusty Smashed Potatoes (page 260), or Winter Squashes Roasted in Chunks (page 270).

2   garlic cloves, crushed

2   tablespoons Dijon mustard

2   tablespoons olive oil

1   tablespoon chopped fresh rosemary

2   tablespoons chopped fresh thyme

$1/2$ teaspoon coarse salt, or to taste

$1/2$ teaspoon freshly ground black pepper, or to taste

1   3–$3^{1}/_{2}$-pound chicken, backbone removed and flattened (see page 193)

Juice of 1 lemon

In a small bowl, combine the garlic, mustard, oil, rosemary, thyme, salt, and pepper.

Place the chicken in a roasting pan, skin side up. Create a space between the skin and flesh of the chicken by gently inserting your finger under the skin at the neck end and working it away from the flesh. Spoon half of the mustard mixture between the skin and flesh, beginning at the neck and moving along the breast and thigh, then rub the remaining mixture onto the skin. (If preparing in advance, cover the chicken loosely with plastic wrap and refrigerate it for 4 hours or up to overnight.)

Set the oven at 400 degrees.

Place the chicken, skin side up, in a roasting pan. Tuck the ends of the wings under the bird. Bend the legs up so the thighs sit high on the breast and protect the bottom of the breast from drying out.

Roast the chicken for 50 to 60 minutes, or until an instant-read thermometer inserted into the thickest part of the thigh registers 170 degrees. Set in a warm place for 5 minutes.

With poultry shears, cut the chicken into 10 pieces (see page 194). Arrange them on a platter, sprinkle with lemon juice and serve.

To Flatten Chicken for Quick Roasting

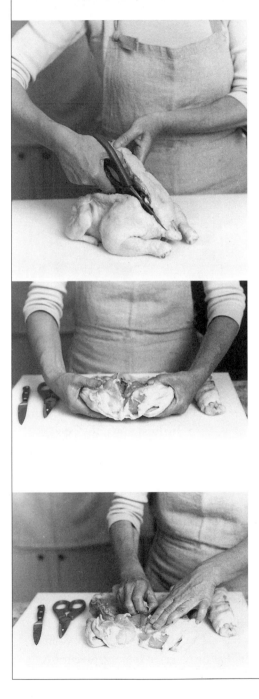

Have on hand several sheets of paper towels, a paring knife, and poultry or kitchen shears. Place a broiling or frying chicken (3 to 3½ pounds) on a cutting board, breast side down. With the shears, cut along either side of the backbone and lift it out (top left). (Freeze it for making stock.) With paper towels, wipe out the cavity, removing any soft pieces clinging to the edge where the backbone was cut away. Trim off and discard the excess fat.

Place a hand on either side of the back where the backbone was, then press down on the chicken so it opens and you can see the breastbone (middle left). With the paring knife, make a ¼-inch incision through the cartilage just above the breastbone until you reach a deep red diamond-shaped bone. Using your hands, fold the breasts toward each other (you'll fold the skin, too), so the reddish bone pops out. Lift the bone out with your fingers (just keep wiggling if it's stubborn; bottom left).

VARIATION Apricot-Glazed Flattened Chicken

Omit the mustard and lemon juice. Roast as directed, letting it cook for only 40 minutes. Remove from the oven.

In a bowl, combine 1 teaspoon olive oil and ¼ cup good-quality apricot preserves. Brush this mixture all over the skin of the bird and return it to the oven. Continue roasting the chicken for 10 to 20 minutes, or until the skin is golden and the thickest part of the thigh registers 170 degrees.

Turn on the broiler. Broil the chicken, watching it carefully, for 1 to 2 minutes, or until golden brown and crisp. Cut it into 10 pieces and serve.

VARIATION Teriyaki Flattened Chicken

Allow at least several hours or as long as a day for the chicken to marinate.

- ¹/₄ cup tamari or soy sauce
- ¹/₄ cup dry sherry
- 2 tablespoons dark brown sugar
- 2 tablespoons dark sesame oil
- 1 tablespoon finely chopped fresh ginger
- 2 garlic cloves, finely chopped
- 1 3–3¹/₂-pound chicken, flattened (see page 193)

In a small bowl, combine the tamari or soy sauce, sherry, brown sugar, sesame oil, ginger, and garlic.

Place the chicken in a baking dish in which it fits snugly. Pour the marinade over it and turn to coat. Cover with plastic wrap and refrigerate for at least 4 hours and for as long as overnight.

Set the oven at 400 degrees.

Transfer the chicken, skin side up, to a roasting pan. Roast for 15 minutes. Turn the heat down to 375 degrees and continue roasting for 35 to 45 minutes, or until the chicken is cooked through and the thickest part of the thigh registers 170 degrees. Set in a warm place for 5 minutes, then cut it into 10 pieces and serve.

To Cut Up a Chicken

With poultry scissors or kitchen shears, cut the wings from the bird, taking a 1-inch piece of breast meat with the wings. Remove the drumsticks from the bird.

Cut off both thighs. Now you have 6 pieces. Cut off the breasts; cut each in half crosswise (to make 4 pieces of breast).

roast cod and vegetables agrodolce

Agrodolce means sweet and sour in Italian. In this recipe, the sweet comes from tomatoes and golden raisins, the sour (though it isn't *really* sour) from balsamic vinegar. The flavors enliven an otherwise plain roasted cod. Serve this with boiled new potatoes.

2 medium zucchini
4 plum tomatoes, peeled and chopped
1 garlic clove, finely chopped
1/3 cup golden raisins, plumped in hot water for 10 minutes
1 tablespoon balsamic vinegar
2 tablespoons chopped fresh parsley, plus more for garnish
1/2 teaspoon coarse salt, or to taste
1/2 teaspoon freshly ground black pepper, or to taste
2 pounds cod, about 1 inch thick, cut into 6 serving pieces
Olive oil, for sprinkling

Set the oven at 425 degrees.

Quarter the zucchini lengthwise and remove the seeds with the tip of a knife. Slice the zucchini thinly.

In a large skillet, combine the zucchini, tomatoes, garlic, raisins, vinegar, parsley, salt, and pepper. Cook the vegetables over medium heat, stirring often, for 8 minutes, or until the zucchini softens.

Place the cod in an oiled baking dish large enough to hold the pieces in a single layer. Add the cod, and sprinkle with oil. Spoon the vegetables and their juices over the fish. Cover the dish with foil, shiny side down.

Roast for 20 minutes. Remove the foil and continue roasting for 10 minutes, or until the cod is opaque and the sauce is bubbling at the edges. Taste the cooking juices for seasoning and add more salt and pepper, if you like.

Spoon the fish and vegetables into deep plates. Sprinkle with extra parsley and serve at once.

chicken and seafood stew with bow ties

This all-in-one dish begins with a rich, dark port-infused tomato sauce in which white fish cooks with steamed mussels, clams, and roasted chicken thighs. The ingredients are added to the pot in stages, and you can eliminate some and still make a fine dish; the recipe is very forgiving. For instance, you can change this to an all-fish or all-chicken dish (use chicken stock instead of fish stock or clam broth if it's entirely poultry) or simply increase the amount of chicken and reduce the fish. Make the tomato sauce and roast the thighs a day ahead, if you like, to save time. The recipe is adapted from Agora restaurant in Providence, Rhode Island.

6 chicken thighs
Olive oil, for sprinkling

1 tablespoon plus 1 teaspoon coarse salt, or to taste

1/2 teaspoon freshly ground black pepper, or to taste

1 tablespoon olive oil

1 Spanish onion, coarsely chopped

2 garlic cloves, finely chopped

1 1/2 cups canned imported tomatoes, crushed in a bowl

2 tablespoons chopped fresh rosemary

2 tablespoons chopped fresh oregano

1/2 teaspoon crushed red pepper

1 cup port

2 cups fish stock or bottled clam broth
Pinch of saffron

2 pounds mussels

12 littleneck clams

1/2 pound dried bow tie pasta

1 1/2 pounds skinless, boneless cusk, pollock, hake, ocean catfish, or other plain white fish, cut into 2-inch pieces

1/2 pound large shrimp, shelled

3 tablespoons chopped fresh parsley

Set the oven at 400 degrees.

Pull off the skin from the chicken thighs. Arrange them in one layer in an 8-inch square baking dish, packing them in tightly. Sprinkle them with the oil, 1/2 teaspoon of the salt, and 1/4 teaspoon of the pepper. Roast for 40 minutes, or until they are cooked through. Remove from the oven and set aside to cool. (If making in advance, cover and refrigerate the chicken thighs separately from the cooking juices in the pan.)

Heat the oil in a large flameproof casserole, and cook the onion over medium heat, stirring occasionally, for 10 minutes, or until it softens. Add the garlic and cook for 1 minute more.

Add the tomatoes, rosemary, oregano, red pepper, and the remaining 1/2 teaspoon salt and 1/4 teaspoon black pepper. Cook, stirring, for 1 minute. Pour in the port, fish stock or clam broth, and saffron. Bring to a boil. Reduce the heat to low and let the mixture simmer for 20 minutes. (If making in advance, let the sauce cool, then transfer to a plastic container, cover, and refrigerate.)

Bring a large pot of water to a boil for the pasta. Add a generous tablespoon of salt and set it aside over low heat so it's ready when you need it.

Skim the fat from the chicken cooking juices and add the juices to the tomato sauce. Let sit over low heat.

Pour 1/4 inch of water into the bottom of a soup pot. Add the mussels and clams, cover with the lid, and set over high heat. Bring to a boil, watching the pot carefully so the liquid doesn't bubble over. Cook for 2 minutes, shaking the pot once or twice, until the mussels and clams open. Discard any that do not open. Lift the shellfish from the pot and transfer them to a bowl.

Line a strainer with several layers of cheesecloth. Strain the shellfish broth and add half of it to the tomato mixture. Add the chicken thighs.

Bring the water for the pasta back to a boil, add the bow ties, and stir well. Cook them for 10 minutes, or until they are tender but still have a bite.

Meanwhile, add the fish and shrimp to the tomato sauce, submerging them in the liquid. Return to a boil, reduce the heat to low, and cook for 3 minutes, or until the fish is cooked through and the shrimp are pink. Add the mussels and clams to the pot, and turn the heat to its lowest setting. If the sauce seems thick, add more mussel broth.

Drain the bow ties into a colander, shake it well, and divide the pasta among six large shallow bowls. Taste the fish mixture for seasoning and add more salt and pepper, if you like. Ladle the chicken, fish, shellfish, and sauce into each bowl, sprinkle with parsley, and serve at once.

shrimp, corn, red potato, and green bean boil with dipping sauces

Perfect for supper on the back porch, this is a takeoff on the New England clambake made with lobsters and clams. Everything goes into one large pot. Spread out newspapers on the table, peel the shrimp as you eat them, and serve one or two dipping sauces on the side. Make Corn Bread Baked in a Skillet (page 161) to accompany it.

❋{ FOR THE SPICY COCKTAIL SAUCE

- 1/2 **cup ketchup**
  Juice of 1 lemon
- 1/2 **cup bottled horseradish**
  Dash liquid hot sauce, or to taste
  Pinch of coarse salt

Combine the ketchup, lemon juice, horseradish, hot sauce, and salt in a small bowl. Stir well. Taste for seasoning and add more hot sauce or salt, if you like. Cover with plastic wrap and refrigerate while you make the Dill Mayonnaise, if using, and the shrimp boil.

❋{ FOR THE DILL MAYONNAISE

- 1/2 **cup mayonnaise**
- 1/2 **cup sour cream**
- 1 **tablespoon red wine vinegar, or more to taste**
- 2 **tablespoons finely chopped red onion**
- 1/2 **cup finely chopped fresh dill**
- 1/2 **teaspoon coarse salt, or to taste**
- 1/2 **teaspoon freshly ground black pepper, or to taste**

In a small bowl, whisk together the mayonnaise and sour cream. Add the vinegar slowly, whisking until smooth. With a spoon, stir in the onion, dill, salt, and pepper. Cover tightly with plastic wrap, and refrigerate to let the flavors mellow. Add more vinegar, salt, and pepper, if you like.

※{ FOR THE BOIL

  4 **quarts water**
  2 **tablespoons pickling spices**
  4 **dried red chili peppers**
  2 **lemons, quartered**
  1 **tablespoon coarse salt, or to taste**
 12 **medium red potatoes, quartered**
  2 **onions, peeled, root ends intact, quartered**
1¹/2 **pounds green beans, trimmed**
  2 **pounds large shrimp (unshelled)**
  6 **ears fresh corn, shucked and cut into thirds**

Bring the water to a boil in a large pot.

Tie together the pickling spices, chilies, and lemons in a large piece of cheesecloth. Place the spices in the water with the salt.

Add the potatoes and onions and bring to a boil. Reduce the heat to medium-low and simmer for 15 minutes.

Add the green beans and return the water to a boil. Reduce the heat to medium-low and simmer the beans for 3 minutes, or until they are almost tender.

Add the shrimp and corn. (It's OK if they're not submerged.) Simmer for 2 to 3 minutes, or until the shrimp are firm and bright pink and the corn is tender.

Remove the cheesecloth packet. Serve the boil right from the pot with a slotted spoon, or arrange the vegetables and shrimp on a large platter. Serve with the cocktail sauce and/or dill mayonnaise.

roast side of salmon

Boneless sides of Atlantic farm-raised salmon are available everywhere year-round, they're consistently good, and they can be prepared simply: roasted in a hot oven. You'll need parchment paper for this recipe, available at some supermarkets or at specialty food shops.

In New England on the Fourth of July, salmon and peas are traditional. We use fresh peas (or sautéed sugar snaps). In the summer, you can also serve Romano Beans with Tomatoes (page 250) and Fresh Corn "Risotto" (page 252). Winter sides might include Casserole-Roasted Fall Vegetables (page 264) or Stovetop Red Cabbage with Apples (page 256).

1   **2–3-pound whole boneless side of salmon**
    Olive oil, for drizzling
1/2 **teaspoon coarse salt, or to taste**
1/2 **teaspoon freshly ground black pepper, or to taste**

1   **tablespoon chopped fresh thyme**
1   **tablespoon chopped fresh parsley**

Set the oven at 450 degrees. Line a rimmed baking sheet with parchment paper.

Set the salmon on the baking sheet skin side down. Drizzle it with oil and sprinkle it with the salt and pepper. Press a piece of parchment paper directly onto the salmon — this keeps the fish moist.

Roast the salmon for 15 minutes, or until the fish flakes easily when tested with the tip of a knife. Remove from the oven, sprinkle it with thyme and parsley, and slide onto a platter (right) to serve.

VARIATION
Maple-Glazed Salmon

A quick 2-hour marinade of maple syrup, mustard, and rum turns the salmon dark and glazes the flesh.

    1 **2-pound piece of boneless salmon (cut from the wide end**
         of the fish)
  ¹/4 **cup maple syrup**
  ¹/4 **cup rum**
    2 **tablespoons Dijon mustard**

Set the fish, skin side down, in a plastic container or shallow baking dish large enough to hold it flat.

In a small bowl, combine the maple syrup, rum, and mustard.

Rub the fish all over with the marinade. Cover and refrigerate for at least 2 hours, turning once or twice.

Roast the salmon as directed on page 200.

salmon and mushroom pot pie

An elegant presentation for leftover salmon (or for salmon that you've roasted special-ly for this dish), this is a cross between the classic Russian coulibiac, in which salmon, mushrooms, and rice are wrapped in a rich pastry, and an old-fashioned pot pie. The filling — salmon and peas in a white sauce — goes into a baking dish and is covered with Rich Pastry, which puffs beautifully and makes a tender, flaky crust.

※{ FOR THE FILLING

- 2 **tablespoons butter**
- 1 **onion, finely chopped**
- 2 **small leeks (white part only), chopped, rinsed, and dried**
- $1/2$ **pound white button mushrooms, finely chopped**
- 8 **large shiitake mushrooms, stems removed and caps finely chopped**
- 1 **teaspoon chopped fresh thyme**
  Pinch of freshly grated nutmeg
  Pinch of cayenne pepper
- $1/2$ **teaspoon coarse salt, or to taste**
- $1/2$ **teaspoon freshly ground black pepper, or to taste**
- 2 **tablespoons all-purpose flour**
- $1^{3}/4$ **cups whole milk**
- 1 **pound cooked salmon, flaked**
- 1 **cup fresh or frozen (not thawed) peas**

- $1/2$ **recipe Rich Pastry (see variation page 145)**
- 3 **tablespoons whole milk, for glazing**

- 1 **bunch watercress, for garnish**

Melt the butter in a large saucepan, and cook the onion over medium heat, stir-ring often, for 8 minutes. Add the leeks and continue cooking, stirring often, for 2 minutes, or until softened.

    Add the button and shiitake mushrooms, thyme, nutmeg, cayenne pepper, salt, and black pepper. Cook, stirring occasionally, for 10 minutes more, or until the mushrooms release their liquid.

    With a wooden spoon, stir in the

flour, and cook, stirring constantly, for 2 minutes. Add the milk, ¼ cup at a time, still stirring constantly, until it is all added. Reduce the heat to low and simmer for 10 minutes.

Fold in the salmon and uncooked peas. Transfer the filling to an 11-by-7-inch or a 9-inch square baking dish or another dish with a 2½-quart capacity. Let cool completely while you prepare the pastry. (The filling can be made ahead, covered and refrigerated for up to 1 day.)

❊⟩ TO ASSEMBLE

Set the oven at 375 degrees.

On a lightly floured counter, roll the pastry slightly larger than the dish.

Lift the dough onto the rolling pin and ease it onto the filling. Fold under the edges to make a hem. Brush the dough lightly with the milk. Using the tines of a fork, press the edges of the pastry into the rim of the dish all around. Using kitchen shears or a sharp paring knife, make four ½-inch slashes through the top of the pastry at regular intervals.

Set the dish on a rimmed baking sheet to catch any drips and bake the pie for 40 to 50 minutes, or until the pastry is golden and the filling is bubbling at the edges. Remove from the oven and set aside for a few minutes so the juices can settle.

Use a small knife to cut the crust into large squares. Place a piece of crust on each of six dinner plates. Spoon some filling onto the pastry, garnish with watercress, and serve.

squash, zucchini, and white bean stew

When you know there will be several vegetarians in the crowd, this stew is ideal. Though intended as an entrée, this dish can be served alongside Roast Side of Salmon (page 200) or Herb-Roasted Flattened Chicken (page 192), if you like, so there's something for everyone. During that fleeting moment in the fall when tomatoes and squash are both on the vines and everything in the pot is locally grown, the flavors are especially beautiful.

 4 medium leeks
 2 large buttercup or butternut squash (3–4 pounds each)
 6 medium zucchini
 2 tablespoons vegetable oil, plus more for sprinkling
 1 teaspoon coarse salt, or to taste
 1/2 teaspoon freshly ground black pepper, or to taste
 6 cups water, plus more as needed
 6 large tomatoes, peeled and cut into eighths
 3 garlic cloves, crushed
 1/8 teaspoon ground allspice
 1/8 teaspoon ground cumin
 1/8 teaspoon crushed red pepper
 3 cans (15 ounces each) cannellini beans, drained and rinsed
     with water
 2 tablespoons chopped fresh oregano
 2 tablespoons chopped fresh rosemary
 2 tablespoons chopped fresh thyme

Set the oven at 425 degrees.

Trim the leeks and cut the white part into thirds. Halve the squash, remove the seeds and stems, and cut the squash into 3-inch pieces. (If the butternut is already peeled, simply cut it up.) Trim the zucchini and cut them in half lengthwise and then cut each long piece into thirds.

Spread the vegetables flesh side up in a large roasting pan, and sprinkle with oil, and the salt and pepper. Add 1 cup of the water to the edge of the pan.

Roast the vegetables for 1 hour, or until they are all very tender when pierced with a skewer. Set aside to cool.

Meanwhile, in a large flame-proof casserole, heat the 2 tablespoons oil and cook the tomatoes over medium-high heat, stirring constantly, for 5 minutes. Add plenty of salt and pepper. Add the garlic, allspice, cumin, and red pepper. Cook, stirring, for 2 minutes.

Add 4 cups of the water and bring to a boil. Reduce the heat to low and simmer for 15 minutes.

When the roasted vegetables are cool enough to handle, halve the leeks lengthwise, then slice them thickly and add them to the tomato sauce. Remove the skin from the squash and add the large pieces of flesh to the sauce. Slice the zucchini thickly and add it to the sauce.

Add the remaining 1 cup water to the pan in which you cooked the vegetables. Set it over medium heat and let the water come to a boil, scraping the bottom to release the caramelized bits. Tip the water into the tomato sauce.

Add the cannellini beans and bring the sauce to a boil. Add more water to the pan if the mixture seems dry; it should be almost soupy. Reduce the heat to low and simmer the vegetables for 10 minutes.

Sprinkle the stew with the oregano, rosemary, and thyme. Taste for seasoning, add more salt and pepper, if you like, ladle into large shallow bowls and serve.

simmering pots

Our notion of a simmering pot is a satisfying stewlike meal that cooks slowly, either on top of the stove or in the oven, and is meant to be served family-style — right from the pot.

We think of these as kitchen suppers, though many are nice enough to go out to the dining room and a tableful of guests.

A simmering pot might be a stew or a chowder or a thick soup, and whatever form it takes, it's always the main event of the meal. Often the supper begins with a salad, and then comes the brimming pot and not much else, except perhaps some steamed broccoli spears or green beans.

In spring, the pot is full of leeks and red potatoes. And it's still chilly enough at night that a bowl of thick vegetable soup is welcome. Because we live in chowder country, we make them year-round. We're partial to bowls of creamy fish chowder, made in Boston for centuries, and we like a bowl of brothy clams as well. Portuguese fishermen taught us to make tomato-based fish and potato chowders, which we love because they're always a little spicy.

In summer, during corn season, we mix the just-picked kernels with chicken. When tomatoes and beans come in, we simmer them with chicken breasts in another stew. By the time the weather cools in the fall, we're thinking about pots full of lamb shanks, veal shoulder, stuffed cabbage, and chuck roast.

Our stews are thinner and often lighter than the same dishes our mothers made. But they're still nourishing and always simmered with lots of vegetables. We love what these dishes do to the house: the kitchen windows get a little steamy in winter, and in spring, when we throw open the back door, guests say that they can catch a hint of what's for dinner as they pull into the driveway.

simmering pots

spring garden stew

On a fine late-spring day, we go out to the garden or to the local farm stand and find the first spring onions and new potatoes, toss them into a pan with lots of leeks, young lettuces, and peas, and make this very green and appealing bowl. You can add finely diced ham to the sautéed leeks, if you like.

2 tablespoons olive oil

4 leeks (white part only), thinly sliced and rinsed well

1 large Spanish onion, coarsely chopped

1 bunch spring onions or 2 bunches scallions (white part only), trimmed and thinly sliced

1 teaspoon coarse salt, plus more to taste

4 medium red potatoes, cut into 1-inch pieces

1 garlic clove, finely chopped

1 quart chicken stock

1 head Boston lettuce, cored and coarsely chopped

2 cups fresh or 1 package (10 ounces) frozen (not thawed) peas

1/2 teaspoon freshly ground black pepper, or to taste

2 tablespoons chopped fresh mint

Heat the oil in a large flameproof casserole and cook the leeks, onion, spring onions or scallions, and 1/2 teaspoon of the salt over medium heat, stirring often, for 10 minutes or until the vegetables soften.

Add the potatoes, garlic, and stock. Bring to a boil, reduce the heat to medium-low, cover, and simmer for 20 minutes or until the potatoes are cooked through.

Stir in the lettuce, peas, the remaining 1/2 teaspoon salt, and pepper, and bring to a boil. Reduce the heat to medium-low and simmer for 2 to 5 minutes, or until the peas are tender (fresh peas take longer to cook). Taste and add more salt and pepper, if you like. Ladle the stew into bowls and sprinkle with mint. Serve at once.

bean and vegetable soup

All winter, this is the pot we make, and it has many variations. Some weeks we use dried beans, sometimes canned beans (one 15-ounce can), other times potatoes. And lots of onions and carrots and some celery are cooked to concentrate the flavor before the green or yellow beans, Swiss chard, a few canned tomatoes or tomato paste, and fresh herbs go into the pot. When the soup is reheated for several nights, it just keeps getting thicker, which is how we like it. You can always add a little water each time you bring the soup to a boil. Allow time to soak the beans overnight. Drain and rinse canned beans and add them to the soup with the Swiss chard.

$1/2$ cup dried cannellini beans

2 tablespoons olive oil, plus more for sprinkling

2 quarts water

1 Spanish onion, coarsely chopped

1 large carrot, coarsely chopped

1 celery stalk, coarsely chopped

$1^1/2$ teaspoons coarse salt, or to taste

1 teaspoon freshly ground black pepper, or to taste

1 garlic clove, finely chopped

2 tablespoons chopped fresh rosemary

6 cups chicken stock or water

1 2-inch piece Parmesan cheese rind

$1/2$ cup canned tomatoes, crushed in a bowl

1 pound green or yellow beans, trimmed and cut into $1/2$-inch pieces

1 bunch Swiss chard, stemmed and coarsely chopped

2 tablespoons chopped fresh parsley, for serving

1 cup freshly grated Parmesan cheese, for serving

In a large bowl, combine the cannellini beans with enough cold water to cover them completely. Set aside to soak overnight.

Drain the beans and transfer them to a large saucepan. Sprinkle them with oil and toss to coat them. Add the 2 quarts water and bring to a boil. Turn the heat to medium-low, cover, and simmer, stirring occasionally, for 1 to 1½ hours (cooking time will vary with the age of the beans), or until tender.

Meanwhile, in a large flame-proof casserole, heat the 2 tablespoons oil. Cook the onion, carrot, celery, ½ teaspoon of the salt, and ½ teaspoon of the pepper over medium-low heat, stirring often, for 10 minutes, or until softened.

Stir in the garlic and rosemary and cook, stirring, for 1 minute more. Add the cooked beans, stock or water, Parmesan rind, tomatoes, green or yellow beans, Swiss chard, the remaining 1 teaspoon salt and ½ teaspoon pepper. Bring to a boil, reduce the heat to low, cover the pan, and simmer, stirring occasionally, for 40 minutes more, or until all the vegetables are tender. Discard the cheese rind (or chop the soft part finely) and taste for seasoning. Add more salt and pepper, if you like.

Spoon the soup into large flat bowls, sprinkle with parsley and Parmesan, and serve.

yellow split-pea soup with linguiça

When the larder is bare and you have split peas and something smoky in the freezer, this is a satisfying bowl. Like the green ones, yellow split peas completely fall apart, so the finished soup is thick. Turkey linguiça is lighter than the pork sausage (which you can certainly use), but we've also made this with a ham bone or a bone from a pork roast and with chicken stock instead of water. Serve with crusty bread.

- 1 **pound (about 2 cups) dried yellow split peas**
- 3 **quarts water**
- 2 **tablespoons olive oil**
- 1 **large Spanish onion, coarsely chopped**
- 2 **garlic cloves, finely chopped**
- 2 **large carrots, coarsely chopped**
- 2 **celery stalks, finely chopped**
- 1/2 **teaspoon coarse salt, or to taste**
- 1/2 **teaspoon freshly ground black pepper, or to taste**
- 1/2 **turkey linguiça (about 6 ounces), halved lengthwise and thinly sliced**

Combine the split peas and water in a large flameproof casserole. Bring to a boil, reduce the heat to medium-low, cover, and simmer for 1 hour, skimming the foam from the liquid as it rises to the surface.

Meanwhile, in a large skillet, heat the oil and cook the onion, garlic, carrots, celery, salt, and pepper over low heat, stirring often, for 15 minutes, or until the vegetables soften.

Add the vegetables in the skillet to the split peas. Stir in the linguiça. Cover the pan and continue to simmer for 2 hours more, or until the peas are almost pureed, skimming off the fat and impurities that rise to the surface. Add more water during cooking if the soup seems too thick.

Ladle the soup into bowls and serve. Leftover soup will thicken as it stands. Add more water, 1/4 cup at a time, as you reheat it, until it is the consistency you like.

fish stew with tomatoes and potatoes

One of the ways to give a simple tomato-based fish stew some bite and depth is to add crushed red pepper and sweet paprika, as the Portuguese do on Massachusetts' Cape Cod. This version, from home cook Arlene DeMelo, can be made with any firm-fleshed white fish you can get. It's the sort of dish you can make an hour before company arrives and serve in any season. If you prefer more bite, use hot paprika.

2	tablespoons vegetable oil
1	Spanish onion, coarsely chopped
4	plum tomatoes, cored and coarsely chopped
2	russet (baking) potatoes, peeled and cut into 1-inch pieces
1	teaspoon paprika
1/2	teaspoon crushed red pepper
4	cups water, plus more if needed
1 1/2	pounds skinless, boneless cod or haddock (or other white fish), cut into 2-inch pieces
1/2	teaspoon coarse salt, or to taste
1/2	teaspoon freshly ground black pepper, or to taste
1/4	cup chopped fresh parsley

Heat the oil in a large flameproof casserole, and cook the onion with a pinch of salt over medium heat, stirring often, for 10 minutes, or until the onion softens. Add the tomatoes and cook, stirring often, for 5 minutes more.

Add the potatoes, paprika, red pepper, and water. Bring to a boil, reduce the heat to low, and cook for 25 to 30 minutes, or until the potatoes are tender.

Add the fish, salt, and pepper. Return the liquid to a boil, then reduce the heat to low and simmer for 5 minutes, or until the fish is tender. Add more water if the stew seems too thick. Stir in the parsley and serve at once.

yankee gumbo

Hot sausage in a tomato-based fish stew makes an appealing bowl of gumbo. Okra is traditional, but people who weren't raised on it often don't like it. So we took the basic premise of the dish and substituted zucchini for the okra, adding red bell pepper, shrimp, a mixture of white fish, and andouille sausage. Ladle the stew over white rice in large shallow bowls.

2	tablespoons vegetable oil
2	tablespoons butter
1/4	cup all-purpose flour
2	celery stalks, chopped
1	Spanish onion, chopped
1	red bell pepper, cored, seeded, and chopped
2	garlic cloves, chopped
1/2	pound andouille or other hot, cooked sausage, thinly sliced
1	can (16 ounces) whole peeled tomatoes, crushed in a bowl
2	cups chicken stock
2	cups bottled clam juice
2	bay leaves
1/2	teaspoon coarse salt, or to taste
1/2	teaspoon freshly ground black pepper, or to taste
	Pinch of cayenne pepper (optional)
2	medium zucchini, halved, seeded, and thinly sliced
1	pound skinless, boneless, white fish, such as cod, pollock, ocean catfish, or monkfish, cut into 2-inch pieces
1	pound medium shrimp, shelled
	Handful fresh Italian parsley leaves, finely chopped, for serving

Heat the oil in a large flameproof casserole, and when it is hot, add the butter. When it melts, add the flour, and cook, stirring constantly, for 10 minutes, or until golden brown.

Stir in the celery, onion, red pepper, and garlic and mix well. Add the sausage, tomatoes, stock, clam juice, bay leaves, salt, black pepper, and cayenne, if using. Bring to a boil, stirring constantly. Reduce the heat to low, cover, and simmer for 30 minutes.

Stir in the zucchini and cook for 25 minutes more. Add the fish and shrimp to the gumbo, cover the pan again, and simmer, stirring once or twice, for 5 minutes, or until they are cooked through.

Taste for seasoning, add more salt and pepper, if you like, and sprinkle with parsley. Serve.

new england fish chowder

We like to serve creamy New England chowders as a main course with a wedge of Corn Bread Baked in a Skillet (page 161) and Montreal Slaw (page 48).

- 2 ¹/4-inch-thick strips slab bacon, coarsely chopped
- 2 large Spanish onions, finely chopped
- 2 teaspoons all-purpose flour
- 1 quart bottled clam broth (four 8-ounce bottles)
- 1 quart water
- 2 russet (baking) potatoes, peeled and cut into ¹/2-inch pieces
- 2 pounds skinless, boneless, firm white fish, such as cod, haddock, pollock, monkfish, halibut, or cusk, cut into 2-inch pieces
- 1 cup heavy cream
- ¹/2 teaspoon coarse salt, or to taste
- ¹/2 teaspoon freshly ground black pepper, or to taste

- 1 tablespoon butter
- 2 leeks (white part only) halved, well washed, and cut into matchsticks

Heat a large flameproof casserole over medium-high heat. Add the bacon and cook, stirring often, for 5 minutes, or until brown. With a slotted spoon, transfer the bacon to a plate lined with paper towels.

Discard all but 1 tablespoon of the bacon fat from the pan. Add the onions and cook over medium heat, stirring often, for 10 minutes, or until they soften. Add the flour and cook, stirring, for 2 minutes.

Add the clam broth and water, stirring constantly, and bring to a boil. Add the bacon and potatoes and cook for 20 minutes, or until the potatoes begin to soften but aren't cooked through.

Add the fish and cook over low heat for 5 minutes, or until cooked through. Add the cream, salt, and pepper, and heat almost to boiling. Add more water if you like a thinner chowder.

While the fish is cooking, melt the butter in a skillet over medium heat. Add the leeks and cook, stirring often, for 1 to 2 minutes, or until they soften slightly.

Ladle the soup into bowls. Garnish with the leeks and serve at once.

legal sea foods' light clam chowder

The legendary Boston restaurant Legal Sea Foods added this light version of chowder to its menu about a dozen years ago. The soup contains no butter, milk, or cream — in fact, nothing to dilute the briny taste of the clams. The secret to the intensity of the broth is the lengthy simmering, which also tenderizes the clams. Like squid, clams should be cooked briefly or for a long time, but nothing in between, or they will not be tender. Meaty quahogs make the best chowder, but try it with other hard-shell clams, too. They're often available at supermarkets, fresh or frozen.

1 medium Spanish onion, finely chopped
2 cups finely chopped fresh or frozen clams
3 cups fish stock or $2^1/2$ cups bottled clam juice mixed with
  $^1/2$ cup water
1 bay leaf
$^1/4$ teaspoon dried thyme
1 celery stalk, finely chopped
1 carrot, finely chopped
1 large russet (baking) potato, peeled and cut into $^1/4$-inch
  pieces
1 garlic clove, finely chopped
Coarse salt and freshly ground black pepper, to taste

1 tablespoon chopped fresh parsley, for serving

Combine the onion, clams, fish stock or clam juice and water, bay leaf, and thyme in a large saucepan. Bring to a boil, reduce the heat to low, cover, and simmer for 45 minutes, or until the broth is briny from the clams.

Add the celery and carrot, cover, and continue cooking for 25 minutes. Add the potato and garlic, cover, and simmer for 20 minutes more (total cooking time is 90 minutes), or until the potato is cooked through.

Taste for salt — the clam broth may already have sufficient saltiness — and add some if necessary. Remove the bay leaf, add plenty of pepper, sprinkle with parsley, and serve.

corn and chicken chowder

We add russet potatoes to our chicken chowder (for their starch) and, because we like color and a little acidity, a few canned peeled tomatoes. Begin the dish by poaching chicken thighs in water so you have a good homemade stock as the base (or use a commercial stock if you're in a hurry). Serve with Corn Bread Baked in a Skillet (page 161).

12 chicken thighs

3 quarts water

1 large carrot, quartered

1 onion, peeled but left whole

1 bunch parsley, stems only

1 bunch dill, stems only

1 bunch celery, leaves only

1 bay leaf

1 teaspoon coarse salt, or to taste

2 peppercorns

2 tablespoons canola oil

1 large Spanish onion, coarsely chopped

1/2 cup canned whole peeled tomatoes, crushed in a bowl

2 large russet (baking) potatoes, peeled and cut into 1/2-inch pieces

4 ears fresh corn, kernels removed (see page 113), or 2 cups frozen corn

2 tablespoons chopped fresh thyme

1/2 teaspoon crushed red pepper (optional)

1/2 teaspoon freshly ground black pepper, or to taste

2 tablespoons chopped fresh parsley

In a large flameproof casserole, combine the chicken thighs, water, carrot, whole onion, parsley, dill, celery, bay leaf, and ½ teaspoon of the salt. Bring the mixture to a boil, skim the surface thoroughly, and add the peppercorns. Reduce the heat to medium-low, cover the pan, and simmer the chicken for 1 hour, or until it is falling off the bone. Remove the chicken from the stock and set both aside to cool slightly.

Remove and discard the skin and bones from the chicken. Shred the meat with your fingers. Skim and discard the fat from the stock. Set the chicken and stock aside.

Heat the oil in a large flameproof casserole. When it is hot, cook the chopped onion over medium heat, stirring often, for 10 minutes, or until softened. Add the tomatoes and cook for 5 minutes more. Add the potatoes and reserved chicken stock and bring to a boil. Reduce the heat to medium-low and simmer for 15 minutes.

Add the corn, thyme, red pepper (if using), remaining ½ teaspoon salt, and black pepper. Continue cooking for 25 minutes, or until the potatoes are very tender and the soup is well flavored. Return the chicken to the pot and heat until hot. Remove the bay leaf. Taste for seasoning and add more salt and pepper, if you like. Add more water if the chowder is too thick.

Stir in the parsley, ladle the soup into deep bowls, and serve.

chicken-meatball soup with swiss chard

More typical for this Italian soup of tiny meatballs with Swiss chard would have been beef or pork meatballs. We've lightened them using ground chicken, mixing it with Parmesan cheese and bread crumbs. The meatballs simmer in chicken stock after the chard has cooked, which makes the broth very flavorful.

FOR THE MEATBALLS

- 1/2 **pound ground chicken**
- 1 **large egg, lightly beaten**
- 1 **garlic clove, chopped**
- 3 **tablespoons chopped fresh parsley**
- 1/2 **cup freshly grated Parmesan cheese**
- 1/4 **cup fresh white bread crumbs (see page 29)**
  Pinch of freshly grated nutmeg
- 1/2 **teaspoon coarse salt, or to taste**
- 1/2 **teaspoon freshly ground black pepper, or to taste**

In a large bowl, combine the chicken, egg, garlic, parsley, Parmesan, bread crumbs, nutmeg, salt, and pepper. Mix thoroughly, cover with plastic wrap, and refrigerate while you make the soup.

FOR THE SOUP

- 1 **tablespoon olive oil**
- 1 **tablespoon butter**
- 1 **large Spanish onion, coarsely chopped**
- $^1\!/_2$ **teaspoon coarse salt, or to taste**
- $^1\!/_2$ **teaspoon freshly ground black pepper, or to taste**
- 1 **bunch Swiss chard, stems removed, leaves coarsely chopped**
- 2 **quarts chicken stock**

- 2 **cups freshly grated Parmesan cheese, for sprinkling**

Heat the oil in a large flameproof casserole. Add the butter and, when it melts, cook the onion with the salt and pepper over medium heat, stirring often, for 10 minutes, or until softened.

Add the Swiss chard and continue cooking, stirring often, for 5 minutes more. Add the stock and bring to a boil. Reduce the heat to low, cover the pan, and simmer for 20 minutes.

Meanwhile, shape the meatballs: Dip your hands into cold water.

Roll a heaping teaspoon of the chicken mixture into a small ball between your hands. Continue until all the chicken is used. With a slotted spoon, lower the meatballs, several at a time, into the soup. Return the liquid to a boil, reduce the heat to low, cover, and simmer for 20 to 25 minutes, or until the meatballs are cooked through.

Ladle the soup into bowls, sprinkle each portion generously with Parmesan cheese, and serve.

cuban stewed chicken

This dish is similar to the classic Cuban arroz con pollo (chicken with rice) but is made without rice. Called *Pollo Guisado*, it includes tomato sauce, sherry, potatoes, olives, and raisins. The recipe comes from a worn cookbook that former Boston teacher Teresa Maranges Abadi carried with her when she left Cuba over thirty years ago in a fishing boat. When she settled in Boston, she found a community of other Cubans who were also alone. "We used to call each other," she says, "and say, 'Come on over, I'm cooking this or that.' " Then, she would open the old book and make this dish.

2	tablespoons olive oil
4	chicken thighs (about 1 pound), skin removed
4	chicken breast halves (about 3 pounds), skin removed
1	green bell pepper, cored, seeded, and cut into thin strips
1	red bell pepper, cored, seeded, and cut into thin strips
1	large Spanish onion, coarsely chopped
2	garlic cloves, finely chopped
1	cup canned tomato sauce
2	plum tomatoes, cored and coarsely chopped
1	cup dry sherry
1	cup water
3	medium russet (baking) potatoes, peeled and quartered
1/2	cup pimiento-stuffed Spanish olives, quartered
1/4	cup dark raisins
1	bay leaf
	Pinch of ground cumin
1/2	teaspoon coarse salt, or to taste
1/2	teaspoon freshly ground black pepper, or to taste

Heat the oil in a large flameproof casserole, and brown the chicken on all sides. Remove it from the pan and add the bell peppers and onion. Cook over medium heat, stirring often, for 10 minutes, or until they soften.

Add the garlic and continue cooking for 1 minute. Stir in the tomato sauce and tomatoes. Bring to a boil and cook for 1 minute. Pour in the sherry and water, then add the potatoes, olives, raisins, bay leaf, cumin, salt, and pepper. Return the chicken to the pan. Bring to a boil, reduce the heat to medium-low, cover, and simmer for 30 to 40 minutes, or until the chicken and potatoes are very tender. If the sauce seems too thick during cooking, add water, a few spoonfuls at a time, to thin it. Remove the bay leaf.

Taste for seasoning, add more salt and pepper, if you like, and serve.

portuguese chicken with rice

Slightly reminiscent of paella, this aromatic chicken and rice is a favorite meal for Arlene DeMelo, a Portuguese home cook in Hyannis, Massachusetts. Because the chicken slowly absorbs its seasonings for 8 hours, you'll need to think ahead.

8   chicken drumsticks (about 2 pounds)
8   chicken thighs (about 2 pounds)
1   teaspoon paprika
$1/2$ teaspoon ground cinnamon
$1/2$ teaspoon crushed red pepper
$1/4$ teaspoon fennel seeds, crushed with a mallet (optional)
$1/2$ teaspoon coarse salt, or to taste
$1/2$ teaspoon freshly ground black pepper, or to taste
    Generous dash liquid hot sauce
2   garlic cloves, finely chopped
2   tablespoons vegetable oil
1   large Spanish onion, finely chopped
$3^1/2$ cups water
1   cup long-grain white rice

Place the drumsticks and thighs, skin side up, in a baking dish large enough to hold them in one layer.

In a small bowl, mix together the paprika, cinnamon, red pepper, fennel, salt, black pepper, and hot sauce. Rub the spice mixture over the chicken, then scatter the garlic on top. Cover the baking dish with plastic wrap and refrigerate for 8 hours or overnight.

In a large flameproof casserole, heat the oil and cook the onion with a pinch of salt over medium heat, stirring often, for 10 minutes, or until softened. Add the chicken and brown it in the onion mixture, turning often. Add $1/2$ cup of the water and cook the chicken, still turning often, for 15 minutes.

Add the remaining 3 cups water and bring to a boil. Turn the heat to medium-low and partially cover the pan. Cook the chicken, turning it occasionally, for 45 minutes, or until it is cooked through. Skim the fat from the cooking liquid several times as it rises to the surface.

Add the rice and cover the pan. Cook over low heat for 20 to 25 minutes, or until the rice is tender. Taste for seasoning, add more salt and pepper, if you like, and serve.

summer chicken stew
with romano beans and tomatoes

Thick, fleshy green beans can be cooked for a long time and still taste wonderful and meaty.

- 2 tablespoons olive oil
- 1 large red onion, coarsely chopped
- 1/2 teaspoon coarse salt, or to taste
- 1 garlic clove, finely chopped
- 4 skinless, boneless chicken breasts (about 2 1/2 pounds)
- 4 ripe plum tomatoes, peeled (see page 9) and finely chopped
- 1/4 teaspoon ground allspice
- 1/4 teaspoon ground cinnamon
- 1/4 teaspoon freshly grated nutmeg
  Pinch of ground cloves
- 1/2 teaspoon freshly ground black pepper, or to taste
- 1/2 teaspoon crushed red pepper
- 1 cup dry white wine
- 1 cup chicken stock
- 1 pound Romano beans, trimmed and halved

- 3 tablespoons chopped fresh parsley

In a large flameproof casserole, heat the oil and cook the onion with a pinch of salt over medium heat, stirring often, for 10 minutes, or until softened. Add the garlic and cook for 1 minute more.

Add the chicken and cook it in the onion mixture, turning often until the chicken looks opaque. It's OK to crowd the pieces in the pan. Transfer the chicken to a platter and set it aside.

Add the tomatoes, allspice, cinnamon, nutmeg, and cloves to the pan. Sprinkle with 1/2 teaspoon salt, black pepper, and red pepper. Cook for 2 minutes, scraping the bottom of the pan to release any onions that stick to it.

Add the wine and bring to a boil. Reduce the wine to 1/2 cup. Add the stock and beans and bring to a boil. Return the chicken to the pan. Reduce the heat to low, partially cover the pan, and cook for 40 minutes, or until the chicken and beans are tender. Remove from the heat, sprinkle with parsley, and serve.

hearty chicken and chickpea stew

Vaguely Middle Eastern, with its seasoning of cumin, ground ginger, and cilantro, this stew features chicken thighs. They're simmered, then cut up and returned to the pot. Serve this with Pita Crackers (page 13).

2	tablespoons olive oil
1	Spanish onion, coarsely chopped
1/2	teaspoon coarse salt, or to taste
6	plum tomatoes, peeled (see page 9) and coarsely chopped
1	red bell pepper, cored, seeded, and chopped
1	garlic clove, finely chopped
12	chicken thighs, skin removed
2	teaspoons ground cumin
1	teaspoon ground ginger
2	carrots, coarsely chopped
3	quarts water
1/2	teaspoon freshly ground black pepper, or to taste
1	can (14 ounces) chickpeas, drained and rinsed with cold water
1/2	pound green beans, cut into 1/4-inch pieces
1/2	cup dark raisins
1/2	bunch cilantro (leaves only), finely chopped (1/4 cup)

Heat the oil in a large flameproof casserole and cook the onion with a pinch of salt over medium heat, stirring often, for 10 minutes, or until softened.

Add the tomatoes, bell pepper, and garlic and cook for 5 minutes more, stirring occasionally, or until the tomatoes soften.

Add the chicken thighs to the pot, along with the cumin and ginger. Cook over medium heat, stirring often, for 10 minutes, or until the chicken looks opaque on the outside.

Add the carrots, water, 1/2 teaspoon salt and pepper. Bring to a boil, reduce the heat to low, and simmer, uncovered, for 30 minutes, or until the chicken is tender.

With tongs, lift the pieces of chicken from the liquid and transfer them to a plate to cool. Pull the meat into bite-sized pieces, discarding the bones. Skim and discard the fat from the surface of the liquid.

Return the chicken to the casserole dish. Add the chickpeas, green beans, and raisins. Bring to a boil, reduce the heat to low, cover, and simmer for 1 hour, or until the vegetables are very tender. Skim the stew as it cooks.

Sprinkle with cilantro and taste for seasoning. Add more salt and pepper, if you like, and serve.

turkey-stuffed cabbage rolls

This is a new version of an old Eastern European dish, in which cabbage is filled with meat (traditionally, stale bread soaked in water or egg was added to stretch the meat). Then the stuffed cabbages are simmered in a tomato-based broth. These cabbage rolls are filled with a mixture of ground turkey and cooked rice. Apricot and peach preserves balance the cider vinegar and lemon juice in the tomato sauce.

FOR THE CABBAGE ROLLS

14 green cabbage leaves, softened (see page 230)
2   pounds ground turkey
1   medium Spanish onion, very finely chopped
1   garlic clove, finely chopped
1/4 cup long-grain white rice (uncooked)
1/3 cup golden raisins, coarsely chopped
1/4 teaspoon ground cinnamon
1/2 teaspoon dried thyme
1/2 teaspoon coarse salt, or to taste
1/2 teaspoon freshly ground black pepper, or to taste

Chop 2 of the cabbage leaves and set them aside.

Combine the turkey, onion, garlic, rice, raisins, cinnamon, thyme, salt, and pepper in a large bowl. Mix well.

Lay the remaining 12 cabbage leaves on the counter, cored end closest to you. Put one portion of the filling along the middle of each leaf and begin rolling them: fold the cored ends over the stuffing, bring the two sides in to the center, then continue rolling. Secure the roll with wooden toothpicks. Continue until all 12 rolls are formed. Set aside while you make the sauce.

※⟩ FOR THE SAUCE

- 1 can (28 ounces) whole peeled tomatoes, crushed in a bowl
- 1/4 cup apple cider vinegar, plus more if needed
- 1/4 cup fresh lemon juice
- 1/4 cup packed dark brown sugar, plus more if needed
- 2 cups water, plus more if needed
- 2 tablespoons apricot preserves
- 2 tablespoons peach preserves
- 1/2 teaspoon ground ginger
- 1/2 teaspoon ground cinnamon
- 1/2 teaspoon coarse salt, or to taste
- 1/4 teaspoon freshly ground black pepper, or to taste

In a flameproof casserole large enough to hold the rolls in one snug layer, combine the tomatoes, vinegar, lemon juice, brown sugar, water, apricot and peach preserves, ginger, cinnamon, salt, and pepper. Bring to a boil, stirring.

Add the chopped cabbage to the pan to prevent the rolls from sticking to the bottom.

Carefully place the cabbage rolls on top. They should fit snugly.

Cover the pan and set it over medium-low heat. Cook, turning the rolls every 30 minutes, for 3 hours. If at any time the dish is boiling too rapidly, turn the heat down or set the pan on a flame diffuser if possible. If the sauce seems dry, add a little extra water. After 2½ hours, taste the sauce for seasoning. Add more sugar, vinegar, salt, or pepper, if you like. Continue to cook until the rolls are glazed on all sides. Serve with some of the tomato sauce spooned over.

To Soften Cabbage for Stuffing

Core the cabbage, making the cut deep enough for the leaves to separate. Place the head of cabbage in a large pot, cored end down. Pour a tea kettle of boiling water over it, and return the water to a boil. Cook the cabbage for 5 to 10 minutes, or until the leaves are soft and separate easily. Lift the cabbage from the water and transfer it to a colander (leave the water on the burner; you'll need it again).

When the cabbage is cool enough to handle, peel the outer leaves. If the inner ones become difficult to separate, repeat the cooking process until you have 14 leaves.

lamb shanks with white beans

Before she braises lamb shanks with a lot of garlic, carrots, and onions, Susan Jasse of Walpole, New Hampshire, roasts them for at least an hour until they caramelize at the edges. Then she deglazes the pan and continues cooking the shanks in water seasoned with fresh herbs and tomatoes for 2 more hours, adding beans before serving.

You can roast the shanks and simmer them up to 2 days in advance, if you like. That way you can skim off all the fat. Soak and cook the beans ahead, too. Then, after reheating the lamb, add the beans. We've made the dish successfully with canned white beans instead of dried and without any beans. In that case, add Crusty Smashed Potatoes (page 260) or Potato Crisps with Fresh Herbs (page 262).

FOR THE LAMB

- 6 **lamb shanks**
- 8 **carrots, quartered**
- 4 **medium onions, quartered**
- 6 **garlic cloves, unpeeled**
  Olive oil, for drizzling
- 1 **teaspoon coarse salt, or to taste**
- 1/2 **teaspoon freshly ground black pepper, or to taste**
- 8 **cups water**
- 6 **plum tomatoes, peeled and chopped**
  Handful fresh oregano, leaves chopped
  Handful fresh rosemary, leaves chopped
- 3 **tablespoons black olive tapenade (available at specialty food stores)**

Set the oven at 450 degrees.

Place the lamb shanks, carrots, onions, and garlic in a large roasting pan. Drizzle them with oil and sprinkle them with the salt and pepper.

Roast the shanks and vegetables for 60 to 70 minutes, turning several times, or until the onions are burned at the edges and the meat has shrunk from the bone.

Reduce the oven temperature to 350 degrees. Remove the lamb and vegetables from the pan.

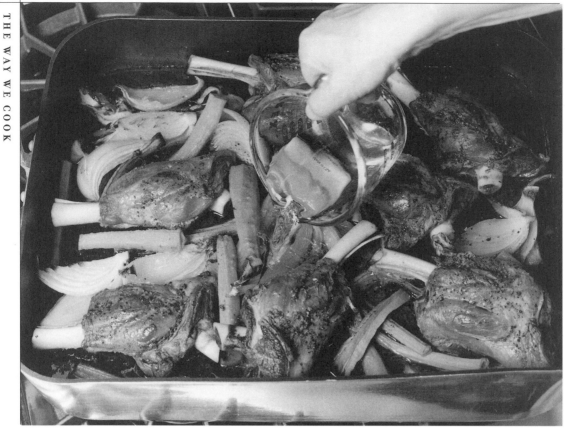

Press the garlic so the pulp slips out of the skins. Discard the skins. Set the roasting pan directly over a burner and turn the heat to high. Holding the pan carefully, pour in 4 cups of the water, and scrape the bottom to remove all the dark sediment. Remove the pan from the heat and add the lamb shanks, vegetables, and garlic, easing them into the liquid.

Add the remaining 4 cups of water, the tomatoes, oregano, and rosemary.

Bring to a boil. Cover the roasting pan with foil. Roast the shanks and vegetables for 1 hour.

Remove the foil, turn the shanks and vegetables, and continue cooking, uncovered, for 1 hour, or until the meat is falling off the bone. (You can prepare the shanks to this point up to 2 days ahead and refrigerate; see note next page). Skim and discard the fat. Stir in the tapenade. Prepare the beans.

note: If you made the shanks ahead, reheat as follows: Set the oven at 350 degrees. Transfer the shanks, vegetables, and liquid to the roasting pan. Warm the shanks for 40 minutes, or until they are very hot. Stir in the tapenade.

⁂⁝ FOR THE WHITE BEANS

    1 **pound dried small white beans (Great Northern or navy beans), soaked overnight and drained**

    1 **medium onion, finely chopped**

    3 **plum tomatoes, peeled (see page 9) and chopped**

      Handful fresh oregano, leaves chopped

      Handful fresh rosemary, leaves chopped

  1/2 teaspoon coarse salt, or to taste

  1/2 teaspoon freshly ground black pepper, or to taste

Put the white beans and onion in a large flameproof casserole. Add enough water to cover the beans by 1 inch. Bring to a boil, reduce the heat to low, and add the tomatoes and half of the oregano and rosemary.

    Cover and simmer for 1½ to 2 hours, or until the beans are tender. Add more water if the beans seem dry.

When the lamb is cooked through, ladle about 1 cup of the lamb-cooking liquid into the beans. Bring to a boil and simmer, uncovered, for 20 minutes, so the beans absorb some flavors from the lamb. Season with salt, pepper, and the remaining oregano and rosemary.

    Serve the shanks with the beans and sauce.

beef stew with butternut squash

Butternut squash replaces the usual potatoes in a beef stew with medium-hot poblano chili peppers. The peppers are broiled until they're blackened all over, which gives them a smoky flavor. Buying ready-peeled squash cuts down on the preparation time. Boston chef Danny Wisel created this stew.

2	poblano or other large, medium-hot peppers
2	tablespoons vegetable oil, plus more for rubbing
1	large Spanish onion, finely chopped
1/2	teaspoon coarse salt, or to taste
2	garlic cloves, finely chopped
2	pounds chuck roast, well trimmed and cut into 2-inch pieces
2	quarts water
1	pound peeled butternut squash, cut into 1/2-inch pieces
1/4	cup long-grain white rice
1	tablespoon dried oregano
	Pinch of crushed red pepper
1/4	teaspoon freshly ground black pepper, or to taste
12	6–7-inch flour tortillas, warmed (see page 235)

Preheat the broiler. Rub the poblano or other peppers with oil and set them on a broiler pan. Broil them, turning them often, until they are blackened all over. You can also hold the peppers over a flame (right). Let them cool. Discard the stems and seeds. Slice the peppers thinly and set them aside.

Heat the oil in a large flame-proof casserole and cook the onion with the salt over medium heat, stirring often, for 10 minutes, or until softened.

Add the garlic and roasted peppers and cook for 5 more minutes.

Add the meat, turn the heat to high, and cook, stirring often, until the meat loses its pink color. Pour in the water and bring to a boil, scraping the bottom of the pan. Reduce the heat to low and partially cover the pan. Simmer, stirring occasionally, for 2½ hours, or until the meat is soft but not falling apart. If the pan seems dry during cooking, add more water. Add the squash,

To Warm Flour Tortillas

Wrap the tortillas in foil, 6 to a package, and set them on a baking sheet. Warm them in a 450-degree oven for 8 to 10 minutes, or until the tortillas in the center of the package are warm. (Open the foil to check.) Quickly fold the tortillas into quarters, arrange them overlapping on a plate, and serve at once.

rice, oregano, and red pepper. Cover and simmer for 20 to 30 minutes, or until the squash and rice are tender.

Season with more salt and black pepper, if you like, and serve with warm tortillas.

braised beef in balsamic vinegar

Old-fashioned chuck roast simmers in a sweet-salty sauce made with onions, balsamic vinegar, soy sauce, white wine, and brown sugar. The recipe comes from Ana Sortun, chef and owner of Oleana restaurant in Cambridge, Massachusetts, who makes it with beef short ribs.

Refrigerate the dish overnight and skim all the fat before serving (right). If you like, add cooked wedges of potato, turnip, and carrot to the edges of the dish when you reheat it. We serve this with Crusty Smashed Potatoes (page 260).

> 2 tablespoons olive oil
> 1 tablespoon butter
> 4 large Spanish onions, halved and thinly sliced
> 1/2 teaspoon coarse salt, or to taste
> 1/2 teaspoon freshly ground black pepper, or to taste
> 2 cups balsamic vinegar
> 1 cup low-sodium soy sauce
> 1/2 cup dry white wine
> 1/2 cup water
> 1/2 cup dark brown sugar
> 1 4-pound boneless chuck roast, tied with string at 4-inch intervals
> 4 garlic cloves, finely chopped
> 2 whole star anise (optional)
> 1 bay leaf

Set the oven at 350 degrees.

In a large flameproof casserole, heat the oil, and when it is hot, add the butter. When it melts, add the onions, salt, and pepper and cook over medium-high heat, stirring often, for 5 minutes. Turn the heat to medium-low and cook the onions for 10 more minutes, or until golden brown. Remove the onions from the pan.

Remove the pan from the heat. Pour in the vinegar, soy sauce, wine, water, and sugar. Set the chuck roast in the liquids and cover it with the onions.

Add the garlic, star anise (if using), and bay leaf. Return the pan to the heat and bring the liquid to a boil. Cover the pan and transfer it to the oven. Cook the meat for 3 hours, turning several times, or until it is so tender that when you lift it with a fork, it falls back into the pan.

Transfer the meat to a large bowl. Pour the liquid into a heatproof bowl. When they are cool, cover and refrigerate both for several hours or overnight.

To serve: Remove the strings from the meat and cut it apart where it falls open. Cut the meat along its natural lines to make large pieces. Trim off any fat.

Carefully lift off and discard the fat from the surface of the cooking liquid. Return the liquid to the casserole. Bring it to a boil and let it bubble until it reduces to a syrupy sauce. Add the meat and let the sauce come to a boil again. Reduce the heat to low and simmer the meat gently for 10 minutes, or until it is hot. Serve.

To Skim Fat from a Dish

All stews improve after being refrigerated. You can leave the dish in the cooking pot (if it's enamel or stainless steel) and cool it before refrigerating, or separate the meat and vegetables from the cooking liquid and refrigerate them separately in plastic containers. When the cooking juices chill, the fat will solidify on top of the liquid, so you can lift it off with a spoon.

If you want to freeze meat in liquid, cut up the meat so it's submerged. Chill the dish, skim the fat, then press a piece of foil or plastic wrap directly onto the surface of the sauce. Cover with the lid and freeze the dish.

beef tsimmes with potato kugel topping

On the Jewish holidays every fall, Myra Kraft, a Boston philanthropist and avid New England Patriots fan (she and her husband, Robert, own the football team), makes this tsimmes of brisket and vegetables. The meat cooks with sweet potatoes, carrots, prunes, apricots, honey, pineapple juice, and orange juice. The following day, after chilling the dish and skimming the fat, Myra adds a kugel — a potato pudding that is usually baked in its own dish — to the top of the meat. It turns brown and crusty in the oven. Begin this tsimmes up to 3 days ahead, but make the kugel just before serving.

FOR THE BRISKET

- 1 **6-pound double brisket of beef**
- 2 **quarts water, or more as needed**
- 1/2 **teaspoon coarse salt, or to taste**
- 1/2 **teaspoon freshly ground black pepper, or to taste**
- 6 **large sweet potatoes, peeled and cut into 2-inch pieces**
- 2 **pounds carrots, peeled and cut into 1/2-inch pieces**
- 1 **cup pitted prunes**
- 1 **cup dried apricots**
- 1 **cup honey**
- 1 **cup pineapple juice**
- 1 **cup orange juice**

Put the meat in a large flameproof casserole and add enough of the water to cover the meat. Sprinkle with the salt and pepper, and bring to a boil. Cover the pot and reduce the heat to low, and simmer for 1½ hours.

During the last 15 minutes of simmering time, set the oven at 300 degrees.

Transfer the meat and liquid to a large roasting pan. Add the sweet potatoes, carrots, prunes, apricots, honey, pineapple and orange juices. Sprinkle with salt, cover with foil, shiny side down, and transfer the pan to the oven.

Cook for 4½ to 5 hours, adding more water to the pan, ¼ cup at a time, if the mixture seems dry, until the meat is very tender.

Remove from the oven and set aside to cool. Cover, refrigerate overnight, and skim the fat from the cooking liquid (see page 237).

Cut the meat on the diagonal into thin slices. Arrange the meat, vegetables, and cooking liquid in a large roasting pan and set aside while you prepare the kugel.

❧ FOR THE POTATO KUGEL

- 4 **large eggs**
- 1 **teaspoon coarse salt, or to taste**
- 1/2 **teaspoon freshly ground black pepper, or to taste**
- 2 **medium Spanish onions, grated**
- 2 **russet (baking) potatoes, peeled and grated**
- 2–3 **tablespoons chicken fat or vegetable oil**
- 2/3 **cup matzo meal**
- 1 1/2 **cups cold water**

Set the oven at 350 degrees.

Combine the eggs, salt, and pepper in a large bowl. With a wooden spoon, stir the mixture for 1 minute. Stir in the onions, potatoes, chicken fat or oil, matzo meal, and water. Cover the bowl and refrigerate for 1 hour, or until it thickens. The mixture may seem watery, but it will thicken as it sits.

Spoon the potato mixture in mounds over the meat in the roasting pan. Bake for 1 hour, or until the kugel topping is golden brown and the meat and vegetables are hot. Serve.

beef daube with tomatoes, anchovies, and oranges

Sheryl learned this recipe in the south of France, where both oranges and green olives aren't uncommon in a stew. The sauce also contains tomatoes, anchovies, and thyme, all of which blend into the aromatic broth during a 4-hour stay in the oven. Even with its red wine sauce, the dish is light enough for a spring dinner, with steamed new potatoes tossed in butter and parsley. If you make this dish a day ahead, the flavors will mellow and the fat can easily be skimmed.

1   tablespoon olive oil
2   tablespoons butter
1   large Spanish onion, coarsely chopped
1/2 teaspoon coarse salt, or to taste
1/2 teaspoon freshly ground black pepper, or to taste
2   garlic cloves, finely chopped
1   5-pound boneless chuck roast, tied with string at 4-inch
      intervals
2   tablespoons all-purpose flour
2   cups dry red wine
2   cups beef stock
1   can (28 ounces) whole imported tomatoes, crushed in a bowl
1/2 cup Picholine or other mild, green olives
2   navel oranges (unpeeled), quartered and thinly sliced
4   anchovy fillets
3   tablespoons chopped fresh thyme

Set the oven at 350 degrees.

Heat the oil and add the butter in a large flameproof casserole. When the butter melts, cook the onion, salt and pepper over medium heat, stirring often, for 10 minutes, or until the onion softens. Add the garlic and meat. Cook the meat on all sides in the onion mixture for 10 minutes.

Remove the meat from the pan and set it aside. Sprinkle the flour over the onions and cook, stirring, for 3 minutes, or until the flour browns slightly.

Pour in the wine and beef stock. Bring the liquid to a boil, scraping any brown bits that cling to the bottom of the pan. Add the tomatoes, olives, oranges, anchovies, and 1½ tablespoons of the thyme. Bring to a boil, return the meat to the pan, and cover. Transfer it to the oven and cook for 3 hours, turning the meat halfway through cooking.

Uncover the pan and continue cooking the meat for 1 hour, or until it is falling apart. (You can prepare the daube to this point up to 2 days ahead. Spoon the juices into a plastic container and transfer the meat and vegetables to another container. Refrigerate; see note.)

Transfer the meat to a cutting board. Skim the fat from the sauce. Discard the strings from the meat and cut it into large chunks along its natural lines.

Return the meat to the sauce, and heat for 10 minutes, or until the meat is very hot. Sprinkle with the remaining 1½ tablespoons thyme, and serve.

note: If you made the daube ahead, reheat as follows: Set the oven at 350 degrees. Transfer the meat and vegetables to a large flameproof casserole. Pour the cooking juices around them. Bring to a boil, cover, and cook for 30 minutes, or until it is very hot and the juices are bubbling at the sides.

veal stew with bacon and potatoes

In France this veal stew, made with a little bacon and some pearl onions, is called *bonne femme* ("good wife"), because every French housewife once had a version. The shoulder is a tough, flavorful cut, good for braising. Perhaps because this dish originated in farmhouse kitchens, it seems strikingly similar to some of the early New England stews of meat, bacon, and onions.

    1   thick slice slab bacon, cut into $1/8$-inch strips
    2   tablespoons butter
   24   pearl onions, blanched and peeled (see page 243)
    2   pounds boneless veal shoulder, well trimmed and cut into
          4-inch pieces
    3   tablespoons all-purpose flour
    1   bottle (750 ml) dry white wine
    2   cups water
    1   garlic clove, finely chopped
  $1/2$ teaspoon coarse salt, or to taste
  $1/2$ teaspoon freshly ground black pepper, or to taste
    3   large russet (baking) potatoes, peeled and cut into 2-inch
          pieces
  $1/4$ cup chopped fresh parsley

Cook the bacon in a large flameproof casserole, turning once, until it is golden brown. With a slotted spoon, transfer it to a double thickness of paper towels and blot it with the towels. Set aside.

With a large spoon, remove all the fat from the pan. Wipe out the pan. Add the butter and cook the onions over medium heat, stirring occasionally, for 5 minutes, or until browned.

Remove the onions from the pan. Add the veal, turn the heat to medium-high, and cook, turning often, for 5 minutes, or until browned.

Sprinkle the veal with flour and cook, stirring, for 2 minutes. Return the bacon and onions to the pan. Pour in the wine and water. Add the garlic and bring to a boil, stirring often, until the sauce is smooth.

Season with salt and pepper and partially cover the pan. Reduce the heat to low, and simmer, stirring occasionally, for 1½ to 2 hours, or until the meat and onions are very tender when pierced with a skewer.

Meanwhile, in a saucepan fitted with a steamer insert, steam the potatoes over several inches of boiling water, covered, over high heat for 10 to 15 minutes, or until they are cooked through, taking care that they don't fall apart.

Add the potatoes to the stew and spoon some of the juices in the pan over the potatoes. Partially cover, and continue to simmer for 15 minutes, or until the potatoes are very tender. Sprinkle with parsley, taste for seasoning, add more salt and pepper, if you like, and serve.

To Peel Pearl Onions

Plunge the unpeeled pearl onions into a saucepan of boiling water. Let them cook for 1 minute. Drain and rinse them with cold water.

Use a small paring knife to cut a very thin slice from the root end of the onions (the root holds the onion together), and peel off the skins (above), leaving the pointed ends intact.

sides

Most people we know change their side dishes the way they do their clothes — with the seasons. If you adjust your menu according to what's locally available — cheating, of course, when you want something else — it's enormously satisfying: greens in spring when the days are longer and the air warmer; denser, filling root vegetables at harvest time.

In summer, we cook a lot on the stove-top, in a skillet, or in a steamer basket. In the fall, we roast more. Roasting not only intensifies the flavor of the vegetable but adds caramelization as well.

Almost everything we do with vegetables involves familiar ingredients. We're trying to keep the integrity of the original, quite humble dishes. We gravitate toward recipes that are strikingly simple or those that, while not necessarily quick, don't require a lot of fussing.

We often serve more than one vegetable on the plate, so they're as celebrated a part of the meal as the main course. The two-vegetable approach also gives you something to offer guests who eat less meat than they used to and are counting on vegetables to fill out the meal.

Cooks sometimes forget the importance of a piquant taste on a plate, and relishes are even quicker to make than salads. They may take a little chopping, then a few hours or a day for the flavors to settle in, but nothing elaborate.

Some of the recipes in this chapter can play a versatile role in the structure of a meal. Pots of White Beans with Swiss Chard can serve as a main dish. Asparagus Cooked for Two Minutes works equally well as a side dish or as an hors d'oeuvre, passed on a platter. If the main course is simple, a beautiful side dish can make the meal.

sides

asparagus cooked for two minutes

A couldn't-be-simpler method of cooking asparagus in a skillet for 2 minutes results in bright-green spears that still have a crisp texture. We like these as an appetizer, served hot or at room temperature.

1   **pound asparagus**
1   **tablespoon olive oil**
    Generous squeeze of ½ lemon
    Coarse salt, to taste
    Freshly ground black pepper, to taste

Bring a deep skillet of salted water to a boil.

Meanwhile, snap off the stem ends of the asparagus spears by bending the spears gently. Break them where they snap naturally. Use a paring knife to trim off any stringy ends on the spears.

Transfer the asparagus to the boiling water and let the water bubble vigorously for 2 minutes, or until the spears are just tender but still bright green. During cooking, use a wide metal spatula to move the spears on the bottom of the skillet to the top. Watch them carefully: they go from bright green to olive green in seconds.

Quickly remove the spears from the hot water, and lay them on paper towels to dry.

On a large platter, arrange the spears every which way (like pick-up sticks, not in perfect rows). Drizzle them with the oil, and sprinkle with the lemon juice, salt, and pepper. Serve.

broccolini with olive oil and lemon juice

Small, slender stalks of broccolini have a taste that is slightly reminiscent of asparagus, with the peppery quality of broccoli rabe. They remind us of the crisp, bright sautéed greens served in all the Italian-American restaurants in Boston, but they're much easier to prepare. The stalks are elegant on a dressy dish or even draped over a chicken stew. Use this method to cook trimmed, quartered stalks of regular broccoli or broccoli rabe.

2　bunches broccolini (about 1 1/4 pounds)
2　tablespoons olive oil
1　garlic clove
　　Juice of 1/2 lemon
　　Coarse salt and freshly ground black pepper, to taste

Have on hand a large bowl filled with ice and water.

Trim the ends of the broccolini and remove any leaves. Bring a large saucepan of water to a boil, add the broccolini, and cook for 3 minutes. Lift out the broccolini with a slotted spoon and transfer them to the bowl of ice water. When they are cold, lay them on paper towels to dry.

Heat the oil in a large skillet, and add the garlic and the stalks of broccolini. Use tongs to toss them in the oil for 3 to 4 minutes, or until they are tender but still have some bite. Sprinkle with lemon juice, salt, and pepper and serve.

harvard beets

Some say these shiny crimson beets were originally named for the official school color of Harvard College, but the sweet-and-sour preparation is made all over the country under different names.

2 **bunches (about 6) large beets, peeled and quartered**
2 **teaspoons cornstarch**
1/2 **cup sugar**
1/4 **cup distilled white vinegar**

Cover the beets with cold water in a large flameproof casserole. Bring to a boil, reduce the heat to medium, and simmer for 25 to 30 minutes, or until the beets are tender.

Remove 1¼ cups of the cooking liquid from the pan and set aside to cool. Drain the beets into a colander.

Mix ¾ cup of beet-cooking liquid and the cornstarch in a small bowl.

Combine the sugar and vinegar in the casserole. Cook over low heat, stirring constantly, just until the sugar dissolves. Add the cornstarch mixture. Increase the heat to medium-high and let the mixture come to a boil. Reduce the heat to medium-low, and cook, stirring often, just until it begins to thicken.

Add the beets and cook them in the sauce for 5 minutes, or until they are hot and glazed. If the sauce seems thick, add a few tablespoons of the remaining beet-cooking liquid. Serve.

romano beans with tomatoes

Romano beans are part of the green bean family, though they're wider and flatter than the ones you usually see in markets. They're similar to Kentucky Wonder beans, but more tender. They taste like green beans used to taste — without the stringiness. Romano beans should always be cooked so they're meltingly tender.

- 2 tablespoons olive oil
- 4 ripe plum tomatoes, peeled (see page 9) and coarsely chopped
- 2 garlic cloves, finely chopped
- 1/2 teaspoon coarse salt, or to taste
- 1/2 teaspoon freshly ground black pepper, or to taste
- 1 1/2 pounds Romano beans, trimmed and cut on the diagonal into 1-inch pieces
- 3/4 cup water, or more if needed
- 2 tablespoons chopped fresh oregano
- 2 tablespoons chopped fresh parsley

Freshly grated Parmesan cheese, for sprinkling

Heat the oil in a large flameproof casserole. Add the tomatoes, garlic, salt, and pepper, and cook over medium heat, stirring often, for 5 minutes.

Add the Romano beans, water and 1 tablespoon oregano. Bring to a boil, reduce the heat to low, and cover. Simmer over medium-low heat, stirring occasionally, for 25 to 30 minutes, or until the beans are very tender. If at any time the beans seem dry, add a little more water, 1 tablespoon at a time. The mixture should be slightly soupy.

Stir in the remaining 1 tablespoon oregano and the parsley. Taste for seasoning and add more salt and pepper, if you like. Transfer the beans to a serving bowl, sprinkle with Parmesan cheese, and serve.

corn on the cob

We have such strong feelings about how corn should be cooked that sometimes, in someone else's house, we have to leave the kitchen when it's done another way. First of all, great corn is picked and eaten on the same day. It's refrigerated as soon as you get home and husked just before you cook it (the husks keep the corn moist). A big pot of water does not work well because it takes too long for the water to return to a boil after the corn is added (though restaurant-style stoves do this well). We prefer to cook corn in a small amount of water and virtually steam it. Since a steamer insert isn't large enough to hold the ears, you'll have to rig up your own system. Make a rack in a deep casserole — the sort you'd pull out to make a stew — by laying two short wooden spoons on the bottom. The shucked corn goes into shallow water, and then it's cooked briefly so it doesn't lose its sweet crunchiness. Wrap the corn in a large, clean cloth napkin to serve it.

8 **ears fresh corn**

4 **tablespoons ($1/2$ stick) butter, for serving**
Coarse salt and freshly ground black pepper, for sprinkling

Bring a large flameproof casserole filled with 2 inches of water to a boil. Lay 2 short wooden spoons or a flat rack in the bottom. Set the corn perpendicular to the spoons or directly on the rack. Cover with the lid. Cook for exactly 2 minutes.

Remove the corn from the hot water and serve at once with butter, salt, and pepper passed separately.

fresh corn "risotto"

When the corn comes in, many families eat it every single night, perhaps because our growing season is so short. Some nights we remove the kernels and stir the corn with a little garlic and butter and cream to make this "risotto." Once the corn is husked and the kernels removed (this is a nuisance, and there are no shortcuts), the dish takes only a few minutes.

      2 **tablespoons butter**
      1 **garlic clove, finely chopped**
     12 **ears fresh corn, husked and kernels removed from the cobs**
         (see page 113)
    1/2 **cup heavy cream**
    1/8 **teaspoon freshly grated nutmeg**
      2 **tablespoons chopped fresh chives**
      2 **tablespoons chopped fresh parsley**
    1/2 **teaspoon coarse salt, or to taste**
    1/2 **teaspoon freshly ground black pepper, or to taste**

Melt the butter in a flameproof casserole. Add the garlic and cook over medium-high heat, stirring, for 1 minute.

Add the corn and cook, stirring occasionally, for 2 minutes. Add the cream and nutmeg and bring to a boil. Reduce the heat to low and cook for 2 to 3 minutes, or until the cream reduces slightly. Stir in the chives, parsley, salt, and pepper, and serve at once.

old-fashioned creamy corn pudding

When you grate corn, you get a delicious-tasting milky liquid. Old-fashioned recipes, in fact, instructed cooks to make pudding from this corn "milk" by adding regular milk and egg yolks. But you don't need the milk or the eggs. If you grate the kernels and add a couple of tablespoons of cream, you have a simple, soft, dreamy corn pudding. Jane Levy Reed of San Francisco discovered this when she began reworking her mother-in-law's corn pudding recipe. Serve with Roast Side of Salmon (page 200), Orange-Marinated Turkey Breast (page 184), or grilled chicken.

12 ears fresh corn, kernels removed from the cobs (see page 113)
2–3 tablespoons heavy cream, or to taste
1/2 teaspoon coarse salt, or to taste
1/2 teaspoon freshly ground black pepper, or to taste

Set the oven at 375 degrees. Generously butter a 9-inch square baking dish or another dish with a 2½-quart capacity.

In a food processor, combine half of the corn kernels with 1 tablespoon of the cream and half of the salt and pepper. Pulse just until the corn is chunky but not pureed. Add enough cream to moisten the mixture without making it too loose. Transfer the corn to a bowl.

Process the remaining corn, cream, salt, and pepper in the same way. Combine the two batches, stir well, and pour the mixture into the baking dish.

Bake for 30 minutes, or until the top is slightly brown. You can slide the pudding under the broiler for half a minute, if you prefer a golden top. Serve at once, spooning the pudding onto plates with a large spoon.

scalloped tomatoes

In this dish, ripe tomatoes — with all their seeds and juices — are baked with a crust of bread crumbs and cheese. This is a splendid dish beside grilled fresh tuna or sword-fish.

3 **tablespoons butter**
1/2 **cup fresh white bread crumbs (see page 29)**
4 **extra-large (about 4 pounds), ripe tomatoes, peeled (see
     page 9)**
1 **teaspoon sugar, or to taste**
1/2 **teaspoon coarse salt, or to taste**
1/2 **teaspoon freshly ground black pepper, or to taste**
   Handful fresh basil leaves, finely chopped
   Handful fresh parsley leaves, finely chopped
1/2 **cup grated Gruyère cheese**

Set the oven at 400 degrees. Use 1 table-spoon of the butter to grease an 11-by-7-inch baking dish or another dish with a 2½-quart capacity.

Sprinkle the bread crumbs on a baking sheet and toast them in the oven for about 5 minutes, turning them several times, until they are pale golden. Watch them carefully. Remove them from the oven, and leave the oven on.

Pile the tomatoes into a bowl and add the sugar, salt, and pepper. Taste the tomatoes for sweetness, and add a little more sugar, salt, or pepper, if you like.

Stir in the basil and parsley. Transfer the mixture to the buttered dish and sprinkle the top with the browned crumbs. Scatter the cheese on top and dot with the remaining 2 table-spoons butter. Set the dish on a rimmed baking sheet to catch any spills.

Bake the tomatoes for 25 to 30 minutes, or until the cheese melts and the tomatoes are bubbling at the edges. Serve.

creamy cabbage in a skillet

Cooking a watery vegetable like cabbage in a little oil and butter over low heat draws out the juices in the vegetable and makes it surprisingly creamy and flavorful. Serve with a simple roast chicken, beside a pork chop, or with broiled fish. We learned to make this dish from Rich Barron, chef and co-owner of Il Capriccio, the Waltham, Massachusetts, restaurant known for its modern Italian cooking. Barron slices the cabbage very thinly before cooking it with carrots and onions.

1   tablespoon olive oil
1   tablespoon butter
1   large Spanish onion, halved and thinly sliced
1   medium head green cabbage, quartered, cored, and thinly sliced
2   medium carrots, grated
1/2 teaspoon coarse salt, or to taste
1/2 teaspoon freshly ground black pepper, or to taste

Heat the oil in a large, heavy skillet. When it is hot, add the butter and cook the onion over medium heat, stirring often, for 10 minutes, or until softened.

Add the cabbage, carrots, salt, and pepper. Cover, reduce the heat to medium-low, and cook, stirring often, for 60 minutes, or until the vegetables turn into a jamlike mixture.

Taste for seasoning, add more salt and pepper, if you like, and serve.

stovetop red cabbage with apples

Similar to the once popular red cabbage pickle, this dish cooks with vinegar, sugar, apples, and thyme. Serve with loin of pork or turkey breast.

- 2 **tablespoons butter**
- 2 **red onions, thinly sliced**
- 1 **garlic clove, finely chopped**
- 1 **large red cabbage, cored, quartered, and thinly sliced**
- 1 **cup chicken stock or water, plus more if needed**
- 2 **cooking apples, peeled, cored, and thinly sliced**
- 2 **tablespoons packed dark brown sugar**
- 2 **tablespoons red wine vinegar**
- 1/2 **teaspoon dried thyme**
- 1 **bay leaf**
- 1/2 **teaspoon coarse salt, or to taste**
- 1/2 **teaspoon freshly ground black pepper, or to taste**

Melt the butter in a large flameproof casserole, and cook the onions over medium heat, stirring often, for 10 minutes, or until they soften. Add the garlic and cook for 1 minute, stirring.

Increase the heat to high and add the cabbage, stock or water, apples, brown sugar, vinegar, thyme, bay leaf, salt, and pepper. Stir well.

Bring the mixture to a boil, reduce the heat to low, and simmer the cabbage very gently, stirring occasionally, for 30 minutes, or until tender. Add more stock or water during cooking if the mixture seems dry. Taste for seasoning, remove the bay leaf, and serve.

Apples for Cooking

When you're choosing apples for the savory table, the ideal choice is a cooking apple — that is, one that has a lot of flavor and will keep its shape during baking. We like Ida Reds, Jonathans, Cortlands, Golden Delicious, Rome Beauties, and Baldwins for sautéing or adding to dishes that will cook on the stovetop or in the oven. You can also use Granny Smiths, which are firm and tart and more widely available.

sautéed apples

In the fall, when apples are everywhere, we cook big wedges of peeled apples in a skillet with a little sugar and butter so they caramelize and spoon them alongside roast chicken. Use an apple that will keep its shape.

  6   **cooking apples (see page 256)**
  3   **tablespoons unsalted butter**
1^{1}/$_{2}$ **tablespoons sugar, or to taste**
      Pinch of coarse salt

Peel and quarter the apples, removing the cores. Cut each quarter in half again.

Heat the butter in a nonstick skillet. When it melts but is not brown, add the apples and cook over medium-high heat for 2 minutes, turning often to brown the cut sides.

Sprinkle the apples with sugar and salt and continue cooking for 5 minutes more, or until the sugar caramelizes and the apples are tender. Serve.

cauliflower in milk with rosemary

Few savory dishes rely on milk. We use it here to tone down the somewhat harsh taste of cauliflower. The cauliflower is cooked in big pieces initially, then drizzled with cream and Parmesan cheese at the end of cooking.

- 1 **tablespoon olive oil**
- 1 **tablespoon butter**
- 2 **shallots, finely chopped**
- 1 **head cauliflower, cored and cut into 4 pieces**
- $1/2$ **cup whole milk**
  Handful fresh rosemary leaves, coarsely chopped
- 2 **tablespoons heavy cream**
- $1/2$ **teaspoon coarse salt, or to taste**
- $1/2$ **teaspoon freshly ground black pepper, or to taste**
- $1/4$ **cup freshly grated Parmesan cheese**

Heat the oil in a large flameproof casserole. When it is hot, add the butter and cook the shallots over medium heat, stirring often, for 5 minutes, or until softened. Add the cauliflower, milk, and rosemary. Bring to a boil, reduce the heat to medium-low, cover, and cook for 15 to 20 minutes, or until the cauliflower is tender.

Use a fork to break the cauliflower into small, irregular pieces. Drizzle the cauliflower with the cream, salt, and pepper, and cook over medium heat for 3 minutes, or until the cream is hot. Transfer the cauliflower and sauce to a serving dish. Sprinkle with the cheese, and serve.

brussels sprouts with honey, mustard, and dried cranberries

Dried cranberries didn't catch on for a long time, but they contribute just the right sweet-tart flavor to Brussels sprouts. Here, the cranberries are plumped in water, as you would raisins, then tossed with the sprouts, and finished with a honey-mustard sauce. This dish is always a hit on the Thanksgiving table.

2 **pounds Brussels sprouts**
2 **tablespoons butter**
1/4 **cup honey**
2 **tablespoons Dijon mustard**
1/2 **cup dried cranberries, soaked in hot water for 10 minutes and drained**
1/2 **teaspoon coarse salt, or to taste**
1/2 **teaspoon freshly ground black pepper, or to taste**

Using a sharp paring knife, trim the stem ends of the Brussels sprouts, removing any wilted or brown leaves. Cut a shallow "X" in the stem end of each sprout to keep the leaves from separating. Soak the sprouts for 10 minutes in a bowl of lightly salted cold water.

In a saucepan fitted with a steamer insert, steam the Brussels sprouts over several inches of boiling water, covered, over high heat for 8 minutes, or until almost tender. Drain and rinse with cold water until the Brussels sprouts turn bright green again. When they are cool enough to handle, cut some into halves and some into quarters (you want different sizes).

In a skillet, melt the butter and cook the sprouts for 1 minute. Mix the honey and mustard together in a small bowl and add them to the pan with the cranberries, salt, and pepper.

Cook over medium-high heat, stirring often, for 5 minutes, or until the Brussels sprouts are tender when pierced with the tip of a knife. Serve.

crusty smashed potatoes

One day, when we were beating hot milk into mashed potatoes, it occurred to us that if we began by simmering the potatoes in milk, which would add richness, we might be able to add less milk later, thereby making the dish lighter. Then, instead of mashing, we would simply smash the potatoes with a fork and let them toast a little in a hot oven. It worked like a charm. The potatoes are creamy, the top is crusty, and you can make the dish several hours in advance, so there's no last-minute worry. Use one of the yellow varieties of potato — Yukon Gold or Yellow Finn — because they're such a good color and just the right fleshy texture for this dish, and don't bother to peel them first. After cooking, mash them roughly on a plate with a fork, pull off the skins with your fingers, add a little potato-cooking water, and layer them with olive oil.

> 5 **Yukon Gold, Yellow Finn, or other yellow potatoes**
>   **($3^{1}/_{2}$–4 pounds), unpeeled and quartered**
> 1 **teaspoon coarse salt, plus more to taste**
> 2 **cups skim or low-fat milk**
> 1 **quart water, or more to cover potatoes**
> 1 **onion, halved**
> 4 **peppercorns**
> 1 **bay leaf**
>   **Olive oil, for drizzling**
> $^{1}/_{2}$ **teaspoon freshly ground black pepper, or to taste**

Set the oven at 400 degrees. Oil an 11-by-7-inch baking dish or another dish with a $2^{1}/_{2}$-quart capacity.

Put the potatoes in a large saucepan and add the 1 teaspoon salt, milk, water, onion, peppercorns, and bay leaf. Add enough additional water to cover the potatoes by 1 inch.

Bring to a boil, reduce the heat to medium, set the cover on askew, and let the potatoes bubble steadily for 20 to 25 minutes, or until they are very tender but not falling apart.

When the potatoes are cooked, use a slotted spoon to remove them from the cooking liquid a few at a time and transfer them to a large plate. Reserve the cooking liquid. Discard the onion, peppercorns, and bay leaf. Smash the potatoes with a fork, just to break them up, pulling off the skins as you work.

Transfer a layer of potatoes to the baking dish and sprinkle with oil, salt, and pepper. Add 2 tablespoons cooking liquid. Add more potatoes, sprinkle them with oil, salt, and pepper, and cooking liquid. (You can make the potatoes up to 2 hours ahead and set aside at room temperature.)

Bake the potatoes for 15 minutes, or until brown and crisp on top. Serve.

potato crisps with fresh herbs

This dish begins with very finely sliced potatoes that are layered in a jelly-roll pan with fresh herbs. As the potatoes brown, you turn them over in clusters, so they end up very crisp, and golden, and charmingly rustic. They have all the appealing qualities of good hash browns, but they're much easier to make and lower in fat. For best results, you need a vegetable slicing machine (see page 263). These are nice with broiled or grilled fish.

> 2 teaspoons chopped fresh rosemary
> 1 tablespoon chopped fresh chives
> 1 teaspoon chopped fresh oregano
> 4 russet (baking) potatoes, peeled and left in cold water
> Olive oil, for sprinkling
> 1 teaspoon coarse salt, or to taste
> 1/2 teaspoon freshly ground black pepper, or to taste

Set the oven at 425 degrees. Oil an 11-by-16-inch jelly-roll pan.

Combine the rosemary, chives, and oregano in a small bowl.

Using a handheld slicing machine or a sharp knife, slice the potatoes as thinly as possible. Layer them in the prepared pan in haphazard layers — don't make them even. Sprinkle each layer with olive oil (right), some of the herb mixture, salt, and pepper.

Roast the potatoes for 20 minutes, or until they are crusty on the bottom, then use a metal spatula to turn them. You will be able to turn only as many potatoes as the spatula will hold, and the layers will break up. That's OK. Continue roasting the potatoes for another 20 to 30 minutes, turning them several more times, until the potatoes are cooked through, golden brown, and crusty on top. Serve.

Handheld Slicing Machines

Although an expensive French mandoline will slice your potatoes beautifully — as will the Japanese slicer available in most Asian markets — our favorite handheld slicing machine is the inexpensive Feemster's Famous Vegetable Slicer (below, beside potatoes). It consists of a wide razor blade of carbon steel set on a platform. You can adjust the machine so it slices very thin (for potatoes, for instance) or wider to cut cabbage for slaw or cucumbers. Feemster's is available in some old-fashioned hardware stores or from M. E. Heuck Co. in Cincinnati, Ohio (1-800-359-3200), for about $6.00, plus $5.00 for shipping and handling.

casserole-roasted fall vegetables

Ever since this recipe was published in the *Boston Globe* a dozen years ago, we have heard from readers who tell us that they make it all the time as an accompaniment to turkey breast or roast beef or a roasted side of salmon. These proportions and vegetables are guidelines; the dish is successful with almost any combination.

We like to include one or two kinds of potato, winter squash, and onion and vary the remaining vegetables with the season. All root vegetables — potatoes, carrots, turnips, parsnips — need to be steamed first to soften them. Leaving part of the root on the onions and leeks helps them keep their shapes. Add something red to the dish, too: bell peppers and radishes, or plum tomatoes, or beets (steam beets first). Roast in a nice-looking ceramic baking dish that goes to the table, and pack the vegetables in as tightly as you can; they'll shrink during roasting, and the dish won't look a bit crowded. The vegetables will be full of good juices at the end of cooking.

6	small red potatoes, unpeeled and left whole
2	sweet potatoes, peeled and thickly sliced
1	bunch (4 medium) leeks, trimmed but with part of the roots intact, halved lengthwise, thoroughly rinsed, and cut into 3-inch lengths
	Olive oil, for sprinkling
1 1/2	teaspoons coarse salt, or to taste
1	teaspoon freshly ground black pepper, or to taste
2	medium red onions, peeled but with part of the roots intact, cut into sixths
1	butternut squash, peeled and cut into wide bands
1/2	pound shiitake mushrooms, stems removed and caps halved
1	red bell pepper, cored, seeded, and cut into 6 pieces
1	bunch radishes, rinsed and stemmed
	Large handful fresh thyme sprigs, leaves stripped and coarsely chopped

Set the oven at 400 degrees. Oil a 9-by-13-inch baking dish or another dish with a 3½-quart capacity.

In a large saucepan fitted with a steamer insert, steam the red potatoes over several inches of boiling water, covered, over high heat for 10 minutes, or until they are almost tender when pierced with a skewer. Remove the potatoes from the pan. Add more water to the pan if the water does not come up to the level of the steamer basket. Steam the sweet potatoes over boiling water for 5 minutes, or until they soften a little but still hold their shape.

Set the leeks on either end of the baking dish. Set half of the sweet potatoes beside them so the slices are standing and overlapping. Halve the red potatoes and arrange them in clusters around the dish. Sprinkle the vegetables lightly with oil, salt, and pepper.

Arrange the onions in the dish in clusters — you should have onions in three different places. Arrange the squash in the dish in clusters. Add the mushrooms, red pepper, and radishes in clusters. Pack the vegetables into the dish as tightly as possible. It's fine if most of them are standing on their sides.

Drizzle all the vegetables lightly with oil, and sprinkle them with salt, pepper, and half of the thyme. Cover the dish with foil.

Roast the vegetables for 1½ hours, or until they are all very tender, basting several times with the juices that accumulate in the dish. Sprinkle with the remaining thyme and serve, spooning the cooking juices over each serving.

roasted onion wedges

These often go onto the table when we make Herb-Roasted Flattened Chicken (page 192), or grill a simple piece of fish or steak. They're also good alongside Yankee Pot Roast (page 128), if you don't want to make the caramelized vegetables, or with fried eggs and toast. The tips of the cut onions brown in the oven, and a coating of mustard, balsamic vinegar, and olive oil tones down their heat and makes them piquant.

2	**Spanish onions, peeled but with part of the roots intact**
1	**large red onion, peeled but with part of the roots intact**
2	**tablespoons olive oil**
2	**tablespoons Dijon mustard**
3	**tablespoons balsamic vinegar**
3	**tablespoons chopped fresh thyme**
1/2	**teaspoon coarse salt, or to taste**
1/2	**teaspoon freshly ground black pepper, or to taste**

Set the oven at 400 degrees.

Halve the onions lengthwise, then cut each half into 3 or 4 wedges, keeping a piece of root on each wedge to hold the layers together.

In a small bowl, mix together the oil, mustard, vinegar, 1½ tablespoons of the thyme, salt, and pepper. Add the onions and toss gently to coat them.

Arrange the onions in a 9-inch square baking dish or another dish with a 2½-quart capacity, points up, packing them in as tightly as possible. Cover with foil and roast for 45 minutes.

Remove the foil and continue roasting the onions for 30 minutes, or until they are golden brown and very tender when pierced with a skewer. Sprinkle with the remaining 1½ tablespoons thyme and serve.

roasted potato and red onion mélange

This makes a grand presentation: several kinds of potatoes roasted together in a large baking dish. You need to steam all the potatoes first, so they become crisp in the oven but remain moist inside. Pack them into a baking dish as tightly as possible, standing them on their edges.

> 2 sweet potatoes, unpeeled and sliced 1/2 inch thick
> 3 Yukon Gold or Yellow Finn potatoes, unpeeled, each cut into
> 6 wedges
> 2 russet (baking) potatoes, unpeeled and sliced into 1/2-inch
> rounds
> 4 red potatoes, unpeeled and halved
> 2 large red onions, peeled and cut into 1/2-inch wedges
> Olive oil, for sprinkling
> 1 teaspoon coarse salt, or to taste
> 1/2 teaspoon freshly ground black pepper, or to taste
> Bunch fresh thyme, leaves removed

Set the oven at 400 degrees. Oil a 9-by-13-inch baking dish or another dish with a 3½-quart capacity.

In a large saucepan fitted with a steamer insert, steam the sweet potatoes over several inches of boiling water, covered, over high heat for 10 minutes, or until the potatoes are just tender. Add more water to the bottom of the steamer when necessary. Remove the sweet potatoes from the steamer and transfer them to a plate.

Steam the remaining potatoes in the same way, adding as many to the steamer as you can fit in. When all the potatoes are tender, cut the red potatoes in half again.

Arrange the potatoes in the baking dish in clusters of three or four, setting the slices on their sides, when possible, so they are almost standing on edge. Set the onions in clusters in two or three places. When all the potatoes are arranged, they should look like a beautiful garden, with sweet potatoes, for instance, in three different places, red potatoes in three different places, and so on.

Sprinkle the potatoes and onions with olive oil, then add salt, pepper, and thyme. Cover with foil and roast for 1½ hours.

Remove the foil and continue roasting for 20 to 30 minutes, or until the potatoes are crusty on top. Serve.

roasted turnips with pears

Until recently, sophisticated cooks paid the homely turnip little attention, though old-fashioned households have always boiled or mashed turnips to serve with corned beef or pot roast. We use ordinary purple-topped turnips, mix them with rutabaga, and roast them at a high temperature with Bosc pears to offset any tang in the roots.

1   large rutabaga, peeled, halved, and cut into $1/2$-inch cubes
2   purple-topped turnips, peeled, halved, and cut into $1/2$-inch cubes
2   Bosc pears, peeled, cored, and cut into $1/2$-inch cubes
2   tablespoons olive oil
$1/2$ teaspoon coarse salt, or to taste
$1/2$ teaspoon freshly ground black pepper, or to taste

Set the oven at 400 degrees. Lightly oil an 11-by-7-inch baking dish or another dish with a $2^1/2$-quart capacity.

In a large bowl, combine the rutabaga, turnips, and pears. Sprinkle with the olive oil, salt, and pepper. Toss gently but thoroughly. Transfer the vegetables and fruit to the baking dish and cover with foil, shiny side down.

Bake for 45 minutes. Uncover and continue baking for 45 minutes more, or until the vegetables are cooked through. Serve.

winter squashes roasted in chunks

Sometimes a recipe is so obvious or so simple that we wonder why everyone doesn't already make it. Yet when we serve these chunks of squash, with their caramelized edges and lightly salted flesh, all our guests wonder what we did. And the answer is: practically nothing. Where most recipes instruct you to set the squash in the baking dish cut sides down, here you cook them cut sides up and blast them in a hot oven. We mix varieties. Winter squash is so meaty that some nights, a plateful of the squash, a big salad, and a glass of red wine are a satisfying supper. On other nights, we mash the chunks with a little butter and serve them beside roast chicken. Sheryl often takes several pieces to work for lunch. At the end of the week, we might simmer what's left with chicken stock, add an onion that we sauté and season with some imported Indian curry powder, then puree the mixture into a soup.

2   delicata squash, halved, seeded, and cut into 3-inch chunks
1   medium buttercup squash, halved, seeded, and cut into 2-inch chunks
1   8-inch piece of blue hubbard squash, seeded, and cut into 2-inch chunks
1/2   cup water, or more if needed
     Olive oil, for sprinkling
1   teaspoon coarse salt, or to taste
1/2   teaspoon freshly ground black pepper, or to taste

Set the oven at 450 degrees.

Place all the squash, cut sides up, on a large, rimmed baking sheet (a sturdy 11-by-16-inch jelly-roll pan works well). Pour the water into the bottom of the pan. Drizzle the squash with oil and sprinkle with salt and pepper.

Roast for 55 minutes, or until tender when pierced with the tip of a knife. They will be ready at different times. Remove the cooked pieces from the oven when they are ready. Transfer the squash to a platter and serve.

Winter Squashes

Cook any of the dozens of winter squash in our markets in the fall and a surprise awaits you. Some are meaty-flavored, others rich. **Spaghetti squash** cooks into pastalike strands that you can coat with a simple tomato sauce. **Butternut squash** is the most widely available variety in farm stands and supermarkets. It's freshest when it's unpeeled, because the skin protects it from deteriorating, but we buy it ready-peeled when we're in a hurry. Dark-green **acorn squash** is perfect for stuffing with all kinds of nutty mixtures. A new variety of **orange acorn squash,** which seems to be sweeter, has appeared in the markets. For years, our favorite winter squash has been **buttercup,** which has a round dark-green bottom with a little hat on top. Like the acorn, buttercup has also been bred in an orange color. **Hubbard**, one of the largest squash available and somewhat less sweet than the others, is so dense that it's often sold cut into 8- or 10-inch pieces. Because of its size, it's wonderful for a crowd. **Delicata squash,** as its name implies, is slightly more delicate than many dense winter varieties, and its skin is tender enough to be eaten.

sweet potatoes
with brown sugar and marmalade

Our concession to the popular sweet potatoes and marshmallows of the 1950s, still offered on celebration tables, is this version, glazed with brown sugar, butter, and marmalade.

- 6   **sweet potatoes, sliced $1/4$ inch thick**
- 1   **teaspoon coarse salt, plus more to taste**
- 2   **tablespoons butter**
- 2   **tablespoons packed dark brown sugar**
- $1/2$ **teaspoon ground cinnamon**
- $1/4$ **teaspoon freshly ground nutmeg**
- $1/2$ **teaspoon freshly ground black pepper, or to taste**
- 1   **cup top-quality marmalade**

Set the oven at 400 degrees. Butter an 11-by-7-inch baking dish or another dish with a $2\frac{1}{2}$-quart capacity.

In a large flameproof casserole, combine the sweet potatoes with enough water to cover the potatoes by 1 inch. Add the salt.

Bring them to a boil, turn down the heat so the mixture barely simmers, and cover the pan. Cook the potatoes for 10 minutes, or until they are almost tender.

With a slotted spoon, lift the potatoes from the water. Arrange half the potatoes overlapping in the baking dish. Dot them with half the butter.

In a small bowl, toss together the brown sugar, cinnamon, nutmeg, salt to taste, and pepper. Sprinkle half the sugar mixture over the potatoes, then spoon half the marmalade on top. Make another layer just like the first one.

Bake the potatoes for 55 minutes, or until they are browned and cooked through. Serve.

white beans with swiss chard

Quick, filling, and inexpensive, this old-fashioned Italian-American dish is still very popular. We know half a dozen Italian families who make it on the nights when there's not much else in the cupboard. Swiss chard, the mildest of the winter greens, has a spinachlike quality, but it's related to the beet family. We often add it to vegetable soups. (If you've ever cooked Swiss chard, you know that big handfuls reduce to spoonfuls once the leaves are heated.)

> 2 **tablespoons olive oil**
> 1 **Spanish onion, finely chopped**
> 1/2 **teaspoon coarse salt, or to taste**
> 1/2 **teaspoon freshly ground black pepper, or to taste**
> 2 **garlic cloves, chopped**
> 1 **can (16 ounces) whole peeled tomatoes, crushed in a bowl**
> 1 **can (15 ounces) cannellini beans, drained and rinsed**
> 1/2 **cup water**
> 1 **tablespoon chopped fresh rosemary**
> 1 **bunch Swiss chard, stems removed and leaves coarsely chopped**
>   **Olive oil, for drizzling**
> 1 **cup freshly grated Parmesan cheese, for serving**

In a large flameproof casserole, heat the oil and cook the onion with salt and pepper over medium heat, stirring often, for 10 minutes, or until softened. Add the garlic and tomatoes and cook for 5 minutes more.

Add the beans, water, and rosemary. Bring to a boil, reduce the heat to low, and simmer, stirring occasionally, for 20 minutes.

Add the Swiss chard and cook, stirring, for 15 minutes more, or until tender. Taste for seasoning and add more salt and pepper, if you like. Drizzle with olive oil and serve with Parmesan cheese.

jasmine rice

Deeply aromatic, jasmine rice will perfume your whole house as it cooks. Served in many Thai restaurants, it's made without peeking into the boiling pot. This ensures perfectly cooked rice (it also prevents any liquid from evaporating). It goes well with spicy or flavorful food.

>   2 **cups jasmine rice**
> $2^2/_3$ **cups water**
> $1/_2$ **teaspoon coarse salt**

Rinse the rice in several changes of cold water. Transfer the rice to a medium pot with a tight-fitting lid. Add the water and salt. Bring to a boil, reduce the heat to low, cover, and simmer for 15 minutes.

Without removing the lid, take the rice off the heat and let it stand for 5 minutes. Taste the rice, and if the grains are not tender, re-cover the pot and let it rest for a few minutes longer. Fluff the rice and serve at once.

basmati rice

Basmati is a long-grain white rice once farmed only in India but now grown in this country, too. It emits a beautiful smell when it's cooking and has a nutty taste. In other recipes, you're often directed to cook the rice in the amount of water the rice will absorb completely. In this method, you use quite a lot of water — like cooking pasta, actually — and then drain the rice when it's done. A lemon half, cooked with the rice, keeps the grains white. If you're making rice for a salad, this is the only way to cook it. The extra water keeps the grains firm and separate.

>   1 **lemon half**
> 1/2 **teaspoon coarse salt, or to taste**
>   2 **cups basmati rice**

Bring a large saucepan of water to a boil (you need at least 10 cups). Add the lemon half and salt.

When the water is at a rolling boil, sprinkle the rice into the pan and stir with a wooden spoon so the rice keeps moving as the water returns to a boil.

Meanwhile, set a colander in the sink.

Lower the heat slightly so the water bubbles steadily. Let the rice cook, stirring several times, for exactly 12 minutes. Pick up a grain of rice on the spoon and taste it. The center of the grain should be cooked. If not, continue cooking, testing the rice every minute.

Drain the rice into the colander, and use the end of the wooden spoon to poke a half-dozen holes in the rice so it drains. Let sit for 3 minutes.

Remove the lemon half from the rice. Transfer the rice to a warm bowl and fluff it with the spoon. Serve at once.

quick couscous

Most packages of couscous call for cooking the grains in boiling water, which turns them mushy. This method lets you soak the couscous in advance and ensures that the grains stay separate: first you soak the couscous, then heat it in the oven just before serving.

> 1   box (10 ounces, or 1¹/₂ cups) quick-cooking couscous
> 1¹/₄ cups cold water

Set the oven at 350 degrees. Butter a 1¹/₂-quart baking dish.

In a bowl, combine the couscous and water. Stir well and set the bowl aside for 10 minutes. If the grains seem dry, add a few more spoonfuls of water and set the couscous aside for a few minutes more. With a fork, gently fluff the couscous. Transfer it to the baking dish and cover with foil.

Heat the couscous for 20 to 25 minutes, stirring once or twice, until it is very hot. Serve.

blue cheese popovers

A little crumbled blue cheese folded into a popover batter becomes mellow and gives the popovers a nice tang. If you have an extra muffin tin, use two pans and fill every other indentation so each one has plenty of room to puff up. But they work well in one pan, too. Serve them quickly. They go well with Tenderloin of Beef with Red Wine Sauce (page 172).

4	**large eggs**
$1^3/4$	**cups milk**
$1^1/4$	**cups all-purpose flour**
$^1/2$	**teaspoon salt**
$^1/2$	**cup crumbled Danish blue, Maytag, or other blue cheese**

Set the oven at 425 degrees. Butter a standard 12-muffin tin (or use two, if you have them).

Whisk the eggs in a large bowl with an electric mixer or by hand for 2 minutes, until they are light and fluffy. Add the milk, flour, and salt and beat for 30 seconds. Stir in the cheese.

Spoon or ladle the batter into the muffin cups. Bake for 20 minutes.

Reduce the heat to 350 degrees and continue to bake for 15 to 20 minutes more, or until the popovers are golden brown and toasted. Do not open the oven until the last few minutes, or you risk deflating the popovers.

Remove the popovers from the oven. Use a blunt knife to gently ease them out of the tin. Serve at once.

noodle pudding

Traditional Jewish noodle puddings (kugels) are made with lots of sugar and raisins, which means they're sweet. Even so, they're intended for the main course, beside a salmon steak or another simple fish dish. Noodle puddings might also appear on the brunch table with stacks of bagels and trays of smoked fish. This one is made with sour cream, cottage cheese, and cream cheese, which makes it quite rich. The mixture comes right to the top of the baking dish. Brenda Cheifetz, a cook in Burlington, Massachusetts, who makes this all the time, advises walking slowly to the oven with it. The squares of baked kugel are high and moist.

- 1/2 **teaspoon coarse salt, to taste**
- 1 **pound broad egg noodles**
- 4 **tablespoons (1/2 stick) butter, melted**
- 1 **package (8 ounces) cream cheese, at room temperature**
- 6 **large eggs**
- 2 **cups (1 pint) sour cream**
- 1 **cup whole milk**
- 1 **cup sugar**
- 1 **teaspoon vanilla extract**
- 1 **teaspoon ground cinnamon, plus more for sprinkling**
- 2 **cups (1 pint) cottage cheese**
- 3 **cups dark raisins**

Set the oven at 350 degrees. Butter a 9-by-13-inch baking dish or another dish with a 3½-quart capacity.

Bring a large pot of water to a boil. Add a pinch of salt and the noodles. When the water returns to a boil, cook the noodles, stirring often, for 5 minutes (they will not be cooked through). Drain in a colander.

Transfer the noodles to a large bowl. Add the butter and toss gently.

Beat the cream cheese in another large bowl with a wooden spoon, to soften it and break it up. Add the eggs, one at a time, stirring well after each addition. Add the sour cream, milk, sugar, vanilla, cinnamon, and salt. Stir thoroughly.

Pour the cream cheese mixture over the noodles and stir gently but thoroughly.

Fold in the cottage cheese and raisins. Transfer the mixture to the prepared dish and sprinkle with cinnamon.

Bake the pudding for 1 to 1¼ hours, or until the noodles are set and the top is golden brown.

Remove from the oven and let it sit for 5 minutes to settle. With a large knife, cut the pudding into 3-inch squares. Serve.

pickled red onions

An instant pickle, these red onions are quite crisp when you eat them. Enjoy them in turkey sandwiches or on hamburgers. Or use them to make the delicious onion sandwich James Beard talked about early in his food-writing career: butter two pieces of toasted bread and pile on onions, salt, and pepper. You don't need anything else for a satisfying lunch. You'll need to start this dish a day ahead.

4 large red onions, thinly sliced
   Coarse salt, to taste
1 teaspoon black peppercorns
6 allspice berries
1 tablespoon sugar
1 cup distilled white vinegar

Layer the onions in a large bowl, with a sprinkling of salt between each layer. Add enough cold water to cover the onions. Set aside for 1 hour.

Tip the onions into a colander and rinse them thoroughly. Transfer the onions to a plastic container. Add the peppercorns and allspice berries. Stir the sugar into the vinegar, and pour the mixture over the onions. Refrigerate for at least 1 day or for up to 1 week before serving.

brazilian onion-jalapeño sauce

Lots of lemon, onions, jalapeños, and garlic go into this *molho*, a sauce that accompanies barbecued pork in Brazil, where Cindy Hoffman, a design editor at *Time* magazine, lived as a child. She learned to make this from her mother, Gladys. Serve with pork, grilled sausages, or roast chicken.

- 2 red or green jalapeños, cored, seeded, and cut into strips
- 4 garlic cloves
- 1/2 cup Champagne vinegar
  Juice of 3 lemons (about 3/4 cup)
- 1/2 cup olive oil
- 3 medium onions, finely chopped
- 1/4 cup chopped scallions
- 1/4 cup chopped fresh parsley
- 1/4 teaspoon coarse salt, or to taste
- 1/4 cup chicken stock or water (optional)

Chop the jalapeños and garlic together.

Whisk together the vinegar, lemon juice, and oil in a small bowl. With a spoon, stir in the onions, scallions, parsley, the jalapeño mixture, and salt.

Taste for seasoning and add more salt, if you like. If the sauce is too strong, add chicken stock or water to thin it before serving.

crisp bread-and-butter pickles

Sheryl's mother, Doris Julian, has been making this pickle every year from a recipe her sister-in-law gave her forty years ago. Unlike most pickles, they can be eaten right away. They're very crunchy, with just enough sugar to balance the vinegar, so they're not sweet. Doris makes them only in the summer, when she can buy cucumbers from her local farmers' market. We use a Feemster's Famous Vegetable Slicer to slice the cucumbers and peppers (see page 263).

   3 **cups distilled white vinegar**
2^1/$_2$ **cups sugar**
   4 **teaspoons coarse salt**
   1 **teaspoon dry mustard**
   1 **teaspoon turmeric**
   9 **unwaxed cucumbers, unpeeled, scrubbed, and thinly sliced**
   3 **red bell peppers, cored, seeded, and thinly sliced**
   4 **medium onions, thinly sliced**

Combine the vinegar, sugar, salt, mustard, and turmeric in a large flameproof casserole over medium heat. Cook, stirring occasionally, for 5 minutes, or until the sugar dissolves. Turn up the heat until the mixture is quite hot — do not let it boil.

Add the cucumbers, peppers, and onions to the vinegar mixture. Heat thoroughly for 5 to 10 minutes, stirring often, but do not let it come to a boil or the cucumbers will be overcooked and lose their crispness.

Ladle the vegetables and their liquid into jars and cover with the lids. Store in the refrigerator for up to 1 month.

corn, yellow pepper, and thyme relish

For generations, cooks all over the country have put up corn relish in August, sealing the jars in a water bath so the relish stayed fresh all winter. This one can be made and served within an hour.

8	ears fresh corn, kernels removed from the cobs (see page 113)
1/4	cup white wine vinegar, or more to taste
2	garlic cloves, very finely chopped
1	teaspoon coarse salt, or to taste
1/2	teaspoon freshly ground black pepper, or to taste
1/8	teaspoon yellow mustard seeds
2	yellow bell peppers, cored, seeded, and very finely chopped
1/4	cup fresh thyme leaves, finely chopped
6	scallions (white part only), very finely chopped

Bring a large saucepan of water to a boil. Add the corn and cook for 2 minutes; the corn should still have some bite. Drain into a colander and shake the colander to remove excess moisture. Set aside for a few minutes.

Transfer the corn to a large bowl and add the vinegar, garlic, salt, pepper, and mustard seeds. Stir thoroughly. Set aside to cool completely.

Add the yellow peppers, thyme, and scallions to the corn and toss thoroughly. Taste for seasoning and add more vinegar, salt, or pepper, if you like. Cover the bowl and refrigerate the relish for at least 1 hour and for up to 2 days before serving.

spicy cranberries and apples

We add apples, gingerbread spices, orange rind, orange juice, and raisins to fresh cranberries, then bake the relish, rather than cooking it on the stovetop, so we don't have to watch it and there's no risk of scorching it. The end result is a lot like a chutney.

- 1 **cup fresh whole cranberries**
- $^1/_2$ **cup golden raisins**
- $^1/_2$ **cup packed dark brown sugar**
- $^1/_2$ **cup sugar**
- 1 **tablespoon grated orange rind**
- $^1/_2$ **cup orange juice**
- $^3/_4$ **teaspoon ground cinnamon**
- $^1/_2$ **teaspoon ground ginger**
- $^1/_8$ **teaspoon ground cloves**
  Pinch of ground nutmeg
- 2 **tablespoons Grand Marnier or other orange liqueur (optional)**
- 4 **large baking apples (see page 256), peeled, quartered, and diced**

Set the oven at 325 degrees.

In an 11-by-7-inch baking dish or another dish with a 2½-quart capacity, combine the cranberries, raisins, sugars, orange rind and juice, cinnamon, ginger, cloves, nutmeg, and orange liqueur, if using. Stir thoroughly and cover with foil, shiny side down.

Bake for 1 hour, stirring occasionally, or until the cranberries are cooked through. Add the apples to the cranberries, stir thoroughly, and continue baking uncovered for 30 minutes, or until the apples are tender.

Remove from the oven and set aside to cool to room temperature. Serve, or transfer to a covered container and refrigerate for up to 1 week.

rise and dine

Breakfast food is wonderful —
sweet breads, smoked fish,
eggy dishes that are perfect
after a late night. We like to spend
lazy weekend mornings reading
the papers and nibbling on
something special — not a whole
spread, but a slice of sweet bread
along with fruit and yogurt, or a
hot dish that takes almost no time
to prepare.

A more formal brunch holds little appeal. It seems to disrupt the day, coming as it does smack in the middle, and when we do go to brunch, all we want to do afterward is nap.

For breakfasts, we keep quick breads in the freezer or make scones the night before and bake them the morning we need them. Many muffin batters can be refrigerated without harm overnight and poured into paper-lined muffin tins the next morning. We might make a hash from leftover sweet potatoes, a frittata from boiled or baked potatoes, quesadillas with quickly assembled tomatoes and peppers.

A luxurious breakfast might include Sour Cream Coffee Cake or warm Prune Plum Kuchen, both with a brown-sugar streusel topping. We're also wild about any kind of smoked fish, either lox and cream cheese on bagels or smoked or roast salmon mixed with rice and curry powder to make the popular English lunch dish Salmon Kedgeree.

There are two secrets to early-morning cooking: having a stash of baked goods in the freezer and pulling them out the night before or doing half the work before you go to bed. If you want to make a frittata, for instance, it'll be a breeze in the morning if the eggs are already in a bowl in the refrigerator, the baking dish oiled, the filling ingredients measured and waiting.

We've brought many of these dishes, either made or ready to assemble, to friends when we stay at their weekend houses, where lazy mornings take on a new definition. When we're that relaxed, of course, we begin thinking about a nap midmorning. Perhaps we shouldn't blame all our sleepiness on brunch.

rise and dine

leek and egg frittata

Many frittata recipes require complicated flipping so the eggs cook on top as well as on the bottom. This one, made with sautéed leeks and a lightly mashed potato, couldn't be simpler: just bake it until it's set. We've used leftover boiled or mashed potatoes for this dish, and you can certainly substitute 3 onions for the leeks; you can practically make it with anything that's around. In summer, serve it with sliced tomatoes; in winter, with sliced oranges; and all year, with warm, crusty bread. The recipe comes from Fran Putnoi, of Cambridge, Massachusetts, who makes a thin version in a buckled aluminum pan she inherited from her grandmother.

- 2 **tablespoons olive oil, plus more for sprinkling**
- 6 **leeks, trimmed at both ends, well washed, halved lengthwise, and thinly sliced**
- 1 **large russet (baking) potato, peeled and quartered**
- 1/2 **teaspoon coarse salt, or to taste**
- 6 **large eggs, lightly beaten**
- 1/2 **cup mixed freshly grated Parmesan and Romano cheeses**
- 1/2 **teaspoon freshly ground black pepper, or to taste**

In a skillet, heat the oil and cook the leeks over medium heat for 20 to 30 minutes, stirring often, or until they are very soft.

Set the oven at 375 degrees. Tip the leeks into a strainer and press out the excess moisture. Set aside.

Put the potato into a medium saucepan and add a pinch of salt and water to cover it. Bring to a boil, lower the heat, and simmer the potato for 15 minutes, or until tender.

On a plate with a fork, lightly mash the potato and transfer it to a large bowl. Stir in the eggs, cheese, salt, pepper, and leeks.

Add enough olive oil to a deep 9-inch pie pan to make a thin film on the bottom and sides. Set the dish in the oven and leave it for 3 minutes, or until the oil is very hot.

Carefully spoon the frittata mixture into the pie pan and press it with the back of a spoon. Bake for 45 to 50 minutes, or until the edges are golden brown and the custard is set in the middle. Cut the frittata into wedges and serve hot or at room temperature.

egg white frittata

Even people who are inclined to turn up their noses at the thought of an all-white frittata like this one. We make it because we keep hearing from high-cholesterol readers who think they shouldn't eat eggs (or rather, egg yolks). Others who worry about their weight won't eat the yolks either. So this filling frittata serves both groups. The dish isn't difficult, but you need to make a kind of chutney from the vegetables, so they become quite flavorful, then simmer them with a little white wine. Julie often makes an instant frittata for lunch using last night's cooked vegetables, some grated cheddar, and egg whites that she buys in the supermarket. For breakfast, serve this with toast.

3 tablespoons olive oil
1 medium red onion, thinly sliced
2 medium zucchini, thinly sliced
4 shiitake mushrooms, finely chopped
1 tablespoon chopped fresh thyme
$^{1}/_{2}$ teaspoon coarse salt, or to taste
$^{1}/_{2}$ teaspoon freshly ground black pepper, or to taste
$1^{1}/_{2}$ cups (about 10) egg whites
$^{1}/_{2}$ cup grated cheddar cheese
2 tablespoons freshly grated Parmesan cheese

In a 10-inch nonstick skillet with a heatproof handle, heat 1 tablespoon of the oil. When it is hot, add the onion, zucchini, mushrooms, thyme, salt, and pepper. Cook over medium-low heat, stirring often, for 45 minutes.

Set the oven at 375 degrees.

Beat the whites in a bowl with a whisk until they are frothy (they'll still be liquid). With a rubber spatula, stir in the vegetables and cheddar cheese.

In the same skillet in which you cooked the vegetables, heat the remaining 2 tablespoons of oil, and when it is hot, pour in the egg mixture. Stir lightly just to distribute the vegetables evenly. Sprinkle with Parmesan cheese.

Cook over medium-low heat for 5 minutes. Transfer the skillet to the oven and bake the frittata for 15 minutes, or until set and cooked through.

Turn on the broiler. Slide the skillet under the broiler for 1 minute just to brown the top slightly. Remove from the oven.

Slip a long metal spatula under the frittata and slide it carefully onto a large platter. Cut it into wedges and serve.

salmon kedgeree

Kedgeree, a warm curried rice dish, is one of England's popular lunch and breakfast dishes. This version has only enough curry powder to season the rice mildly. The dish is traditionally made with smoked haddock, though kippered salmon (cured with a hot-smoke process) also lends kedgeree a good smoky flavor. To use smoked fish, simply flake it and discard any bones. It's stronger than fresh fish, so you'll need less. When we can't find it, we make the dish with roast salmon. Serve kedgeree with hard-cooked eggs and lots of toast. Sheryl learned this recipe years ago at the Cordon Bleu School in London.

1	pound kippered salmon (see above) or smoked haddock, or
	2 pounds fresh salmon fillet
	Vegetable oil, for rubbing
1/4	teaspoon coarse salt, or to taste
1/4	teaspoon freshly ground black pepper, or to taste
8	tablespoons (1 stick) unsalted butter
1 1/2	tablespoons curry powder
	Pinch of cayenne pepper
2	cups heavy cream
1	cup chicken stock
2	cups cooked Basmati Rice (page 275) or other long-grain white rice
1/4	cup chopped fresh parsley
4	eggs, hard-cooked (see page 293), quartered or coarsely chopped

Set the oven at 450 degrees.

Flake the kippered salmon or smoked haddock, if using. Or, lay the fresh salmon fillet in a baking dish skin side down. Rub it with oil, and some salt and pepper. Press a piece of parchment paper directly onto the salmon.

Roast the salmon fillet for 15 minutes, or until it is cooked through but still moist. Set aside to cool, then flake it into 2-inch pieces.

In a deep 12-inch skillet, melt the butter and stir in the curry powder and cayenne pepper. Cook for 1 minute, stirring. Add 1 cup of the cream and the chicken stock. Bring to a boil.

To Hard-Cook Eggs

The cardinal rule for hard-cooking eggs is that they should never be subjected to rapidly boiling water. A hard boil makes the whites tough. This method uses a gentle boil and also eliminates the unpleasant gray circle around the yolks that is caused by overcooking.

Bring a large saucepan of water to a boil (large enough to hold the eggs in one layer with plenty of room to spare). Using a straight pin, prick the rounded end of the eggs. Use a slotted spoon to lower the eggs carefully into the water and stir them with a spoon until the water returns to a boil, which centers the yolks. Reduce the heat to medium and cook the eggs, uncovered, for exactly 12 minutes.

With the slotted spoon, lift the eggs from the water and transfer them to a bowl of ice water. Use the back of a spoon to crack the shells. Peel a strip of shell off each egg to let the cold water into the shell. Leave the eggs until they are cold. Peel the eggs and use as directed.

Stir in the rice and cook over medium heat for 1 minute. Add ¼ teaspoon of the salt and pepper. Add the haddock or the kippered or roast salmon, parsley, and the remaining 1 cup cream. Stir over medium heat until the mixture bubbles at the edges. Cook for 2 minutes, or until the fish is hot and flavored with curry. Taste for seasoning, and add the remaining ¼ teaspoon salt, if you like.

Arrange the kedgeree on a platter, surround it with the eggs, and serve at once.

breakfast quesadillas with peppers, tomatoes, and cheese

Crisp and very cheesy, these quesadillas can be assembled and baked in a few minutes. They also make a good light supper, along with a bowl of Old-Fashioned Vegetable Soup (page 102) or Chicken and Corn Chili (page 121).

8 small (6–7-inch) flour tortillas

6 ripe plum tomatoes, peeled, seeded, and finely chopped (see page 9)

4 scallions, finely chopped

1 jalapeño or other small hot chili pepper, cored, seeded, and finely chopped

3 tablespoons chopped fresh cilantro

1/2 teaspoon coarse salt, or to taste

1/2 teaspoon freshly ground black pepper, or to taste

4 ounces Jack cheese, cut into 4 slices

4 ounces sharp cheddar cheese, grated (1 cup)

Set the oven at 400 degrees.

Place 4 tortillas on a rimmed baking sheet. Warm them in the oven for 3 minutes. Remove from the oven; leave the oven on.

Combine the tomatoes, scallions, jalapeño or chili pepper, cilantro, salt, and pepper in a small bowl.

Divide the Jack cheese among the warm tortillas, then top it with the tomato mixture. Add the cheddar cheese and cover each one with a tortilla.

Return the tortillas to the oven and bake them for 8 to 10 minutes, or until the cheese melts at the edges and the top tortilla is slightly crisp. Cut each quesadilla into quarters and serve.

sweet potato and ham hash

Fleshy sweet potatoes almost beg for something smoky, which makes this ham hash, topped with soft-cooked eggs, especially appealing. Unlike white potatoes, sweet potatoes don't turn as crusty in the skillet. Instead, they lend the hash their earthy taste.

3 large sweet potatoes (unpeeled), cut into $^1/_4$-inch cubes
3 tablespoons canola oil
1 large onion, finely chopped
$^1/_2$ teaspoon coarse salt, or to taste
$^1/_4$ teaspoon freshly ground black pepper, or to taste
2 thick slices ($^1/_2$ pound total) ham, very finely chopped

4 soft-cooked eggs (see page 55)

In a large saucepan fitted with a steamer insert, steam the sweet potatoes over several inches of boiling water, covered, over high heat for 8 minutes, or until they are tender. Lift the steamer from the saucepan and set the potatoes aside.

Heat the oil in a large nonstick skillet, and cook the onion with the salt and pepper over medium heat, stirring often, for 10 minutes, or until softened. Add the ham and sweet potatoes, stir well, and press the mixture into the pan.

Cook over medium heat, without stirring, for 10 minutes, or until the hash is browned on the bottom (use a wide metal spatula to lift an edge to look at it). Turn the hash over in clumps and press it into the pan. Continue cooking for 10 minutes, or until the bottom is browned at the edges.

Spoon the hash onto each of four plates and add an egg to each one. Serve at once.

ham, egg, and cheese pudding

Made from rich white toasting bread layered with eggs, cheddar cheese, and ham, this pudding is assembled and left overnight in the refrigerator before baking. While it sits, the bread absorbs all the liquid in the dish and puffs gloriously in the oven. Somehow, it doesn't seem as if you're eating bread at all but, rather, an airy, cheesy, soufflé-like mixture. This is one of those recipes that was passed from household to household in the 1950s until everyone had a version.

1	loaf (1 pound) rich white toasting bread, such as challah or brioche, cut into thick slices
6	large eggs
1 1/2	cups whole milk
1/2	teaspoon coarse salt, or to taste
1/2	teaspoon freshly ground black pepper, or to taste
1/2	pound flavorful ham, such as Black Forest or Westphalian, finely chopped
8	ounces sharp cheddar cheese, grated (2 cups)

Butter a 2-quart soufflé or similar deep baking dish.

Remove the crusts from the bread. Cut each slice into fourths.

Whisk the eggs in a large bowl and gradually add the milk, salt, and pepper.

Lay one third of the bread in the baking dish, overlapping the pieces. Add half of the ham and half of the cheese. Make another layer using one third of the bread and the remaining ham and cheese. End with a layer of bread neatly overlapping the pieces on top.

Ladle the egg mixture onto the bread, letting it trickle down the edges of the bread into the bottom of the dish.

Cover the dish tightly with plastic wrap and refrigerate for at least 8 hours or up to 2 days. Remove from the refrigerator 1 hour before baking.

Set the oven at 400 degrees.

Remove the plastic wrap, and bake for 50 to 55 minutes, or until the pudding is puffed and brown. Serve at once.

VARIATION
Mushroom Bread Pudding

Make the Ham, Egg, and Cheese Pudding as directed (page 296), substituting mushrooms for the ham and reducing the quantity of cheese to 1 cup.

- 2 tablespoons butter
- 1 1/2 pounds white button mushrooms, finely chopped
- 1 teaspoon coarse salt, or to taste
- 1/2 teaspoon freshly ground black pepper, or to taste
- 2 tablespoons chopped fresh thyme

Heat the butter in a large skillet, and when it melts, add the mushrooms with the salt and pepper. Cook over medium heat, stirring occasionally, until the mushrooms release their liquid.

Turn up the heat to high and continue cooking, stirring constantly, until the liquid evaporates. Set aside to cool completely. Stir in the thyme.

Follow the instructions for the Ham, Egg, and Cheese Pudding, adding the mushroom mixture instead of the ham when you layer the mixture in the dish.

Cover the dish, chill, and bake as directed.

warm cheese pie

Julie's mother, Ghita, often made this pie for Sunday brunch, and now so do we. The farmer-cheese-and-lemon filling reminds Julie of the filling inside cheese blintzes. The base is more like a cake batter than pastry, and it's spread, rather than rolled. It's a little homely, but comforting with a spoonful of sour cream. If you like, prepare it in advance but don't bake it, then slip it into the oven when your guests have assembled.

FOR THE BASE

- 8 tablespoons (1 stick) butter
- 1/2 cup sugar
- 2 large eggs
- 1 cup all-purpose flour
- 1 teaspoon baking powder
- 1/2 teaspoon salt

Butter a deep 9½-inch pie pan.

Cream the butter and sugar in a medium bowl with an electric mixer for 1 minute, or until they are light-colored. Add the eggs, one at a time, and beat for 1 minute more. With the mixer set on its lowest speed, beat in the flour, baking powder, and salt.

Using a long metal palette knife, spread the batter just on the bottom of the pie pan. Set aside while you make the filling.

✳ FOR THE FILLING
  1 **pound pot or farmer cheese**
  ¹/4 **cup sugar**
  3 **large eggs**
  ¹/4 **cup whole milk**
    Grated rind of 1 lemon
  2 **tablespoons fresh lemon juice**
  ¹/2 **teaspoon coarse salt**

  1 **cup sour cream, for serving**

Set the oven at 350 degrees, with a rack in the center.

Cream the pot or farmer cheese in a large bowl with an electric mixer. Beat in the sugar. Add the eggs, one at a time, beating well after each addition. Stir in the milk, lemon rind and juice, and salt.

Pour the filling into the pie pan and smooth the top with a metal spatula.

Bake in the center of the oven for 45 minutes, or until the filling is firm to the touch. It will not brown. Remove the pie from the oven, let it settle for a few minutes, then cut into slices and serve warm with sour cream.

cornmeal currant scones

These handsome cornmeal triangles are studded with currants and flavored with orange rind. They're slightly crumbly and a little chewy and very satisfying. The recipe comes from Boston professional baker Suzanne Lombardi.

- 3¹/₂ cups all-purpose flour
- 1¹/₂ cups yellow cornmeal
- ¹/₂ cup sugar
- 2¹/₂ teaspoons baking powder
- 1¹/₄ teaspoons baking soda
- 1¹/₄ teaspoons salt
- 1¹/₄ cups (2¹/₂ sticks) unsalted butter, cold
- 1 cup dried currants
- 2 tablespoons grated orange rind
- 1¹/₄ cups buttermilk

Set the oven at 375 degrees, with a rack in the center. Line a baking sheet with parchment paper.

In a large bowl, combine the flour, cornmeal, sugar, baking powder, baking soda, and salt.

Cut the butter into small pieces. Add them to the flour mixture. Working quickly, use your fingertips to rub the butter into the flour mixture until it resembles coarse crumbs.

Add the currants and orange rind. With a rubber spatula, toss them in the cornmeal mixture to distribute them evenly.

Make a well in the center of the mixture. Add the buttermilk and stir with the spatula until all the buttermilk is absorbed. The mixture will look dry.

Turn the dough out onto a clean work surface. Knead the dough several times until it forms a rough ball. Shape the dough into an 8-inch round that is 1¹/₂ inches thick. With a chef's knife, cut the round in half. Then cut each half into 5 even-sized triangles.

Set the scones on the parchment paper, allowing 1 inch between each one. Bake in the center of the oven for 30 minutes, or until the scones are lightly browned. Transfer them to a wire rack to cool slightly. Serve warm or at room temperature.

To Freeze Unbaked Scones and Pastries

Many scones and cookies freeze just as well unbaked as they do baked. To make the dough in advance and freeze it, mix and cut the scones, but do not bake them. Spread them on a baking sheet lined with parchment paper (below) and freeze them, uncovered, until they are frozen solid. When they're hard, transfer the frozen scones to a zipper freezer bag.

To bake frozen scones, do not defrost. Bake as directed, but allow 5 minutes more baking time.

blueberry muffins

Fresh blueberries practically melt inside a batter, so when you open a warm muffin, you see giant dots of berries and little sunbursts of blue around each one, where the berry juices mixed with the buttery crumb. Warm blueberry muffins are one of America's great confections. These, with their sugary tops, are high and domed.

12 tablespoons (1¹/₂ sticks) unsalted butter, at room
       temperature
1¹/₄ cups sugar, plus more for sprinkling
   3 large eggs
 ¹/₂ cup whole milk
2¹/₂ cups all-purpose flour
1¹/₂ teaspoons baking powder
 ¹/₂ teaspoon salt
1¹/₂ pints (3 cups) fresh or frozen (not thawed) blueberries,
       picked over

Set the oven at 400 degrees, with a rack in the center. Line a standard 12-cup muffin tray with paper cups.

Beat the butter with the sugar in a large bowl with an electric mixer until light-colored. Add the eggs, one at a time, and beat for 30 seconds after each addition.

Beat in the milk. With the mixer set on its lowest speed, beat in the flour, baking powder, and salt. Use a rubber spatula to fold in the berries.

Divide the batter among the paper liners and sprinkle with sugar.

Bake in the center of the oven for 35 minutes, or until the muffins are firm and golden brown. Let them settle in the pan for a few minutes. Ease the muffins out of the pan. Set them on a rack to cool slightly. Serve.

irish soda bread

Soda breads are offered in all Irish bakeries in Boston, and the business is brisk. The breads take hardly any time to put together, and the result is a light and flavorful loaf. Like most soda breads, this one contains buttermilk and baking soda, with a handful of golden raisins. Serve with butter and jam.

- 4 **cups all-purpose flour, plus more for sprinkling**
- 1/3 **cup sugar**
- 1 **teaspoon baking soda**
- 1 **teaspoon salt**
- 1 1/3 **cups buttermilk**
- 2 **large eggs, lightly beaten**
- 4 **tablespoons (1/2 stick) butter, melted**
- 2 **cups golden raisins**

Set the oven at 350 degrees, with a rack in the center. Line a baking sheet with parchment paper.

Stir together the flour, sugar, baking soda, and salt in a large bowl. Add the buttermilk, eggs, butter, and raisins and stir well with a wooden spoon just until the batter is moist; it will be sticky.

Turn the dough out onto a lightly floured counter and knead it gently until it is smooth. Divide it in half. Form each piece into a 5-inch round that mounds slightly in the center. With a knife, mark a 3/4-inch-deep "X" on top of each round. Set the dough rounds on the baking sheet.

Bake in the center of the oven for 45 minutes, or until the breads are golden brown and sound hollow when tapped on the bottom. Transfer to a wire rack to cool slightly. Cut them into thick slices and serve.

banana bread

Every accomplished or aspiring baker should have a good banana bread in the reper-toire. This one is so simple that after you make it several times, you'll probably memo-rize the proportions. It's the sort of quick bread that you can whip up if you think someone might be coming over and you want something on hand. For breakfast, make it the night before, and if you're seeing off houseguests, wrap up a few slices for them to take on the road. Julie and her mother have been making this bread for many years.

2	**large eggs**
3/4	**cup sugar**
1/2	**cup canola oil**
1	**teaspoon vanilla extract**
1	**cup mashed bananas (from 2 medium ripe bananas)**
1 1/2	**cups all-purpose flour**
1	**teaspoon baking soda**
1/4	**teaspoon salt**

Set the oven at 350 degrees, with a rack in the center. Grease an 8½-by-4½-by-2½-inch loaf pan. Line the bottom with a piece of parchment paper that fits it exactly. Grease the paper and dust the pan with flour, tapping out the excess.

Beat the eggs, sugar, oil, and vanilla in a large bowl with an electric mixer until they are thoroughly mixed.

Add the bananas and beat well.

In a medium bowl, mix together the flour, baking soda, and salt. With the mixer set on its lowest speed, beat in the flour mixture; traces of flour can remain in the batter. Do not overmix. Use a rubber spatula to finish mixing the bat-ter to eliminate any flour pockets. Pour the batter into the pan and smooth the top.

Bake in the center of the oven for 50 to 55 minutes, or until the top springs back when lightly pressed with a fingertip. Remove from the oven and set the pan on a wire rack to cool slightly.

Turn the bread out onto the rack and set it right side up to cool complete-ly. Cut it into thick slices for serving.

sour cream coffee cake

Firm-textured and nutty, this classic sour cream coffee cake is the best version we've tried. It has just the right balance of batter to streusel. Karen Dobkin, a colleague from the *Boston Globe*, gave the recipe to Sheryl twenty years ago. The sour cream batter is layered in a tube pan with a cinnamon-walnut streusel, which is swirled through the batter very gently. Make this cake the day before you want to serve it, then cover it with waxed paper and a clean kitchen towel.

#{ FOR THE TOPPING

- 4 **ounces walnuts, finely chopped (1 cup)**
- 1/3 **cup light brown sugar**
- 1 **teaspoon ground cinnamon**

Combine the nuts, sugar, and cinnamon in a small bowl. Set aside while you make the cake batter.

#{ FOR THE CAKE

- 1 **cup (2 sticks) unsalted butter, at room temperature**
- 1 1/2 **cups sugar**
- 4 **large eggs**
- 2 **teaspoons vanilla extract**
- 3 **cups all-purpose flour**
- 2 **teaspoons baking powder**
- 1 **teaspoon baking soda**
- 1/2 **teaspoon salt**
- 1 **pint sour cream**

Set the oven at 350 degrees, with a rack in the center. Grease a 10-inch tube pan. Line the bottom with parchment paper cut to fit it exactly. Grease the paper, then dust the pan with flour, tapping out the excess.

Cream the butter in a large bowl with an electric mixer until it is soft and light. Beat in the sugar gradually until the mixture is smooth. Add the eggs, one at a time, beating well after each addition. Beat in the vanilla.

In a medium bowl, combine the flour, baking powder, baking soda, and salt. With the mixer set on its lowest speed, beat the flour into the batter in three portions, alternating with the sour cream, beginning and ending with the flour and scraping down the sides of the bowl when necessary.

Spoon half of the batter into the pan. Sprinkle half of the walnut topping over the batter. Spoon the remaining batter into the pan and sprinkle on the remaining topping.

Use a long metal spatula or blunt table knife to cut through the batter several times, but do not touch the sides or bottom of the pan.

Bake in the center of the oven for 60 to 65 minutes, or until a skewer inserted into the cake comes out clean.

Let the cake cool in the pan on a wire rack for 30 minutes, then turn it out and set it right side up on the rack to cool completely. Cut into thick slices for serving.

blueberry loaf cake

There are plenty of blueberries in this cake, which is neither too rich nor too sweet. It has a lovely sugary crust. Let it cool before serving so the texture firms up. You can use frozen blueberries without defrosting them. If you freeze the loaf after baking, defrost it open on a platter so air can circulate around it.

8 tablespoons (1 stick) unsalted butter, melted and cooled to lukewarm

1 cup sugar, plus more for sprinkling

2 large eggs

2 cups all-purpose flour

1 teaspoon baking powder

$1/4$ teaspoon salt

$1/2$ cup whole milk

2 cups fresh or frozen (not thawed) blueberries, picked over and left to dry on paper towels

Set the oven at 350 degrees, with a rack in the center. Grease an $8^{1}/_{2}$-by-$4^{1}/_{2}$-by-$2^{1}/_{2}$-inch loaf pan. Line the bottom with a piece of parchment paper cut to fit it exactly. Grease the paper and dust the pan with flour, tapping out the excess.

Beat the butter and sugar in a large bowl with an electric mixer until fluffy. Add the eggs, one at a time, beating well after each addition.

In a medium bowl, combine the flour, baking powder, and salt.

With the mixer set on its lowest speed, add the flour mixture to the batter alternately with the milk, beginning and ending with the flour. Do not over-beat — it's OK if there are traces of flour in the batter.

Use a rubber spatula to fold the blueberries into the batter as gently as possible. Spoon the batter into the pan, smoothing the top. Sprinkle the top with sugar.

Bake in the center of the oven for 1 to $1^{1}/_{4}$ hours, or until a skewer inserted into the middle of the cake comes out clean.

Set the pan on a wire rack to cool slightly, then turn the cake out of the pan and set it right side up on a rack to cool completely.

Let the cake sit for 2 hours before cutting into slices. (The cake can be made up to 3 months in advance and frozen, well wrapped.)

prune plum kuchen

Prune plums, which are firmer and less juicy than regular plums, are ideal for baking. You can set them on a cake, cut sides up, and sprinkle them with brown sugar and cinnamon to form a pretty pattern. When the batter is just the right consistency, the plums settle into the cake and make it deliciously moist, almost like a pudding.

4 tablespoons (1/2 stick) unsalted butter, at room temperature
3/4 cup sugar
2 large eggs
1/2 cup canola oil
Grated rind of 1 lemon
Juice of 1/2 lemon
1 teaspoon vanilla extract
11/2 cups all-purpose flour
11/2 teaspoons baking powder
1/2 teaspoon salt
1 pint (1 pound) prune plums, quartered and pitted
3 tablespoons dark brown sugar
1 tablespoon ground cinnamon

Set the oven at 350 degrees, with a rack in the center. Butter an 8-inch square cake pan, dust it with flour, and tap out the excess.

Beat the butter and sugar in a large bowl with an electric mixer until the batter is light-colored. Add the eggs, one at a time, and beat for 30 seconds after each addition. Beat in the oil, lemon rind and juice, and vanilla.

With the mixer set on its lowest speed, beat in the flour, baking powder, and salt. Pour the batter into the pan.

Arrange the plums in rows on top, cut sides up, placing them on the batter as close together as possible.

In a small bowl, combine the brown sugar and cinnamon. Sprinkle the mixture on the plums.

Bake in the center of the oven for 40 to 45 minutes, or until the sides of the cake are firm and golden brown. Set the pan on a wire rack to cool. Serve warm, cut into squares.

if you love to bake

It's been said that the world is divided into bakers and cooks. If that's the case, then we're anomalies, enjoying cooking and baking equally.

Perhaps the explanation for why we love to bake lies in the kind of confections we do — or, rather, don't do: we don't make difficult pastries, multilayered cakes, little tartlets, or fussy petits fours. We do bake old-fashioned cakes, cookie-jar cookies (the sort you see at school bake sales), and pies — the kind that were once on diner menus.

We've been collecting these desserts for a long time from good bakers we've known our whole lives and from some we've met recently. We hardly fiddle with anyone's formula, except perhaps to streamline a method so it will work every single time. Our pies have crisp, rich crusts and plenty of fruit; our pound cakes have a fine crumb and bake high in the pan; our cakes are moist and slice beautifully; our cookies are packed with flavor and good ingredients.

Both of our mothers are good bakers, and all these recipes have been in our family — or someone else's family — for many years. Julie's Mother's Apple Cake is made by almost everyone we know. Our readers fell hard for a crisp, chewy ginger cookie that won a *Boston Globe* cookie contest, and we keep getting rave notices about a sumptuous chocolate bread pudding and chip-filled Congo Bars for the lunch box.

If you want to make génoise or another fancy cake, you won't find that here. But you may find a cake just like one you ate as a child, or one your grandmother made. We didn't choose these recipes for nostalgia's sake. It just happens that no one has improved upon these old-fashioned desserts, and we're not about to try. If you're spending time in the kitchen baking, we think you should smile when you see the results.

if you love to bake

strawberry shortcakes

We make strawberry shortcakes with Buttery Pound Cake (page 322) and with the cake that goes into Boston Cream Pie (page 330), and with Lemon-Yogurt Picnic Cake (page 329). But biscuits with a sugary coating make the best bases. When you split the biscuits and spoon the juicy berries and cream on top, the fruit sinks into the crumb, which is just what you want. These biscuits come from the former Cafe Luna in Chestnut Hill, Massachusetts. We also use them to make little sandwiches (see Rosemary Biscuits with Smoked Turkey and Cranberry Relish on page 16). They take no time to mix in a food processor.

❋⟩ FOR THE SHORTCAKES

3½ cups all-purpose flour, plus more for rolling
1 tablespoon baking powder
1½ teaspoons salt
12 tablespoons (1½ sticks) unsalted butter, cut into pieces
3 tablespoons sugar, plus more for sprinkling
1¼ cups whole milk

Set the oven at 425 degrees, with a rack in the center. Line a baking sheet with parchment paper.

Put the flour, baking powder, and salt in a food processor, and pulse once just to combine.

Add the butter and pulse until the mixture resembles coarse crumbs. Add the sugar and pulse once. Remove the processor lid and sprinkle the milk over the flour. Pulse just until the mixture forms large clumps; do not let it come together to form a dough.

Dust a counter with flour. Turn the clumps out onto the counter and cut through them half a dozen times with a pastry scraper or a blunt table knife until they come together to form a dough. Gently, with your hands, shape the dough into a ball, then flatten the ball to make a cake.

With a floured rolling pin, roll the dough to a ¾-inch thickness. Use a 3½-inch cutter to stamp out 5 rounds, setting the cutter down each time as close to the previous cut as possible.

Collect the scraps, re-roll the dough, and stamp out 3 more rounds. You can collect the scraps again and stamp out 1 more round (this is for the cook). Set them on the baking sheet.

Sprinkle the shortcakes with sugar. Bake in the center of the oven for 18 minutes, or until they are lightly browned.

Transfer them to wire racks to cool while you prepare the filling.

❊〉 FOR THE FILLING

2 quarts fresh strawberries, hulled

1/4 cup sugar

1 cup heavy cream, softly whipped with 2 tablespoons confectioners' sugar

Halve the strawberries, and if they're large, cut the halves in half again.

In a medium bowl, layer the berries with the sugar. Cover loosely with plastic wrap and set aside at room temperature for 20 minutes to 1 hour.

Holding a serrated knife parallel to the counter, split the shortcakes in half. Spoon berries onto the bottoms of the cakes, add whipped cream, and set the tops on at a slant. Serve at once.

lemon pudding cake

This kind of cake, in which a sauce forms in the bottom of the baking dish so each serving is part cake and part pudding, has been around since the 1940s. Pudding cakes are probably the result of a baking mistake, but the dessert is charming. Judy Mattera, a pastry chef from Swampscott, Massachusetts, who has worked in some of Boston's finest kitchens, makes this simple lemon-flavored pudding cake for her family. Use a baking dish nice enough to go to the table. We make it in a French soufflé dish.

4 tablespoons ($1/2$ stick) unsalted butter, at room temperature
$3/4$ cup plus 2 tablespoons sugar
4 large eggs, separated
$1/4$ cup all-purpose flour
$3/4$ cup milk
    Grated rind of 1 lemon
    Juice of $2^{1}/2$ lemons (enough to make $1/2$ cup juice)
    Pinch of salt

    Confectioners' sugar, for sprinkling

Set the oven at 325 degrees, with a rack in the center. Butter a $1^{1}/2$-quart baking dish and set it in a deep roasting pan.

Cream the butter and $3/4$ cup of the sugar in a large bowl with an electric mixer. Add the egg yolks, one at a time, beating well after each addition.

With the mixer set on its lowest speed, blend in the flour, milk, lemon rind and juice.

In another bowl with clean beaters, beat the egg whites with the salt and the remaining 2 tablespoons sugar until the whites form soft peaks. Stir one fourth of the whites into the lemon batter. Fold in the remaining whites as lightly as possible.

Spoon the batter into the dish. Carefully pour hot tap water around the dish to come halfway up the sides. Bake the pudding in the center of the oven for 45 minutes, or until the top is set.

Let cool for 20 minutes. Lift the dish from the water and wipe the bottom with a cloth. Sprinkle with confectioners' sugar. Spoon the cake onto plates, giving each person some of the firm edge and some of the saucy bottom.

note: To reheat, set the dish in a roasting pan or large skillet. There should be 1 inch of space all around the dish. Carefully pour boiling water into the pan to come halfway up the sides of the dish. Let the pudding sit for 10 minutes. Remove from the pan and serve.

blueberry gingerbread for a crowd

This large gingerbread is a very moist, oil-based cake with buttermilk and spices. It completely fills the pan and is best baked at a low temperature for a long time. Cut it into large squares and serve it warm with whipped cream.

5	cups all-purpose flour
1	teaspoon baking soda
1	teaspoon baking powder
1	teaspoon salt
1	tablespoon ground cinnamon
1	tablespoon ground ginger
1/2	teaspoon ground nutmeg
1/4	teaspoon ground cloves
1	cup canola oil
2	cups sugar, plus more for sprinkling
4	large eggs
1/2	cup molasses
2	cups buttermilk
2	cups fresh blueberries or 1 package (10–12 ounces) frozen (not thawed) blueberries
1 1/2	cups heavy cream, softly whipped with 3 tablespoons confectioners' sugar

Set the oven at 325 degrees, with a rack in the center. Grease a 9-by-13-inch baking dish. Dust the pan with flour, tapping out the excess.

Sift together the flour, baking soda, baking powder, salt, cinnamon, ginger, nutmeg, and cloves in a medium bowl.

Beat the oil and sugar in a large bowl with an electric mixer until thoroughly mixed. Add the eggs, one at a time, beating after each addition. Beat in the molasses. With the mixer set on its lowest speed, beat in the buttermilk alternately with the flour and spice mixture in three additions, beginning and ending with the dry ingredients. Fold in the blueberries with a rubber spatula.

Pour the batter into the pan and sprinkle extra sugar on top.

Bake in the center of the oven for 1 hour and 30 minutes, or until the cake is firm on top and pulls away from the edges of the pan. It may look done earlier, but the center won't be cooked through.

Let the cake cool on a rack until it is still warm. Cut into 12 large squares and use a large metal spatula to remove the squares from the pan. Serve warm with softly whipped cream.

pumpkin bread with raisins and walnuts

Oil-based quick breads are moist but not rich. When you add grated or pureed fruits or vegetables to the batter — zucchini, carrots, applesauce, or pumpkin, in this case — you're guaranteed a beautiful texture. These are studded with golden raisins and walnuts. After baking, let the breads sit overnight to mellow. The recipe comes from Dolly Gerry, who, with her husband, Joseph, owns a vegetable farm in Brockton, Massachusetts.

4	large eggs
2	cups sugar
3/4	cup canola oil
3/4	cup orange juice
1	can (15 ounces) pumpkin puree
3	cups all-purpose flour
1 1/2	teaspoons baking soda
1/2	teaspoon baking powder
1	teaspoon salt
1	tablespoon ground cinnamon
3/4	teaspoon ground nutmeg
1/2	teaspoon ground allspice
2	cups walnut halves, toasted (see page 149)
3/4	cup golden raisins

Set the oven at 350 degrees, with a rack in the center. Grease two 8½-by-4½-by-2½-inch loaf pans. Line the bottoms with a piece of parchment paper cut to fit them exactly. Grease the papers and dust the pans with flour, tapping out the excess.

Beat the eggs and sugar in a large bowl with an electric mixer for 1 minute. Add the oil, orange juice, and pumpkin and beat just to mix.

Sift the flour, baking soda, baking powder, salt, cinnamon, nutmeg, and allspice into a medium bowl. With the mixer set on its lowest speed, add the dry ingredients to the egg mixture and mix just until it forms a smooth batter.

With a rubber spatula, stir the nuts and raisins into the batter. Pour the batter into the pans.

Bake in the center of the oven for 1 hour and 10 minutes to 1 hour and

15 minutes, or until a skewer inserted into the bread comes out clean. If the breads are browning too much on top, cover them with a piece of foil, shiny side down.

Set the pans on a rack to cool slightly, then turn the breads out of the pans and set them right side up to cool completely. Cover the breads with wax paper and a clean towel and let stand overnight to mellow before cutting into thick slices for serving.

buttery pound cake

Julie's neighbor Susan Welch gave her this cake several years ago, and both of us — and many people who found it in our column — make it all the time. The cake contains very little baking powder, which is one of its appealing points, because there's no chemical aftertaste. In that sense, it closely resembles the old-fashioned pound cakes, which rose because the cook beat air into the butter and sugar. The texture, too, is just right. Use fresh nutmeg, if you can. Scrape a small, sharp knife across the nutmeg and let the shavings fall right into the batter. The baking technique is an old method in which you place the cake in a cold oven, then turn the oven on so the batter warms very slowly. This method makes the crust quite tender. Bake it a few hours ahead so it can cool completely.

3   **cups all-purpose flour**

1/2   **teaspoon baking powder**

    Pinch of salt

1 1/2   **cups (3 sticks) unsalted butter, at room temperature**

2   **cups sugar**

5   **large eggs**

1   **teaspoon vanilla extract**

1/2   **teaspoon freshly ground nutmeg**

1   **cup whole milk**

Butter a 10-inch Bundt pan thoroughly. Dust it with flour. Turn the pan upside down on the counter and rap it hard once to remove the excess flour. If you see any spots that are not buttered, butter and flour them again.

    Sift the flour, baking powder, and salt into a medium bowl; set aside.

    Cream the butter and sugar in a large bowl with an electric mixer for 2 minutes, scraping down the sides of the bowl, until light and fluffy.

    Add the eggs, one at a time, beating well after each addition. With the mixer set on its lowest speed, beat in the vanilla and nutmeg. Pour in the milk slowly, beating, then beat in 1 cup of the flour mixture. Add in the remaining flour, beating only until smooth.

    Pour the batter into the pan and

transfer it to a cold oven, on the center rack. Turn the heat to 350 degrees and bake for 1 hour, or until a skewer inserted into the middle of the cake comes out clean.

Set the pan on a wire rack to cool for 20 minutes. Invert the wire rack onto the cake pan, and turn the cake upside down onto the rack. Lift off the pan, turn the cake right side up, and

cool the cake completely before cutting it into thick slices.

note: To store, wrap in several layers of foil, seal the edges, and keep the cake at room temperature for up to 5 days or freeze for 1 month.

julie's mother's apple cake

For the past thirty years or so, this apple cake has circulated around all the communities where apples are grown. We sometimes call it a "community cake" because we know so many people who make a version. It's a sturdy oil-based, orange-flavored batter, layered with sliced apples and cinnamon-sugar. The cake improves if allowed to sit before serving.

3 **cups all-purpose flour**

1½ **cups sugar**

1 **tablespoon baking powder**

½ **teaspoon salt**

1 **cup canola oil**

4 **large eggs**

¼ **cup orange juice**

1 **tablespoon vanilla extract**

4 **baking apples, peeled, quartered, cored, and thinly sliced (see page 340)**

1 **tablespoon ground cinnamon mixed with 5 tablespoons sugar**

Confectioners' sugar, for sprinkling

Set the oven at 350 degrees, with a rack in the center. Grease a 10-inch tube pan. Line the bottom with a piece of parchment paper cut to fit it exactly. Grease the paper and dust the pan with flour, tapping out the excess.

Sift together the flour, sugar, baking powder, and salt in a large bowl. Add the oil, eggs, orange juice, and vanilla, and beat with an electric mixer just until smooth, scraping down the sides of the bowl.

Spoon one third of the batter into the pan. Smooth the top of the batter with a long metal spatula. Gently press half of the apples into the batter, taking care that the apples do not touch the sides of the pan. It's OK to overlap them. Sprinkle them with half of the cinnamon-sugar.

Spoon another third of the batter into the pan, followed by the remaining apples, and the remaining cinnamon-sugar. End with the batter.

Smooth the top with the spatula. It may not cover the apples completely, but that's OK.

Bake it in the center of the oven for 1 hour to 1 hour and 10 minutes, or until a skewer inserted into the middle of the cake comes out clean. (If the skewer feels sticky, it may have gone into some apples, but it should not be covered with batter.)

Remove the cake from the oven and cool on a wire rack for 30 minutes. With a knife, cut around the inside and outside edges of the cake to release it from the pan. Turn the cake out onto the cooling rack and then set it right side up. Let the cake cool completely.

Sprinkle with confectioners' sugar before serving.

carrot cake with cream cheese frosting

Baked in a rectangular pan, then halved and frosted, this cake looks high and grand. It's perfect for a birthday party. It's particularly moist because of a cup of crushed pineapple, which disappears into the batter so you can't distinguish the taste. Make the cake in advance, then frost it and let it sit overnight, which helps during the crunch time of a party.

FOR THE CAKE

- 2 3/4 cups all-purpose flour
- 2 tablespoons ground cinnamon
- 1 teaspoon baking powder
- 1 teaspoon baking soda
- 1/2 teaspoon salt
- 1 cup canola oil
- 1 1/2 cups sugar
- 4 large eggs
- 1 teaspoon vanilla extract
- 2 cups grated carrots (from 4–5 large carrots)
- 1 cup canned crushed pineapple, drained
- 2 cups walnut pieces

Set the oven at 350 degrees, with a rack in the center. Grease a 9-by-13-inch pan and dust the pan with flour, tapping out the excess.

Sift together the flour, cinnamon, baking powder, baking soda, and salt in a medium bowl; set aside.

Beat the oil and sugar in a large bowl with an electric mixer for 1 minute. Add the eggs, one at a time, beating well after each addition and scraping down the sides of the bowl when necessary. Beat in the vanilla. Add the carrots and

pineapple to the batter and beat just until combined. With the mixer set on low speed, add the flour mixture to the batter and mix just until the dry ingredients are moistened.

With a rubber spatula, fold in the walnuts. Pour the batter into the prepared pan.

Bake in the center of the oven for 45 to 50 minutes, or until a skewer inserted into the middle of the cake comes out clean.

Set the pan on a wire rack to cool for 30 minutes. With a knife, cut around the edges of the cake to release it from the pan. Turn the cake out onto a rack, turn it right side up, and let it cool completely while you make the frosting.

*} FOR THE FROSTING

8 **ounces cream cheese, at room temperature**
3 **tablespoons unsalted butter, at room temperature**
3 **tablespoons orange juice**
3 **cups confectioners' sugar**

Beat the cream cheese and butter in a large bowl with an electric mixer on medium speed until smooth, scraping down the sides of the bowl when necessary. Beat in the orange juice and confectioners' sugar just until thoroughly combined.

*} TO FROST THE CAKE

Cut the cake in half to make two smaller rectangles 4½ by 6½ inches. Set one piece, right side up, on a cutting board. Set the other piece, right side up, on top of the first. Trim the hard edges of the cake (these are treats for the baker).

Remove the top piece of cake. Set it right side up on a cake stand or large rectangular platter.

Use a long metal spatula to spread the cream cheese frosting on the top and sides of the cake. Set the other piece, right side up, on top of the first. Frost the two pieces together and serve.

note: You can let the cake sit for several hours in a cool place before serving or it can sit overnight in a cool place without harm.

chocolate sour cream cake

The trick to a fudgy cake is to bake it just until the top is firm to the touch, but not hard. It will still be moist inside if tested with a cake tester. As the cake cools, the chocolate hardens again. This batter is enriched with sour cream and flavored with light brown sugar.

      4 ounces unsweetened chocolate, chopped
 1¼ cups water
  ¾ cup (1½ sticks) unsalted butter, at room temperature
      2 cups packed light brown sugar
      1 cup sugar
      3 large eggs
      1 tablespoon vanilla extract
      1 cup sour cream
 1½ teaspoons baking soda
  ½ teaspoon salt
 3¼ cups all-purpose flour

Set the oven at 350 degrees, with a rack in the center. Butter a 10-inch Bundt pan thoroughly. Dust it with flour. Turn the pan upside down on the counter and rap it hard once to remove the excess flour.

In a medium saucepan, melt the chocolate in the water until the mixture is smooth. Remove from the heat and let sit until cool but still liquid.

Cream the butter in a large bowl with an electric mixer until it is soft and light. Add the sugars and beat until fluffy. Add the eggs, one at a time, beating well after each addition. Beat in the vanilla, then the chocolate.

In a small bowl, combine the sour cream, baking soda, and salt. The mixture will begin to froth and bubble; work quickly.

With the mixer set on its lowest speed, add the flour to the batter alternately with the sour cream mixture, beginning and ending with the flour. Pour the batter into the pan.

Bake for 55 minutes in the center of the oven, or until the cake springs back when pressed gently with a fingertip and pulls away from the sides. The cake will still be moist inside.

Remove from the oven and set the cake on a wire rack for 30 minutes. Turn it out of the pan onto the rack, set it right side up, and cool completely before serving.

lemon-yogurt picnic cake

The grated rind of three lemons gives this cake a great citrus taste. Grate the lemons first, then squeeze them, because you need the juice as well. This makes a big cake with an even top that cuts up nicely into large squares. Boston cooking teacher and baker Suzanne Lombardi likes to make it the day before she takes it to a picnic. Serve it with a bowl of fresh strawberries.

    4 cups all-purpose flour
    2 teaspoons baking powder
    1 teaspoon baking soda
    1 teaspoon salt
1^1/$_2$ cups (3 sticks) unsalted butter, at room temperature
2^1/$_2$ cups sugar
    6 large eggs
    1 teaspoon vanilla extract
  ^{1}/$_2$ cup whole milk
    1 cup whole-milk plain yogurt
       Grated rind of 3 lemons
  ^{1}/$_4$ cup fresh lemon juice

Set the oven at 325 degrees, with a rack in the center. Butter a 9-by-13-inch baking pan and dust it with flour.

Sift the flour, baking powder, baking soda, and salt into a medium bowl. Beat the butter in a large bowl with an electric mixer until creamy and light-colored. Add the sugar and beat for 5 minutes, scraping down the sides of the bowl several times, until fluffy and almost white.

With the mixer set on its lowest speed, add the eggs, one at a time, beating well after each addition. Beat in the vanilla. Beat in half of the flour mixture, then the milk, yogurt, lemon rind and juice. (The batter may look curdled.) Add the rest of the flour mixture and beat just until incorporated. Scrape up the batter from the bottom a few times with a rubber spatula to make sure it is well mixed. Pour the batter into the pan.

Bake in the center of the oven for 1 hour and 15 minutes to 1 hour and 20 minutes, turning it around once halfway through baking, or until a skewer inserted into the middle of the cake comes out clean.

Set the cake on a wire rack to cool completely. Cover it with foil and let it sit at least half a day or overnight before cutting it into squares.

boston cream pie

There are all kinds of theories about why this one-hundred-year-old cake is called a pie. Among those we think plausible is that the cake was originally made in a pie pan (we use a springform pan). The dessert consists of a simple white cake that is split, layered with a rich egg custard, and then frosted with dark chocolate. Make the cake and pastry cream a day ahead, then assemble the cake and frost it up to half a day before serving. This is as much fussing as we'll do over any dessert, but it's everyone's favorite.

FOR THE CAKE

- 2 **cups all-purpose flour**
- 1 **teaspoon baking powder**
   Pinch of salt
- 14 **tablespoons (1¹/₂ sticks plus 2 tablespoons) unsalted butter, at room temperature**
- ³/₄ **cup sugar**
- 4 **large eggs, lightly beaten**
- 1 **teaspoon vanilla extract**
- ¹/₂ **cup whole milk**

Set the oven at 350 degrees, with a rack in the center. Butter a 9-inch springform pan. Dust the pan with flour, tapping out the excess.

Sift the flour, baking powder, and salt into a medium bowl.

Cream the butter in a large bowl with an electric mixer until it is light and fluffy. Beat in the sugar gradually. Add the eggs, one at a time, beating well after each addition. Beat in the vanilla.

With the mixer set on its lowest speed, beat in the flour mixture in three additions, alternating with the milk, beginning and ending with flour. Pour the batter into the pan and spread it evenly, making the edges slightly higher than the middle.

Bake in the center of the oven for 50 minutes, or until the top of the cake springs back when pressed with a fingertip. Cool the cake in the pan for 20 minutes, then turn it out onto a wire rack. Set it right side up to cool completely.

note: You can prepare the cake a day ahead, wrap it in foil, and store it at room temperature, if you like.

Meanwhile, prepare the pastry cream.

❊{ FOR THE PASTRY CREAM

4   **large egg yolks**
¹/₃ **cup sugar**
3¹/₂ **tablespoons cornstarch**
1¹/₂ **cups whole milk**
2   **teaspoons vanilla extract**

Whisk the yolks, sugar, cornstarch, and ¼ cup of the milk in a medium bowl.

In a heavy-bottomed saucepan, scald the remaining 1¼ cups milk. Whisk the hot milk into the yolk mixture a little at a time, then return the yolk mixture to the saucepan.

Cook the pastry cream over medium heat, stirring constantly, until it comes to a boil. Reduce the heat to low and simmer the cream for 1 minute, still whisking.

Remove the pastry cream from the heat and whisk in the vanilla. Transfer the mixture to a mixing bowl, and press a piece of plastic wrap directly onto the surface of the cream. Cool to room temperature. (You can refrigerate the pastry cream overnight at this point, if you like.)

❊{ TO ASSEMBLE

Set the cake on the counter. Holding a serrated knife parallel to the counter, cut the cake horizontally into thirds. Set the bottom layer on a platter.

Spread one half of the pastry cream on the bottom layer. Set another round of cake on top. Cover it with the remaining pastry cream, then set the top of the cake in place. Set aside while you prepare the frosting.

❊{ FOR THE CHOCOLATE FROSTING

1   **cup heavy cream**
6   **ounces semisweet chocolate, chopped**
4   **tablespoons (¹/₂ stick) unsalted butter, cut into pieces**

Combine the cream and chocolate in a heavy-bottomed saucepan over medium heat, stirring, until the chocolate melts and the cream is quite hot. Stir the mixture with a whisk — the chocolate may separate from the cream and turn into a mass at the bottom, but the mixture will eventually come together.

Remove from the heat and whisk in the butter a little at a time, letting each piece melt before adding another. Transfer the chocolate mixture to a deep bowl and set it inside a roasting pan filled with ice. Whisk the mixture gently until it starts to thicken. It can stiffen all of a sudden over the ice, so don't let it sit on the ice unattended.

When the chocolate is spreadable, remove the bowl from the ice, wipe the bottom, and use a long metal spatula to frost the top and sides of the cake. Let the cake sit for at least 1 hour and for up to half a day to mellow. Cut into wedges and serve.

pear clafouti

Made with what is essentially a pancake batter, clafoutis are not terribly sweet and can include all kinds of fruits. This one uses ripe pears. It's a good fall and winter dessert.

4	large eggs
1	cup whole milk
1	cup heavy cream
1	teaspoon vanilla extract
$1^1/4$	cups all-purpose flour
1	cup sugar
$^1/4$	teaspoon baking powder
$^1/2$	teaspoon salt
6	ripe Anjou or Bosc pears, peeled, halved, cored, and thinly sliced

Confectioners' sugar, for sprinkling

Set the oven at 350 degrees, with a rack in the center. Butter a deep 9-by-13-inch baking dish or another dish with a $3^1/2$-quart capacity.

Beat the eggs in a large bowl with an electric mixer for 1 minute. Add the milk, cream, and vanilla, and continue beating for 1 minute more.

In a medium bowl, stir together the flour, sugar, baking powder, and salt. Gradually add the flour mixture to the liquid, beating just until they are thoroughly incorporated.

Arrange the pears in the bottom of the baking dish. Pour the batter on top. Bake the clafouti in the center of the oven for 1 hour to 1 hour and 5 minutes, or until it is puffed, the edges are browned, and the mixture is just set in the middle.

Sprinkle with confectioners' sugar and serve warm.

perdix's chocolate bread pudding

Dark and luscious, this pudding is made with challah bread, bittersweet chocolate, and lots of cream, an ideal dessert for a special occasion. Bread puddings sit overnight before baking until the custard — in this case, a rich chocolate custard — is completely absorbed by the bread. The next day, when the pudding is baked, you can't really tell it's bread anymore. Perdix, a restaurant in Jamaica Plain, one of Boston's neighborhoods, gave us this sought-after recipe.

1	**loaf (1 pound) challah or other egg bread, thickly sliced**
1/2	**cup dried cherries or cranberries**
7	**ounces bittersweet or semisweet chocolate, chopped**
2	**cups heavy cream**
1	**cup half-and-half**
5	**tablespoons unsalted butter, cut into pieces**
3/4	**cup sugar**
1/2	**teaspoon salt**
4	**large eggs**
1	**teaspoon vanilla extract**
1/8	**teaspoon ground cinnamon, mixed with 1 tablespoon sugar**

Butter an 11-by-7-inch baking dish or use another dish with a 2½-quart capacity. Set it aside.

Remove the crusts from the bread. Cut the slices into quarters. Line the bottom of the dish with the bread, add a layer of cherries or cranberries, and continue layering, ending with the bread.

In the top of a double boiler over hot, but not boiling, water (or in a saucepan set into a deep skillet of hot water), combine the chocolate, cream, half-and-half, butter, sugar, and salt. Cook, stirring with a wooden spoon, just until the chocolate and butter melt.

Remove from the water, wipe the bottom of the pan, and set aside until it is warm but not hot.

Beat the eggs and vanilla in a large bowl with an electric mixer for 1 minute. With the mixer on low speed, slowly beat in the chocolate mixture so it warms the eggs (be sure the chocolate is

not too hot, or the mixture will curdle).
Slowly pour the chocolate mixture over
the bread, pressing the custard into
the bread with your hand or a rubber
spatula.

Sprinkle the pudding with the
cinnamon sugar. Cover the dish with
plastic wrap and refrigerate for 8 hours
or overnight. Remove the pudding from
the refrigerator 1 hour before baking.
Lift off the plastic wrap.

Set the oven at 350 degrees,
with a rack in the center.

Bake the pudding in the center
of the oven for 40 minutes, or until the
top is crusty and the custard doesn't
wiggle when you shake the pan. Don't
overcook the pudding; it should be
moist.

Spoon the pudding onto plates
and serve.

free-form apple tart

The easiest tart is simply a round of dough with sliced apples on top. If the pastry is flaky and the apples hold their shape during cooking, you get moist fruit and crisp mouthfuls of buttery tart. This pastry is made in a food processor with an egg beaten into the dough, so it rolls nicely. Susan Jasse, who owns an apple orchard in Walpole, New Hampshire, with her husband, Bob, makes this tart several times a week. You can omit both the Chinese five-spice powder and the warmed cider jelly, if you like, or make individual tarts (this amount makes 6). Serve with sweetened whipped cream or ice cream.

FOR THE PASTRY

- 2 **cups all-purpose flour, plus more for rolling**
- 1/2 **teaspoon salt**
- 8 **tablespoons (1 stick) unsalted butter, cut into pieces**
- 1 **large egg, lightly beaten with 1/4 cup ice water**

Line a rimless baking sheet with parchment paper.

Combine the flour and salt in a food processor, pulsing once. Add the butter and pulse again until the mixture resembles coarse crumbs.

Sprinkle the egg mixture on top of the flour and pulse just until the dough forms large, moist clumps; it should not come together to form a ball.

Turn the clumps out onto a lightly floured counter and knead them to form a dough. Flatten the dough into a round cake, wrap it in foil, and refrigerate it for 20 minutes.

Dust the counter with flour. Roll the pastry into a 12-inch round or rectangle — it's not necessary to make it even. Lift it onto the rolling pin and ease it onto the baking sheet.

Set the oven at 400 degrees, with a rack in the center.

Set the pastry aside while you prepare the apple filling.

FOR THE APPLES

  4–5 **medium baking apples (see page 340)**
    2 **tablespoons unsalted butter**
  1/4 **cup sugar, plus more for sprinkling**
  1/8 **teaspoon Chinese five-spice powder (optional)**

    4 **tablespoons cider jelly, heated until hot**

Peel, halve, and core the apples. Set the apples, flat sides down, on a cutting board and slice them thinly perpendicular to the core. Arrange them overlapping tightly on the pastry, allowing a 2-inch border around the edge.

Dot the apples with the butter. Mix the sugar and five-spice powder, if using. Sprinkle it onto the apples. Fold the edges of the pastry over onto themselves to make a neat border that covers the edge of the apples. Sprinkle the edge of the dough with extra sugar.

Bake in the center of the oven for 50 to 60 minutes, or until the apples are tender and the edges of the pastry are crisp and golden brown.

Brush the apples with the hot cider jelly and let the tart cool slightly. Cut it into large pieces and serve.

granny fanny's apple pie

A great apple pie has a beautiful crust, one that turns golden and flaky in the oven. And the filling should boast handsome slices of apples that taste faintly lemony and are hardly sweetened. Julie's Granny Fanny used this formula every week for decades, making her high, domed pies with Cortland apples, which don't discolor as quickly as other apples. The water content of apples varies greatly, depending upon the variety. Begin with 2 tablespoons flour the first time you use a new apple, and then see if you need more thickening later. Our modern version whirs the pastry in a food processor. The egg and distilled white vinegar make the pastry easy to roll and tender. Serve warm with heavy cream or ice cream.

❧ FOR THE TWO-CRUST PASTRY

- 2 1/2 cups all-purpose flour, plus more for rolling
- 1/2 teaspoon baking powder
- Pinch of salt
- 6 tablespoons (3/4 stick) unsalted butter, cut into pieces
- 6 tablespoons solid vegetable shortening, cut into pieces
- 2 tablespoons sugar
- 1 large egg, lightly beaten
- 1 tablespoon distilled white vinegar
- 3 tablespoons ice water

Combine the flour, baking powder, and salt in a food processor and pulse once. Add the butter and shortening and pulse again until the mixture resembles coarse crumbs. Add the sugar and whir just to mix.

In a small bowl, combine the egg, vinegar, and water. Mix well. Sprinkle the egg mixture on top of the flour and pulse just until the dough forms large, moist clumps. It should not come together to form a ball. If necessary, sprinkle a little water on the dough.

Turn the clumps out onto a lightly floured counter and knead them gently to form a dough. Divide the dough into two pieces, one slightly larger than the other. Flatten the pieces into round cakes, wrap them in foil, and refrigerate for 20 minutes.

Dust the counter with flour. Roll out the larger piece of dough to an 11-inch round. Lift it onto the rolling pin and ease it into a 9-inch pie pan, letting the extra hang over the edges. Use scissors to trim the edges of the pastry so there is an even ½-inch overhang all around the pie. Turn under a hem to make a thick edge. Press it along the rim of the pan.

Set the oven at 400 degrees, with a rack in the center.

Set the pastry aside while you make the filling.

※} FOR THE FILLING

- **8 medium baking apples (see page 340)**
- **3/4 cup sugar, or to taste, plus more for sprinkling**
- **2 tablespoons fresh lemon juice**
- **2 tablespoons all-purpose flour**
- **Pinch of salt**

Whole milk, for brushing

Peel, quarter, and core the apples. Slice them thinly.

In a large bowl, toss the apples with the sugar. Taste them for sweetness and, if they seem tart, add another 1 tablespoon sugar, if you like. Add the lemon juice, flour, and salt and toss well. Transfer the mixture to the lined pie pan, mounding it slightly in the middle.

To roll out the remaining pastry and assemble: On a lightly floured board, roll the remaining piece of dough to a 10-inch round. Lift it onto the rolling pin and ease it onto the apples. Turn the edges under all around the pie so they're even with the bottom crust.

With a fork, make impressions around the edge of the pie to seal the top and bottom crusts together.

Brush the pastry with milk and sprinkle it with sugar. With a paring knife, make six 1-inch slits in the crust to allow steam to escape.

Set the pie on a rimmed baking sheet. Bake in the center of the oven for 15 minutes. Turn the oven temperature down to 350 degrees. Continue baking for 50 minutes, or until the juices begin to bubble through the vents and the apples feel tender when pierced with a skewer through the vent holes. (The baking time will vary with the type of apples used. If at any time the crust is turning brown before the apples are ready, turn the oven down to 325 degrees.)

Remove from the oven and transfer to a rack to cool for 30 minutes. Serve warm.

Choosing Apples for Pies and Tarts

The important characteristic of a pie apple is that it holds its shape. McIntosh, which are crisp and widely available during the fall, are not good for pies, because they turn watery during baking and soak the bottom crust. Granny Smith, a crisp eating apple, is widely available and popular for pies.

We prefer Jonagolds, Cortlands, Rome Beauties, Baldwins, Northern Spys, Fujis, and Galas, if you can find them. Golden Delicious, also suitable for pies, are often available when these varieties are not.

blueberry pie

This blueberry pie is mounded high and is quite runny — but you need some juices from the blueberries to mix with the vanilla ice cream.

Two-Crust Pastry (see page 338)
4 pints fresh blueberries, rinsed and picked over
3/4 cup sugar, or to taste, plus more for sprinkling
1/3 cup all-purpose flour
1 1/2 tablespoons fresh lemon juice
1 tablespoon unsalted butter

Whole milk, for brushing

Set the oven at 375 degrees, with a rack in the center.

Roll out half of the pastry dough and set it into a 9-inch pie pan as directed on page 338.

Mix the blueberries with the sugar in a medium bowl. Taste the berries and, if they are tart, add more sugar, 1 teaspoon at a time, until the berries taste just right. Stir in the flour and lemon juice. Pour the fruit into the pastry-lined pie pan. Dot the top with butter.

Roll out the remaining dough as directed on page 339, cover the pie with the crust, and turn the edges under. Brush the pastry with milk and sprinkle it with sugar. With a paring knife, make six 1-inch slits in the crust to allow steam to escape.

Set the pie on a rimmed baking sheet. Bake in the center of the oven for 40 to 50 minutes, or until the juices from the berries are oozing at the edges and the crust is golden brown.

Remove from the oven and transfer to a cooling rack. Serve it while it is very warm, cut into slices, with vanilla ice cream.

pumpkin chiffon pie

The filling of this pie is a classic chiffon, in which stiffly beaten whites are folded into a pumpkin-spice mixture, which is set lightly with gelatin. The crust is made from gingersnap cookies. It's the sort of heavenly pie that used to be served in diners and at lunch counters. It was given to us by *Boston Globe* graphic designer Susan Levin, who got it from her grandmother Sarah Mazick.

FOR THE CRUST

- 2 cups crushed gingersnaps (about 10 ounces, or 43 cookies)
- 1/3 cup sugar
- Pinch of salt
- 1/4 teaspoon ground ginger
- 6 tablespoons (3/4 stick) unsalted butter, melted

Set the oven at 325 degrees, with a rack in the center. Butter a deep 9-inch pie pan.

Set aside 2 teaspoons gingersnap crumbs for decorating the pie. Combine the remaining gingersnaps, sugar, salt, ginger, and butter in a medium bowl. Press the mixture into the pie pan with the back of a spoon, making the top edge even all around.

Line the crust with a piece of foil, pressing it directly onto the crust. Bake in the center of the oven for 8 to 10 minutes, or until set and lightly browned. Meanwhile, prepare the filling.

FOR THE FILLING

- 1 envelope gelatin
- 1/2 cup packed dark brown sugar
- 1 teaspoon ground cinnamon
- 1/2 teaspoon salt
- 1/2 teaspoon ground nutmeg
- 1/2 teaspoon ground ginger
- 1/2 cup milk
- 3 large eggs, separated
- 1 can (15 ounces) pumpkin puree
- 1/4 cup sugar

- 1 cup heavy cream, softly whipped with 2 tablespoons confectioners' sugar

In a medium heavy-bottomed saucepan, stir together the gelatin, brown sugar, cinnamon, salt, nutmeg, ginger, milk, and egg yolks. Set over medium heat and cook, stirring gently, until the mixture thickens slightly. Do not let it boil or even bubble at the edges.

Remove from the heat and set aside to cool. Stir the pumpkin puree into the gelatin mixture. Refrigerate, stirring occasionally, until it thickens enough to form mounds.

Beat the egg whites and sugar in a medium bowl with an electric mixer until they form stiff peaks. Stir a few spoonfuls of the whites into the pumpkin mixture, then fold in the remaining whites as lightly as possible, making sure no pockets of white show.

Pour the filling into the cooled crust and refrigerate for several hours.

Just before serving, spoon the whipped cream on top, spreading it to form a mound with a peak in the middle. Garnish the top with the reserved crushed gingersnaps and cut into wedges to serve.

ice cream pie

There are some meals that demand an ice cream dessert — particularly on a warm summer night. This is one that you can put together with children. Ordinary chocolate wafers form the crust, vanilla ice cream is packed into it, and a hot fudge sauce goes onto each serving.

1 **package (8 ounces) thin chocolate wafers**
8 **tablespoons (1 stick) unsalted butter, melted**
1 **quart vanilla ice cream**

Bailey's Hot Fudge Sauce (page 345)

Set the oven at 350 degrees, with a rack in the center.

Pulse the chocolate wafers in a food processor until they form crumbs. Transfer them to a medium bowl. Add the melted butter and stir thoroughly. With the back of a metal spoon, press the mixture into a 9-inch pie pan, making the top edge a little thicker than the bottom.

Line the crumb mixture with foil, pressing it against the crust with your hand. Bake in the center of the oven for 10 minutes, or until it is set and lightly browned. Remove from the oven. Leave the foil in place and cool completely on a rack.

Let the ice cream sit at room temperature for 10 minutes, if necessary, so it's soft but not melted. Spread the ice cream in the crust, smooth the top, and freeze the pie for 1 hour, or until the ice cream is solid again.

Cut the pie into wedges and serve with Bailey's Hot Fudge Sauce.

bailey's hot fudge sauce

Chocolate connoisseurs will love this dark, intense fudge sauce. It comes from Bailey's, an old Boston chain of ice cream parlors.

- 4 **ounces unsweetened chocolate**
- 8 **tablespoons (1 stick) unsalted butter**
- 1 **box (1 pound) confectioners' sugar**
- 1 **can (12 ounces) evaporated milk**
- 1¹/₂ **teaspoons vanilla extract**

In a heavy-bottomed saucepan, melt the chocolate and butter over low heat. Remove from the heat. Add ¹/₂ cup of the sugar, then a little of the milk, and continue alternating the sugar and milk until they are all added.

Set the pan over medium heat and cook until small bubbles appear on the sides of the pan, then let the mixture bubble steadily, stirring occasionally, for 8 minutes.

Stir in the vanilla. The sauce may look curdled, but it will become smooth later. Remove from the heat and let cool for 10 minutes, stirring occasionally, until the fudge sauce is no longer burning hot and has thickened slightly.

note: Reheat leftover sauce over low heat, stirring constantly.

creamy dark chocolate tart

There are many wonderful things about this tart. The first is the pastry, which is a dream to roll and makes a thick shortbreadlike crust. The filling, which has been a favorite of ours for years, combines bittersweet chocolate and cream; it's rich but not too sweet. You can heap it with whipped cream or simply cover the top with shaved chocolate. The pastry comes from chef Delphin Gomes of Marblehead, Massachusetts.

❈〉 FOR THE PASTRY

- 10 tablespoons (1 stick plus 2 tablespoons), unsalted butter, cut into pieces
- 1/3 cup sugar
- 1 large egg, plus 1 egg yolk
- 2 cups all-purpose flour, plus more for rolling
- 1/2 teaspoon baking powder
- 1/2 teaspoon salt

Cream the butter in a large bowl with an electric mixer. Slowly beat in the sugar and mix until combined. Beat in the egg and yolk.

Combine the flour, baking powder, and salt in a small bowl. Beat them slowly into the butter and mix just to form large clumps.

Turn the clumps out onto a lightly floured counter and knead them lightly to form a dough. Shape the dough into a flat disk. Wrap the disk in foil and refrigerate for 10 minutes.

Set the oven at 375 degrees, with a rack in the center.

Roll the dough out on a lightly floured board to a 9-inch round. Lift it onto the rolling pin and ease it into a

10-inch tart pan with a removable base. Press it into the bottom and sides with your fingers. With a fork, prick the dough all over. Press a piece of parchment paper into the dough and fill it with dried beans.

Bake in the center of the oven for 15 minutes. Remove the parchment paper and beans, and continue baking for 15 minutes, or until the pastry is golden brown. Meanwhile, prepare the filling.

Remove the tart from the oven and cool on a wire rack. Place the tart on a small bowl and let the rim of the pan fall away. Slide the tart shell onto a large, flat platter.

❊❧ FOR THE FILLING

- 8 tablespoons (1 stick) unsalted butter, cut into pieces
- 11 ounces bittersweet chocolate, chopped
- 1 ounce unsweetened chocolate, chopped
- 2 cups heavy cream
- 1/2 cup sugar
- 1 tablespoon vanilla extract

1/2 cup heavy cream, stiffly whipped with 2 tablespoons confectioners' sugar, or 2 cups shaved chocolate (see above), for serving

In the top of a double boiler over simmering water (or in a bowl set over a larger saucepan of simmering water), combine the butter, chocolates, and 1/4 cup of the cream.

Cook, stirring, until the chocolate and butter melt. Remove the double boiler top or bowl from the heat, wipe the bottom with a cloth, and transfer the chocolate mixture to a large bowl. Stir occasionally for 15 minutes, or until the mixture cools to room temperature but does not start to set.

Beat the remaining 1¾ cups of cream with the sugar and vanilla in a large bowl with an electric mixer and cold beaters until the mixture holds soft peaks. Fold one quarter of the cream into the cooled chocolate mixture to lighten it, then fold in the remaining cream until no patches of white show.

Spoon the chocolate filling into the tart shell, smoothing the top and mounding it slightly in the center. Refrigerate for at least 2 hours and as long as 6 hours, or until the chocolate sets. Spread the whipped cream on top or decorate with shaved chocolate.

Cut into wedges and serve.

hermits

These classic cookies are chewy and laden with gingerbread spices, molasses, and raisins. Hermits are baked in long, flat strips, then cut into bars. They keep well, which makes them great for a cookie jar. We make them when we want to have something on hand for weekend guests or if we're taking a tin of cookies to a hostess for a gift. Because they're spicy, they're nice with crunchy apples or oranges. The recipe comes from baking teacher Norman Myerow.

    4 **cups all-purpose flour**
$1^1/2$ **teaspoons salt**
    1 **teaspoon baking soda**
  $^1/2$ **cup canola oil**
  $^1/3$ **cup molasses**
  $^1/4$ **cup light corn syrup**
  $^1/4$ **cup water**
    2 **tablespoons milk**
    2 **large eggs**
$1^1/2$ **cups sugar, plus more for sprinkling**
    2 **teaspoons ground ginger**
    2 **teaspoons ground allspice**
    2 **teaspoons ground cinnamon**
    2 **cups dark raisins**

    1 **large egg, lightly beaten, for the glaze**

Set the oven at 400 degrees, with racks in the middle and upper third of the oven. Line two baking sheets with parchment paper.

    Sift the flour, salt, and baking soda into a medium bowl.

    Combine the oil, molasses, corn syrup, water, milk, and eggs in a large bowl, and beat with an electric mixer until blended.

    Beat in the $1^1/2$ cups sugar, ginger, allspice, and cinnamon.

    With the mixer set on its lowest speed, add the flour mixture to the batter, and beat just until combined. With a wooden spoon, stir in the raisins.

With a large metal spoon, spoon one quarter of the batter into a 12-inch-long strip down one side of one baking sheet. Do the same with the remaining batter, making 3 more strips and setting them 2 to a sheet, 4 inches apart. Use a metal palette knife dipped in water (or your wet hands) to shape the strips so they are flat and smooth. Brush with the egg and sprinkle them with sugar.

Bake for 8 minutes. Reduce the oven temperature to 375 degrees and continue baking for 12 to 15 minutes, reversing the baking sheets from front to back and from top to middle halfway through to ensure even browning, until the hermits are puffed and set in the center.

Slide the parchment papers onto wire racks, and let the hermits cool for 10 minutes.

Slip the papers onto a cutting board. Using a sawing motion with a serrated knife, cut the strips at 2-inch intervals to make 6 bars from each band. Let them cool completely. Store in an airtight container for up to 1 week.

congo bars

These bars, which are very easy to make, are dense with chocolate chips and use ingredients that most bakers have on hand. Sheryl's son, Asher, took a bar to school every day for ten years. The recipe came from St. Mary's of the Assumption Parish, in Brookline, Massachusetts, whose mothers compiled a cookbook.

3/4 cup (1½ sticks) unsalted butter, melted
1¾ cups packed light brown sugar
3 large eggs, lightly beaten
1 teaspoon vanilla extract
2 cups all-purpose flour
2 teaspoons baking powder
1/4 teaspoon salt
1 package (12 ounces) semisweet chocolate chips
1 cup chopped walnuts or 1 more cup chocolate chips

Set the oven at 350 degrees, with a rack in the center. Butter a 9-by-13-inch baking pan.

Cream the butter and brown sugar in a large bowl with an electric mixer for 1 minute, or until thoroughly blended. Beat in the eggs, one at a time, beating well after each addition. Beat in the vanilla.

Sift together the flour, baking powder, and salt in a medium bowl. With the mixer set on its lowest speed, add the flour mixture to the butter mixture just until the dry ingredients are blended thoroughly.

Use a wooden spoon to stir the chocolate chips and nuts, if using, into the batter. Spoon the batter into the pan and use a metal palette knife to smooth the top of the batter.

Bake in the center of the oven for 22 minutes for a moist bar, 25 for a slightly drier version. Set the pan on a wire rack and cool completely.

Cut into 24 bars. Store them in an airtight tin, layered with waxed paper, for up to several days. Freeze for up to 1 month.

fudgy chocolate-chip brownies

With their fudgelike centers and intense taste, these brownies are a chocolate lover's dream. Bake them in a foil-lined pan, refrigerate them overnight, and then turn them out of the pan the following day to cut them up. The recipe, from Susie Heller of Napa, California, who runs her own production company and was a caterer for many years, makes professional-looking brownies. You can, of course, cut them in the pan the way regular people do.

1 cup (2 sticks) unsalted butter
4 ounces unsweetened chocolate, coarsely chopped
4 large eggs
2 cups sugar
1 cup all-purpose flour
1/4 teaspoon salt
1 package (6 ounces) semisweet chocolate chips

Set the oven at 375 degrees, with a rack in the center. Butter a 9-by-13-inch baking pan. Line the bottom and sides with foil and butter the foil.

Melt the butter and unsweetened chocolate in a large saucepan over low heat. Stir with a wooden spoon until smooth. Remove the saucepan from the heat and let cool.

Add the eggs and beat well with the wooden spoon. Add the sugar, then stir in the flour, salt, and chocolate chips.

Spoon the batter into the pan. Bake in the center of the oven for 30 minutes, or until the top is just set; do not overbake or the brownies won't be moist.

Set the pan on a wire rack to cool completely. Cover with foil and refrigerate overnight.

Slide a long metal spatula all around the sides to loosen the brownies from the pan. Tip the pan upside down on the counter so the whole rectangle falls out. (If this does not work, halve the rectangle and use a wide metal spatula to lift out the two pieces.)

Peel off the foil. Turn the rectangle right side up and make 2 vertical cuts and 5 horizontal cuts to make 18 brownies. Store in an airtight container for up to 1 week or freeze for up to 2 months.

chocolate chip cookies

Every accomplished home baker has a chocolate chip cookie that he or she thinks out-shines all others. This is Julie's: dense, chewy, dark, and so full of chips that there's just enough batter to hold them together.

1	cup (2 sticks) unsalted butter, at room temperature
1	cup packed dark brown sugar
1/2	cup sugar
2	large eggs
2	teaspoons vanilla extract
2 3/4	cups all-purpose flour
1	teaspoon baking soda
1/2	teaspoon salt
2	cups (12 ounces) semisweet chocolate chips
1	cup (6 ounces) milk-chocolate chips
1	cup (6 ounces) white-chocolate chips
2	cups pecans or walnuts (optional)

Set the oven at 375 degrees, with racks in the middle and upper third. Line two baking sheets with parchment paper.

Cream the butter and sugars in a large bowl with an electric mixer. When the mixture is fluffy, beat in the eggs, one at a time, followed by the vanilla. Beat for 30 seconds just to mix the ingredients thoroughly.

With the mixer set on its lowest speed, beat in the flour, baking soda, and salt. With a wooden spoon, stir in the chocolate chips and nuts, if using.

Use a soup spoon to drop heaping spoonfuls of dough onto the prepared sheets, leaving 2 inches between each one.

Bake for 12 to 14 minutes, reversing the sheets from front to back and from top to middle halfway through to ensure even cooking, until the cookies are golden at the edges. Do not over-bake or they won't be chewy.

Remove the cookies from the oven and let sit for a few minutes, then transfer to a wire rack to cool completely.

note: To store, pack the cookies into an airtight container and store at room temperature for up to 1 week or freeze for up to 1 month. To defrost, remove the cookies from the container and spread them out on a platter.

oatmeal raisin cookies

Oatmeal cookies should be crisp outside but chewy in the centers, as these are. Brown sugar gives the batter a caramel taste, raisins add moisture, and the texture comes from old-fashioned rolled oats. We like a cookie late at night with a cup of tea, and these are always on hand when we're expecting any of our boys to come home.

   2 cups all-purpose flour
   1 teaspoon salt
   ½ teaspoon baking powder
   ½ teaspoon baking soda
   2 cups old-fashioned rolled oats
   1 cup (2 sticks) unsalted butter, at room temperature
   1 cup packed dark brown sugar
   ½ cup sugar
   2 large eggs
   1 teaspoon vanilla extract
   2 cups dark raisins
   1 cup chopped walnuts (optional)

Set the oven at 350 degrees, with racks in the middle and upper third. Line two baking sheets with parchment paper.

Sift the flour, salt, baking powder, and baking soda into a large bowl. Stir in the oats and set aside.

Cream the butter in another large bowl with an electric mixer. When it is light, add the sugars. Beat well.

Add the eggs, one at a time, then the vanilla. With the mixer set on the lowest speed, add the flour and oat mixture. Add the raisins and walnuts, if using, and mix to combine. With a wooden spoon, dip into the bottom of the batter and mix it with the top of the batter so the raisins are evenly distributed.

Use a soup spoon to drop heaping spoonfuls of batter onto the prepared sheets, leaving 2 inches between each one. Bake for 18 to 20 minutes, reversing the baking sheets from front to back and from top to middle halfway through to ensure even browning, until the cookies are lightly browned.

VARIATION
Oatmeal Dried-Cranberry White-Chip Cookies

Make the Oatmeal Raisin Cookies as directed, but omit the raisins and walnuts. Instead, add 8 ounces dried cranberries and 1 package (10 ounces) white-chocolate chips. Use ¼ cup sugar and ¾ cup dark brown sugar. Shape and bake as directed.

note: To store, pack the cookies into an airtight container and store at room temperature for up to 1 week, or freeze for up to 1 month. To defrost, remove cookies from the container and spread them on a platter.

ginger cookies

These cookies are made with chopped crystallized ginger in addition to a generous sprinkling of ground ginger. Because the batter is rolled in sugar, the cookies are quite crisp on the outside, but tender inside. They're perfectly round (you roll them first in your palms) and have just the right balance of spices, molasses, and sugar. Joanie Daniels of Bolton, Massachusetts, sent them in to a *Boston Globe* cookie contest, and everyone was crazy about them. (She won.)

2^1/4 **cups all-purpose flour**
    2 **teaspoons baking soda**
^{1}/2 **teaspoon salt**
    1 **tablespoon ground ginger**
    1 **teaspoon ground cinnamon**
^{3}/4 **cup (1^1/2 sticks) unsalted butter, at room temperature**
    1 **cup sugar, plus more for rolling**
    1 **large egg**
^{1}/4 **cup molasses**
    4 **tablespoons chopped crystallized ginger**

Set the oven at 350 degrees, with racks in the middle and upper third. Line two baking sheets with parchment paper.

Sift the flour, baking soda, salt, ground ginger, and cinnamon into a medium bowl.

Cream the butter and sugar in a large bowl with an electric mixer until light and fluffy. Beat in the egg, followed by the molasses. With the mixer set on its lowest speed, beat in the flour mixture, followed by the crystallized ginger.

Sprinkle a plate with sugar. Roll the batter into 1-inch balls in the palms of your hands, then roll the balls in the sugar.

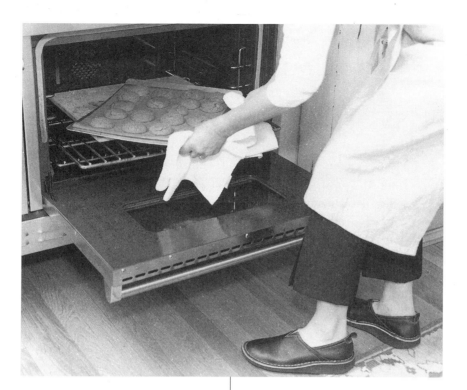

Transfer the balls to the baking sheets, setting them 2 inches apart. Bake for 12 to 15 minutes, reversing the baking sheets from front to back and from top to middle halfway through to ensure even browning, until the cookies are crisp at the edges but slightly soft on top.

Cool on the baking sheets for a few minutes, then transfer the cookies to wire racks to cool completely.

mandelbrot

Mandelbrot means "nut bread," and in some families, these cookies are called "mandel bread." Originally from Germany, they've become traditional on Jewish tables. Because they are made with oil, not butter, they can be served after a meal without violating the dietary laws, which prohibit the mixing of meat and dairy products. Julie ate them as a girl at Annie Stein's house in Montreal and makes them all the time for friends. She slips them into a cellophane bag and fastens the top with an oak tag label. Like biscotti, mandelbrot are baked twice: first in the shape of a log, which is sliced, and then again on their cut sides. The vegetable oil makes them much more tender than their Italian look-alikes.

3 cups whole unblanched (with skins) almonds
4 large eggs
1 cup sugar
3/4 cup canola oil
2 teaspoons vanilla extract
3 cups all-purpose flour
1 teaspoon baking powder
1/4 teaspoon salt

Set the oven at 375 degrees, with a rack in the center. Line a baking sheet with parchment paper.

On another rimmed baking sheet, toast the almonds for 12 to 15 minutes, stirring occasionally, until they begin to brown. Transfer them to a plate to cool.

In a food processor, chop the almonds coarsely.

Beat the eggs in a large bowl with an electric mixer for 1 minute. Add the sugar and continue beating for 1 minute more. Beat in the oil and vanilla just until combined.

With the mixer set on its lowest speed, beat the flour, baking powder, and salt into the batter. Add the almonds and mix well. The dough will be thick and sticky and hard to manage.

Using a large metal spoon, place large dollops of half of the dough down the length of one side of the baking sheet to form a rough log. Place dollops of the remaining dough to form another long log, spacing it about 4 inches from the first log. Use a metal palette knife to shape the logs so they are 2½ inches wide and 13 inches long, and flatten them slightly with the knife.

Bake in the center of the oven for 30 minutes, or until the logs are light brown and firm. Remove from the oven and slide the parchment paper onto a wire rack to cool the logs for 30 minutes.

Turn the oven down to 300 degrees. With a wide metal spatula, remove the logs from the parchment paper and transfer them to a cutting board. With a serrated knife, cut the logs on an extreme diagonal into ¾-inch-thick slices (below). Set the slices, cut sides down, on the parchment paper.

Bake for 30 minutes, or until the mandelbrot are crisp and dried. Remove from the oven and transfer to a rack to cool completely. Store in an air-tight container for up to 1 month.

double-chocolate refrigerator cookies

These cookies are rich and delightfully crunchy, splendid with strawberries or peaches or other soft fruits. In winter, serve them with Oranges in Caramel (page 370) or with a bowl of clementines.

2 cups all-purpose flour

$1/2$ teaspoon salt

1 cup confectioners' sugar, plus more for sprinkling

1 cup sugar

$1/2$ cup unsweetened cocoa powder

1 cup (2 sticks) unsalted butter, at room temperature

1 teaspoon vanilla extract

4 ounces semisweet chocolate, coarsely chopped

Put the flour, salt, sugars, and cocoa powder in a food processor and pulse to combine.

Add the butter, vanilla, and chocolate. Pulse again for 2 to 3 minutes, or until the dough resembles chocolate cement; it will not look like cookie dough. Stop the machine twice, to scrape down the sides.

Turn the dough out onto a counter. Using a plastic pastry scraper to scrape the dough off the counter, if necessary, shape it into a smooth mound. Divide the dough in half. Set each half on a 20-inch sheet of strong plastic wrap. Bring up the long sides and roll the dough in the plastic wrap, under your palms, to form 2 logs that are 2 inches across. Secure the ends. Refrigerate the dough for half a day or for up to 1 week.

Set the oven at 350 degrees, with racks in the middle and upper third. Line two baking sheets with parchment paper.

Use a thin, sharp knife to slice the cookies $1/4$ inch thick. Transfer them to the baking sheets, setting them close, but not touching (they don't spread very much during baking). Bake them for 12 minutes, reversing the baking sheets from front to back and from top to middle halfway through to ensure even browning.

Let the cookies sit on the sheets for a few minutes to firm up, then transfer them to wire racks to cool completely. Store in an airtight container, layered with waxed paper, for up to 1 week, or freeze for up to 1 month.

Sprinkle the cookies with confectioners' sugar before serving.

simple fruit desserts

Sometimes you just want the fruit. You're looking for a little more than a bowl of fresh fruit and a little less than a blueberry pie.

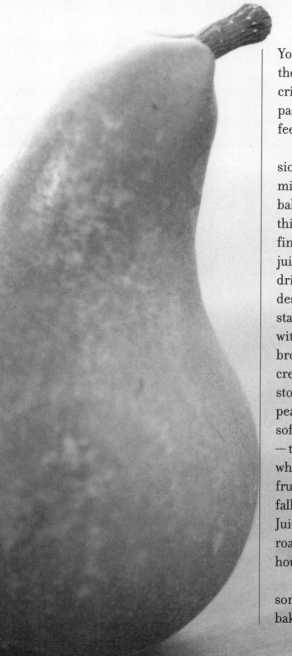

You've got peaches that are so fresh, they still have fuzz on their skins or crisp apples, and you don't want to make pastry or a cake batter or anything that feels like a production.

This is what we do for those occasions. We resist the urge to take out the mixer and soften the butter and begin baking because we're looking for something that will show off the fruits. If we find navel oranges that are firm and juicy, we slice them into a glass bowl and drizzle them with a caramel syrup, a dessert that is one of Sheryl's winter standbys. Beautiful peaches are baked with brown sugar and glazed under a broiler with a few spoons of heavy cream, which Julie makes after she's stopped at the farm stand where the peaches are handpicked. Berries and soft summer fruits are similarly glazed — this time with a vanilla custard sauce, which browns in patches and bathes the fruit in its rich vanilla taste. And for the fall, Whole Roasted Apples with Orange Juice sends wafts of cinnamon and roasting-apple aromas through the house.

As divine as fruit and pastry can be, sometimes you have to know when *not* to bake.

simple fruit desserts

whole roasted apples with orange juice

People say that you should make an apple pie before showing your house to prospective buyers to create a cozy atmosphere. Make this instead. The apples are stuffed with a walnut-cinnamon mixture and roast slowly, basted with orange juice, perfuming your house. Serve them hot, drizzled with heavy cream or beside vanilla ice cream. Sometimes we whisk low-fat plain yogurt or vanilla-flavored yogurt in a bowl, which makes the consistency saucelike, then spoon it over the apples. You'll need an apple corer to remove the cores without cutting the apples.

6	large baking apples (see page 256)
1/4	cup packed dark brown sugar
1/4	cup coarsely chopped walnuts
1	teaspoon ground cinnamon
2	tablespoons butter
1/2	cup orange juice

Set the oven at 350 degrees. Butter a 10- to 12-inch baking dish or another dish that will hold all the apples in one layer.

Core the apples without peeling them. Set them in the baking dish, stemmed ends up.

Combine the brown sugar, walnuts, and cinnamon in a small bowl. Use a small spoon to press some of the wal-nut mixture into each apple. Dot the top with butter. Carefully pour the orange juice over the apples to moisten them.

Bake for 40 to 50 minutes, basting them with the juices that accumulate in the pan, until the apples are tender when pierced with a skewer. Serve.

apple crisp

A great apple crisp has a thick, crunchy topping that covers tender, flavorful apples tossed with just a little sugar and some lemon juice. The crisp is wonderful hot from the oven, drizzled with heavy cream or with ice cream spooned onto it, so it melts at the edges. This is the quickest route to apple pie filling without having to make a crust.

❖{ **FOR THE APPLES**

8 **medium baking apples (see page 340), peeled, cored, and
thinly sliced**
Juice of 1/2 lemon
1/4 **cup sugar**

Set the oven at 350 degrees with a rack in the center of the oven. Butter an 8-inch square baking pan or use another pan with a 2-quart capacity.

Toss together the apples, lemon juice, and sugar in a large bowl. Pour the apples into the baking dish; it should be very full. Set aside while you make the topping.

❖{ **FOR THE TOPPING**

2/3 **cup all-purpose flour**
1/2 **cup old-fashioned rolled oats**
3/4 **cup packed dark brown sugar**
1/4 **cup sugar**
1 **tablespoon ground cinnamon**
8 **tablespoons (1 stick) unsalted butter, cut into pieces**
3/4 **cup coarsely chopped walnuts (optional)**

Heavy cream or vanilla ice cream, for serving

Combine the flour, oats, sugars, cinnamon, and butter in a medium bowl. Work the mixture with a fork or your

fingertips until it is thoroughly mixed and resembles crumbs. Stir in the walnuts, if using.

VARIATION
Blueberry Crisp

Make the Apple Crisp (page 366) as directed (without the cinnamon or walnuts), substituting the following filling for the apple filling. Use an 8-inch square dish or another dish with a 2-quart capacity.

$4^{1}/_{2}$ **pints blueberries, rinsed and picked over**
$^{1}/_{4}$ **cup sugar**
Juice of $^{1}/_{2}$ lemon
$^{1}/_{4}$ **cup all-purpose flour**

Toss together the blueberries, sugar, and lemon juice in a large bowl. Sprinkle the mixture with the flour and toss gently but thoroughly.

Follow the baking instructions for Apple Crisp.

VARIATION
Strawberry-Rhubarb Crisp

Make the Apple Crisp (page 366) as directed (without the walnuts), substituting the following filling for the apple filling. Use an 8-inch square dish or another dish with a 2-quart capacity.

1 **quart strawberries, hulled and sliced**
8 **large stalks rhubarb, thinly sliced**
$^{3}/_{4}$ **cup sugar**
Juice of 1 lemon
$^{1}/_{2}$ **cup all-purpose flour**

Toss together the strawberries, rhubarb, sugar, and lemon juice in a large bowl. Sprinkle the mixture with the flour and toss gently but thoroughly.

Follow the baking instructions for Apple Crisp.

Sprinkle the topping all over the apples. Set the dish on a rimmed baking sheet to catch any spills.

Bake in the center of the oven for 50 to 55 minutes, or until the crisp is golden brown and the apples are bubbling at the edges. Let the crisp settle for 15 minutes. Serve with a pitcher of heavy cream or vanilla ice cream.

summer fruits gratinéed with vanilla custard sauce

Vanilla-scented custard sauce is versatile. It can be served with fruit desserts, poured over pound cake or used as a glaze for fruit, as it is here. Blueberries, raspberries, and nectarines are spread in a baking dish, covered with the sauce and a coating of sugar, and then browned under the broiler. The heat doesn't cook the fruit, but warms the sauce. Choose a baking dish that will withstand the broiling element and looks good enough to go straight to the table. Save the 8 egg whites that are left over from making the custard sauce for an Egg White Frittata (page 290).

FOR THE CUSTARD SAUCE
- 8 large egg yolks
- 1/3 cup sugar, plus more for sprinkling
- 3 cups whole milk
- 1 teaspoon vanilla extract

Beat the yolks and sugar in a large bowl with a wooden spoon until the mixture is thick. Scald the milk in a heavy-bottomed saucepan. Remove from the heat.

Gradually stir half of the hot milk into the yolk mixture, then stir the yolks into the remaining hot milk in the pan.

Over medium-low heat, stir the mixture constantly with the wooden spoon until the custard thickens slightly and a clear trail remains when you draw a finger across the back of the custard-coated spoon. Do not boil or the mixture will curdle.

Strain the custard sauce through a fine-mesh strainer and stir in the vanilla.

(The sauce can be refrigerated for several hours or overnight at this point. If you do that, sprinkle with sugar to prevent a skin from forming and let stand until cool; cover tightly with plastic wrap and refrigerate.) Set aside while you prepare the fruit.

❉⟩ FOR THE FRUIT

1 **quart blueberries**

1 **pint raspberries**

3 **ripe nectarines, pitted and sliced**

Sugar, for sprinkling

Butter a 9-by-13-inch baking dish or another dish with a 3½-quart capacity. Scatter the blueberries, raspberries, and nectarines in the pan so they are evenly distributed. Set aside.

Just before serving, turn on the broiler. Pour the sauce over the fruits and dust the dish generously with sugar. Slide the dish under the broiler for 1 to 2 minutes; watch carefully so the sauce doesn't curdle. Serve at once.

oranges in caramel

Sliced oranges in a glass bowl make a splendid midwinter dessert. You can sprinkle them with kirsch, which is a mild cherry-flavored liqueur, drizzle them with cream or make a caramel syrup. The syrup is very simple. It bubbles madly and, when you add water to it, splatters, which is normal. Proceed with confidence.

> 6 **navel oranges**
> 1/2 **cup sugar**
> 1/2 **cup water, or more if necessary**
> **Squeeze of fresh lemon juice**

Using a slender serrated knife, cut a slice from each end of an orange. Set the orange cut side down on a board. Cutting vertically in a sawing motion, cut a curved slice of rind from the orange, and continue in this way until all the rind and pith is removed. Do this with the remaining oranges. Set the oranges on a plate and use the knife to cut across the sections and make thick slices.

Arrange the oranges in overlapping layers in a serving bowl.

Combine the sugar, 1/4 cup of the water, and the lemon juice in a heavy-bottomed medium saucepan. Let cook over low heat, without stirring, until the sugar dissolves.

Increase the heat to high and let the syrup simmer steadily, without stir-ring, until it turns a rich brown caramel color. It will bubble and begin to turn golden at the edges before the center is ready.

When the syrup is ready, remove it from the heat, avert your eyes, and pour the remaining 1/4 cup water into the pan. It will splutter and bubble up for a minute.

Return the pan to the heat and cook over low heat, stirring, until the hardened pieces of caramel dissolve. If they don't dissolve, add more water 1 teaspoon at a time, letting each addition of water heat before adding more. Remove from the heat and cool completely.

Just before serving, pour the cool syrup over the oranges.

baked peaches in brown sugar

You can't go wrong with three ingredients, two of which are brown sugar and heavy cream. The sugar is sprinkled over peaches, which are baked until they are tender, then glazed under a broiler with cream. Choose a baking dish that will withstand the broiling element. Serve the peaches with vanilla ice cream or frozen yogurt, or offer a plate of Ginger Cookies (page 356) or Hermits (page 348).

6　ripe peaches, unpeeled
3　tablespoons dark brown sugar
3　tablespoons heavy cream

Set the oven at 350 degrees, with a rack in the center. Butter a 9-inch square baking dish or another dish with a 2½-quart capacity.

Cut the peaches into thick slices. Arrange them in the dish, letting them overlap slightly. Sprinkle them with brown sugar. Bake in the center of the oven for 30 minutes, or until the peaches are tender and golden.

Turn on the broiler. Drizzle the peaches with the cream. Slide the dish under the broiler for 1 minute, watching the peaches closely, or until the edges are just beginning to turn quite brown. Serve.

Peaches in Red Wine

Set half a glass of red wine in front of you. Slice a ripe peach directly into the wine. Use a spoon to eat the peach, and then sip the wine that remains. The wine makes the peach taste divine.

index